Who Killed Berta Cáceres?

Who Killed Berta Cáceres?

*Dams, Death Squads and an
Indigenous Defender's Battle for the Planet*

Nina Lakhani

VERSO
London • New York

First published by Verso 2020
© Nina Lakhani 2020

All rights reserved

The moral rights of the author have been asserted

1 3 5 7 9 10 8 6 4 2

Verso
UK: 6 Meard Street, London W1F 0EG
US: 20 Jay Street, Suite 1010, Brooklyn, NY 11201
versobooks.com

Verso is the imprint of New Left Books

ISBN-13: 978-1-78873-306-9
ISBN-13: 978-1-78873-308-3 (US EBK)
ISBN-13: 978-1-78873-309-0 (UK EBK)

British Library Cataloguing in Publication Data
A catalogue record for this book is available from the British Library

Library of Congress Cataloging-in-Publication Data

Names: Lakhani, Nina, author.
Title: Who killed Berta Cáceres? : dams, death squads, and an indigenous defender's battle for the planet / Nina Lakhani.
Description: London ; Brooklyn, NY : Verso Books, 2020. | Includes bibliographical references and index. | Summary: 'Drawing on years of familiarity with Cáceres, her family, her vibrant movement, and with Central America generally, as well as chilling interviews with company and government officials, Lakhani paints an inti- mate portrait of a remarkable woman. Berta Cáceres fought for her ideals in a country beholden to corporate-military control and US power, becoming a role model for acti- vists the world over.' – Provided by publisher.
Identifiers: LCCN 2020001756 (print) | LCCN 2020001757 (ebook) | ISBN 9781788733069 (hardback) | ISBN 9781788733083 (ebk)
Subjects: LCSH: Cáceres, Berta, 1973?–2016. |
  Murder – Investigation – Honduras. | Trials (Murder) – Honduras. | Political corruption – Honduras. | Business enterprises – Corrupt practices – Honduras. | Lenca Indians – Honduras – Government relations. | Environmentalists – Honduras – Biography. | Lenca Indians – Honduras – Biography.
Classification: LCC HV6535.H66 L35 2020 (print) | LCC HV6535.H66 (ebook) | DDC 364.152/3092 – dc23
LC record available at https://lccn.loc.gov/2020001756
LC ebook record available at https://lccn.loc.gov/2020001757

Typeset in Sabon LT by Hewer Text UK Ltd, Edinburgh
Printed in the UK by CPI Group (UK) Ltd, Croydon CR0 4YY

For all the defenders and truth-tellers fighting to save our planet.
And for my grandmother (baa), Narabda Sanchdev, who would have been very proud.

You can't kill the truth.

Contents

Prologue	1
1. The Counterinsurgency State	11
2. The Indigenous Awakening	37
3. The Neo-liberal Experiment	51
4. The Dream and the Coup	65
5. The Aftermath	85
6. The Criminal State	109
7. The Threats	139
8. Resistance and Repression	161
9. The Investigation	183
10. The Trial	233
Afterword	277
Notes	285
Acknowledgements	321
Index	323

Prologue

The final few months of Berta Cáceres's life were filled with ominous signs. Just before Christmas 2015, she confided in her sister Agustina that her life was in danger. 'The messages never stop, the harassment never stops, they have me under surveillance. They don't care that I have children. Those sons of bitches are going to kill me.'

Berta was involved in numerous land and water struggles alongside indigenous Lenca communities across western Honduras. But the battle to stop construction of a hydroelectric dam on the Gualcarque River, in the community of Río Blanco, had her more worried than usual. Berta told her children she was scared, and that they should take the threats seriously. 'Mum said there was a group of dangerous *sicarios* [hit men] attacking the Río Blanco community and asking about us, her daughters,' said Laura, twenty-three, the youngest, home from midwifery college for the Christmas break. 'I knew the threats were serious because she wouldn't leave me alone in the house, not even for a night.'

Berta had reasons to suspect the hit men were hired by DESA, the dam construction company. DESA's trumped-up criminal charges against her and other leaders of the Council of Popular and Indigenous Organizations of Honduras (COPINH) had failed to silence them. Was it now it was pursuing other means to stop the opposition?

Her sense of unease intensified on 12 February 2016. Douglas Bustillo, a thuggish former army lieutenant and DESA's ex-security chief, messaged her COPINH deputy, Tomás Gómez Membreño, out of the blue, accusing Berta of cashing in on the Río Blanco struggle to win the prestigious Goldman Environmental Prize.

'You don't have the same support as before, it seems like you've sold out your conscience and ideals. And you've left the people of La Tejera [in Río Blanco] alone ... you only used them for your boss's prize and didn't help them, not even with a maternity centre even though she got almost 4 million. Now the people have realized, and they're not going to support you.'

Tomás forwarded the message to Berta, who sent it back to Bustillo, and then texted him:

'You never tire of being a frontman for DESA ... repeating everything they say.'

'Hahaha. I'm no frontman, I've forgotten all about that company,' Bustillo replied.

Four days later, driving out of Río Blanco, Berta's car was shadowed by two SUVs carrying armed locals she knew were linked to DESA.

On 20 February, Berta led a convoy to the Gualcarque, a river considered sacred by the Lenca people, to make a stand against the company's attempt to circumvent indigenous land rights by moving the dam across the shore. DESA was warned about the demonstration via its network of paid informants, and summoned its political and security allies to wreck the event. First, COPINH's buses and cars were detained at a checkpoint where everyone was forced out and the men and women were separated, registered and photographed by police and military officers. Then, a small crowd threw stones and insults. 'You old witch, you'll never come back here!' screamed the pro-dam deputy mayor at Berta.

As the crowd jeered, Sergio Rodríguez, DESA's communities and environmental manager, politely greeted Berta before warning her to turn back. 'There are armed men at the river, we won't be responsible if something happens to you.'

'We're not leaving, we have a right to be here,' retorted Berta, and marched on.

But the public road to the river was blocked by company machinery, so Berta set off on foot in the blistering sun towards the dam encampment. Waiting along the gruelling unshaded track were hired thugs and armed security guards and police officers, including some Tigres – an elite US-backed special weapons and tactics (SWAT) team trained for urban combat.

A drone buzzed overhead taking photographs as COPINH protesters threw rocks at the company machinery. DESA's security chief, former police major Jorge Ávila, appeared with a grisly warning: '*En unos días, ustedes van a comer el hígado de una persona*' (In a few days, you'll be eating someone's liver), he said.

Still undeterred, Berta continued with the exhausted group to the river, where they sat on the shady bank to rest and connect with the Gualcarque's sacred spirit. When they finally left it was dark, and Berta's car was pelted with beer bottles and rocks, smashing the rear window.

Less than a week later, around midday on 26 February, a double-cabin pickup truck with polarized windows drove up the narrow dead-end street leading to the COPINH head office in the city of La Esperanza. A tall man with a military-style haircut got out and asked for Berta, while the driver kept the engine running. When asked to identify himself, he jumped into the car and sped off.

These incidents made Berta even more nervous, and she arranged to stay at Utopía, COPINH's bustling training centre in La Esperanza, so as not to be at home alone when Laura returned to university in Buenos Aires.

She also contacted her friend Brigitte Gynther, a researcher at the School of Americas Watch (SOAW), who catalogued threats against COPINH. 'I need to talk to you,' she wrote in a text message on 29 February. 'I have news.' Brigitte was working in rural Colombia, but they agreed to speak later.

On the morning of 1 March, Berta drove Laura to Toncontín airport on the outskirts of the capital, Tegucigalpa. 'I'm proud of you,' she said. 'Enjoy life, make the most of it, but remember this is where you belong, in Honduras, fighting to make this a better place.'

Just before Laura went through security Berta hugged her youngest child one more time. 'This country is fucked, but if anything happens to me, don't be afraid.'

Laura assumed she was worried about being arrested again. 'My mum was so well known that I really doubted anything serious would happen to her. I thought meeting the pope and winning the Goldman Prize would protect her.'

At 2:08 p.m., Sergio Rodríguez sent a WhatsApp message, using a group chat named Security PHAZ (Proyecto Hidroelectrico Agua Zarca). Addressing DESA shareholders and senior managers, among them company president David Castillo, a US-trained former military intelligence officer, he confirmed that Berta would be in La Esperanza the following day.

Laura's plane took off just as Berta's old friend Gustavo Castro, a politically astute Mexican environmentalist, was landing at San Pedro Sula international airport on the other side of the country. Berta had invited Gustavo to give a workshop on alternative energy for COPINH members. The pair, who went way back, hadn't seen each other in several years and spent the evening catching up at Berta's new house in Colonia Líbano, a gated community on the southern edge of La Esperanza.

Berta told him about the turmoil generated by the campaign to stop the dam, a construction project backed by members of one of the country's most powerful clans, the Atala Zablah family, as well as international banks. 'It was strange, as she never sent me any ideas for the workshop, just the ticket; but I had no idea how much pressure she was under,' Gustavo would recall.

They were both tired, so Berta suggested calling it a night and offered to take Gustavo to his lodgings, but he was worried about her safety. 'It's so dark and isolated here, will you be alright driving back alone so late?' he asked. '*Cheque, hermano* [Okay, brother], I'll be fine. But why don't you come and stay here with me from tomorrow night? I've got internet, so we can work here together.'

The next day, Tuesday 2 March, Berta opened the workshop in Utopía before heading to the outdoor kitchen area, carrying her three constantly chiming mobile phones and customary notebook and pen. She messaged Laura, telling her not to worry as Gustavo would be staying at the house. She also called her close colleague Sotero Chavarría, who'd gone to Tegucigalpa for medical treatment. '*Hermano*, I need you back here, come soon, I have to tell you something, it's important,' she said.

Shortly after, Sotero received another call: security chief Ávila and a dozen Río Blanco locals aligned with DESA were approaching La Esperanza in a dark Toyota pickup truck.

What business did they have that day, were they coming to keep tabs on Berta? On his way back to La Esperanza, Sotero noticed the police checkpoint at the city entrance was unmanned. This was so unusual that he mentioned it to colleagues.

Later that morning, Lilian Esperanza, the COPINH finance coordinator, arrived at Utopía with a handful of cheques and a donor letter that needed Berta's signature. 'We need to change the signature,' Berta said. 'What if something happens to me? I could be jailed or killed. If you have problems accessing money, then what would happen to COPINH? I keep on reporting the threats, but no one takes any notice.'

'Don't be silly. Nothing's going to happen to you,' Lilian insisted.

Why was Berta acting as if time was running out?

It was late morning when she left the workshop with Gasper Sánchez, COPINH's young sexual diversity coordinator, heading for the central market. Berta had spent several nights with the vendors occupying the ramshackle ninety-year-old site, contesting the mayor's plan to replace it with a shopping mall. 'She was tired, but they called asking for her help, so we went, and Berta encouraged them to keep fighting,' Gasper told me later.

They met Sotero and one of Berta's brothers at the market, and together went for lunch at their mother's house. Berta still didn't tell Sotero what was so urgent, saying they'd talk later.

In the car on their way back to the workshop, Gasper interviewed Berta for COPINH's community radio station. 'Energy is not just a technical issue,' she explained. 'It's a political issue to do with life, territories, sovereignty and the right to community self-determination. We believe this is the moment to profoundly debate capitalism and how energy is part of the domination of indigenous communities and violation of their rights . . . That's what Lenca communities like Río Blanco are living through right now. In this forum we want to explain the impact of capitalism on Honduras, and work out a community proposal on how we're going to fight this battle . . . to leave behind the logic of consumerism and privatization and think about alternative energy as a human right, part of the process of liberation and emancipation.'

It would be her last interview.

Berta then called her friend Ismael Moreno, a Jesuit priest known as Padre Melo, to confirm Gustavo would guest on his radio show. 'She was scared, but it was Camilito she was most worried about,' Melo said: Berta had recently received an anonymous message threatening to chop her only grandchild into pieces.

Back at the workshop, Berta messaged SOAW's Brigitte Gynther at 4:44 p.m., asking when she'd be back from Colombia. 'I never found out what she wanted to tell me,' said Brigitte. 'But I knew something was wrong. She only contacted me when something was seriously wrong.'

After the workshop, Berta messaged a Swiss journalist who was interested in mining struggles in Honduras. 'We've not allowed mines to enter [Lenca territory], but there are communities under threat,' she texted him at 7 p.m., promising they would speak the following day.

Berta and Gustavo then left Utopía, popping in to visit her mother again before heading to her favourite downtown eatery, El Fogón, for dinner and a beer. Just before 9:30 p.m., a black double-cabin Toyota Hilux with polarized windows and no number plates was seen by a neighbour outside her mother's house. Berta and Gustavo arrived back at her place just after 9:30 p.m.

Berta's green and gold bungalow stands amid a scattering of garishly painted houses, some still empty or under construction, enclosed by a mishmash of wire and white wooden fencing, with views of a lake and distant pine-forested hills. The bungalow is on an unsurfaced road about 150 metres from the security gate, which is operated by two guards working in twelve-hour shifts.

The layout is unusual, with the front door leading into the open-plan lounge and a flimsy wooden back door leading into the kitchen. She and Gustavo sat on the front patio talking for half an hour or so, enjoying the breeze. Then he smoked a cigarette, while Berta finished working on a document. A couple of cars drove past behind the wire perimeter fencing.

Gustavo retired to the guest bedroom nearest the lounge. Berta's room was at the other end of the narrow hallway. After changing into an olive-green t-shirt and black shorts trimmed in red and white, she sat on her bed, legs stretched out, and kept working. At 11:25 she sent a message to Juan Carlos Juárez, the police liaison officer charged with overseeing her protection. 'Wherever you are, I wish you well. Please be careful. *Besos* [kisses].'

At around 11:35, Gustavo heard a noise. Tap! Tap! Tap! He thought it was Berta cleaning or fetching something from the kitchen, and barely looked up from his laptop. A minute or less later there was a louder, duller sound. Thud! Gustavo assumed Berta had dropped something in the kitchen. Then he heard her call out: 'Who's there?'

'It was then I realized that someone was in the house and something bad was going to happen,' Gustavo recalled. Seconds later, a tall, dark-skinned youth with cropped hair, wearing a black top and white scarf, kicked open the bedroom door and aimed a gun at his head from about two metres away. He heard the fuzzy sound of a walkie-talkie. Seated on the bed, Gustavo was looking straight at the gunman, when he heard Berta's bedroom door being forced open. It sounded as if she was struggling to push someone away. Then he heard three shots. Bang! Bang! Bang! Berta's legs gave way and she fell backwards. She tried to defend herself and scratched at the gunman as he bent over her. But she was weak, and the killer stamped on her bleeding body until she could no longer resist.

Gustavo jumped up off the bed and in a split second lifted his left hand to protect his face as the gunman fired a single shot. Bang! The bullet grazed the back of his left hand and the top of his left ear. Gustavo lay completely still on the floor as blood oozed from the wounds. The gunman was convinced and left, but still Gustavo dared not move. He didn't hear a car drive away – what if the assassins were still inside the house? Moments later he heard Berta's voice. 'Gustavo! Gustavo!'

He ran to her and saw his friend sprawled on her back between the bedroom door and the wooden closet, struggling to breathe. Her curly black hair was sticky with the blood from three bullet wounds, spreading across her shorts and t-shirt.

Gustavo squeezed through the small gap between the door and her shivering body. He knelt down and wrapped his arms around her, trying to keep her warm and alive. 'Don't go, Berta! Don't die! Stay with me,' he begged. But Berta Cáceres was bleeding to death.

'Get my phone,' she murmured. 'On the table.' At around a quarter to midnight Berta uttered her last words. 'Call Salvador! Call Salvador!'

Then she was gone.

Berta Cáceres had been murdered. Killed in her bedroom

less than a year after winning the foremost prize for environmental defenders.

Gustavo survived. But would his eyewitness evidence be enough to identify the gunmen? And who was behind this bold execution? Could there ever be justice for someone like Berta in a country like Honduras, where impunity reigns supreme?

Would we ever know who killed Berta Cáceres?

1

The Counterinsurgency State

Río Blanco, April 2013

Dressed in her customary getup of slacks, plaid shirt and wide-rimmed sombrero, Berta Cáceres stood on top of a small grassy mound shaded by an ancient oak tree to address the crowd of men, women and children who'd walked miles from across Río Blanco to discuss the dam. 'No one expected the Lenca people to stand up against this powerful monster,' she proclaimed, 'and yet we indigenous people have been resisting for over 520 years, ever since the Spanish invasion. Seventy million people were killed across the continent for our natural resources, and this colonialism isn't over. But we have power, *compañeros*, and that is why we still exist.'

Río Blanco is a collection of thirteen *campesino* or subsistence farming communities scattered across hilly, pine-forested terrain in the department of Intibucá, a predominantly Lenca region in south-west Honduras. Here, extended families work long days, farming maize, beans, fruit, vegetables and coffee on modest plots of communal land which are mostly accessible only on foot or horseback. Chickens and scraggy dogs dart in and out of every house. Some families also raise cattle, pigs and ducks to eat, not to sell, as there are few paved roads or transport links connecting the communities with market towns. Since being given the land by a former president in the 1940s, these communities have largely been ignored by successive governments – despite election promises to deliver basic health and education services and paved roads.[1] With few public services, the communities rely on the Gualcarque River, which flows north to south, skirting the edge of Río Blanco. The sacred river is a source of spiritual and physical nourishment for the Lenca people. It provides fish to eat, water for their animals to drink, traditional medicinal plants, and fun: with no electricity, let alone internet, the children flock to the river to play and swim. The communities live in harmony with the river and with each other. Or at least they used to.

The pro-business National Party government licensed the Agua Zarca hydroelectric dam in 2010, ignoring the legal requirement for formal consultation *before* sanctioning projects on indigenous territory. Not only that, the environmental licences and lucrative energy contracts were signed off at breakneck speed without proper oversight, suggesting foul play by a gaggle of public officials and company executives. In Honduras this wasn't unusual: the Gualcarque River was sold off as part of a package of dam concessions involving dozens of waterways across the country in the aftermath of the 2009 coup – orchestrated by the country's right-wing business, religious, political and military elites to oust the democratically elected President Manuel Zelaya. Not just dams: mines, tourist developments, biofuel projects and logging concessions were rushed through Congress with no consultation, environmental impact studies or oversight, many destined for indigenous lands. The process was rigged against communities; the question was how high did the corruption go.

The hydroelectric project would dissect the sacred river and divert the water away from local needs, generating electricity to be sold to the national energy company (ENEE). The Lenca people knew that without the river, there could be no life in Río Blanco.

That's why, a few days before Berta's visit, community members had set up a human barricade blocking road access to the Gualcarque in a last-ditch effort to stop construction going ahead.

Berta addressed the crowd that April day just a stone's throw from the makeshift roadblock, which was manned in shifts by families utterly fed up with being treated like intruders on their own land. The blue and white flag of Honduras hung between two wooden posts obstructing the gravel through-way. The community had first sought help from COPINH several years earlier. Berta and other COPINH leaders helped them petition local and national authorities, the dam building company Desarrollos Energéticos SA (DESA) and its construction contractor, the Chinese energy giant Sinohydro, making it crystal clear that they did not want the river they relied upon for food, water, medicines and spiritual nourishment to be dammed. Lavish promises by DESA to build roads and schools turned out to be empty. The people held meetings, voted, marched on Congress and launched judicial complaints against government agencies and officials.

But the mayor of Intibucá, Martiniano Domínguez, claimed resistance was futile. The dam was backed by the president, he said, and they should be grateful to DESA, which promised jobs and development for the neglected community. Domínguez green-lighted construction in late 2011, after falsely claiming that most locals favoured the dam. A crooked consultation deed – filled with the names and signatures of people overtly against the dam, and others who couldn't read or write – was used as proof of community support to shore up permit applications and investments. When heavy machinery rolled in, cables connecting a solar panel to the school's internet and computer servers were destroyed, fertile communal land was invaded, and maize and bean crops on the riverbank were ruined, while well-trodden walking paths were blocked off. Signposts appeared around the construction site: 'Prohibited: Do Not Enter the Water'. For many, this humiliation was the last straw.

Berta only found out later, perhaps too late, that the dam project was backed by members of one of the country's most powerful clans, the Atalas, and that the president of DESA and its head of security were US-trained former Honduran military officers, schooled in counterinsurgency. This doctrine had long been used across Latin America to divide and conquer communities resisting neo-liberal expansion. But Berta grew up during the Dirty War, and by the time of her address at El Roble she had twenty years of community struggle under her belt. She understood the risks of opposing big business interests, and wanted to make sure the people of Río Blanco understood them too.

'Are you sure you want to fight this project? Because it will be tough,' she told them from the grassy mound beneath the oak tree. 'I will fight alongside you until the end, but are *you, the community*, prepared – for this is a struggle that will take years, not days?' A sea of hands rose into the air as the crowd voted to fight the dam.

Standing nearby was the figure of Francisco 'Chico' Javier Sánchez, a squat, moustachioed community leader in a black cowboy hat. 'Berta warned us that opposing the dam would mean threats, violence, deaths, divisions, persecution, infiltrators, militarization, police, *sicarios*, and that everything would be done to break us. COPINH was ready to support us in peaceful protests and actions, but it had to be *our* decision, the community's, because it was us who would suffer the consequences. We were totally ignorant, but she was very clear. Everything she told us that day came true, and worse.'

Three years later, five Río Blanco residents were dead, and so was Berta Cáceres.

Role Models

Berta's mother, Austra Berta Flores López, is a staunchly Catholic, no-nonsense matriarch and was the most important role model in Berta's life. Born in 1933 in La Esperanza, Doña Austra is a nurse, midwife, activist and Liberal Party politician, descended from a long line of prominent social and political progressives who were maligned and persecuted as communists during a string of repressive dictatorships. I interviewed the straight-talking Doña Austra several times, before and after Berta's murder – always at the spacious single-storey colonial-style house she built in the early 1970s, and always while drinking sweet black coffee in her legendary parlour adorned with religious knick-knacks and old photos. It's in this room that Doña Austra has, over the past four decades, hosted a motley crew of colourful characters including Salvadoran guerrilla commanders, Cuban revolutionaries, Honduran presidents and American diplomats. If walls could talk!

La Esperanza, which means 'hope' in Spanish, is a picturesque place in the hills surrounded by sweet-smelling pine forests and dozens of small villages. Lying 120 miles west of the congested concrete capital, Tegucigalpa, at the end of a snaking road riddled with potholes, it is the coolest and most elevated town in Honduras. Politically the set-up here is slightly odd, as La Esperanza merges seamlessly with the city of Intibucá; they are divided by a single street but administered by separate municipal governments. Intibucá is the older of the twin cities, and traditionally Lenca. La Esperanza houses the newer mestizo or ladino community; Berta's maternal great-grandparents (from Guatemala and the neighbouring department of Lempira) were among the first mid-nineteenth-century settlers. Growing up, Doña Austra witnessed the strict ethnic apartheid that banned indigenous inhabitants of Intibucá from entering mestizo schools and churches in La Esperanza.

As a little girl, Austra travelled on horseback to visit her father in El Salvador where he was intermittently exiled during the dictatorship of General Tiburcio Carías Andino (1933–49). 'We'd load one beast with food like dried meat and tortillas, the second one my mother and me would ride for two days to reach my father,' she recalled. 'I come from a family of guerrillas. Some ended up in chains as political prisoners, others were exiled or killed. My family has always fought for social change, and for that we were labelled communists.'

Austra Flores was widowed at the age of fifteen, after three years of marriage to a much older man. Then she trained as a nurse, and later as a midwife. In those days she was often the only health professional in town, so patients would walk miles to the house and wait on benches lined up on the shaded front porch and back patio. Many were impoverished campesinos who brought a hen, some firewood or a sack of maize as payment in kind. 'We didn't have much money, but there was always enough to eat,' said Doña Austra, who even now keeps her leather medical bag handy for when patients turn up. Some still walk miles, and they still wait on the very same wooden benches.

By the mid-70s, student rebellions were part of a burgeoning human rights scene in which Berta's older brother Carlos Alberto, Austra's fifth child, from a different relationship, played a role. Elected student leader of the La Esperanza teacher training college, the Escuela Normal Occidente, he led a hunger strike to oust the abusive and ineffective director. When he was shot in the left shoulder by soldiers deployed to evict striking students at the college, Doña Austra rushed him to Tegucigalpa for surgery.

The injury inspired Carlos to be more than a local student activist. He led nationwide strikes forcing a string of rotten head teachers to resign, and convoked clandestine meetings at the family home to organize hands-on support for leftist guerrilla groups in neighbouring El Salvador and Nicaragua. His belligerent leadership was noted, and the family became targets for the feared state intelligence service, the Dirección Nacional de Investigación (DNI).

'The house would be surrounded by *orejas* [Spanish for ears, meaning informants], it was always under surveillance and we'd hear boots on the roof. Soldiers and DNI men would come in and search the house, but they never looked in there,' said Austra, showing me the wooden wardrobe in the bedroom where they once hid books and pamphlets considered subversive. 'If the DNI had found those, we would have been taken away to the 10th Battalion base [located in nearby Marcala] where Salvadorans looking for supplies or safety were locked up and disappeared.'

Several of Carlos's friends, other student leaders, were disappeared during the 1970s, by which time Austra's house was the de facto socialist (with a small 's') headquarters, used to store medicines and food for the Salvadoran guerrillas and hide their commanders. She also hid young men, boys really, seeking to avoid the military conscription that wasn't abandoned until 1995. Francisco Alexis, her eighth child, was jailed, starved and tortured at the 10th Battalion base after he too tried to escape military service. 'Francisco was so traumatized by the barbarities inflicted on him, we sent him to live in the US,' said Austra. He was smuggled out using fake ID.

After graduating as a teacher, Carlos joined the Communist Party and moved north to the Bajo Aguán region, to work with campesino banana cooperatives campaigning for land redistribution. According to Doña Austra, he got involved in the armed student guerrilla group Los Cinchoneros, also known as the Popular Liberation Movement, founded in rebellious Olancho in eastern Honduras. Carlos moved to Russia with a scholarship to study history and political science. He was later in Nicaragua, defending the Sandinista revolution against the US-armed Contras. For Berta, Carlos was a real-life revolutionary idol.

Berta Isabel Cáceres Flores was born on 4 March 1971, a chubby, placid baby Doña Austra's twelfth and last child. Her father José Cáceres Molina (biological father of the four youngest siblings), from the nearby coffee-growing town of Marcala, was an abrasive ex-infantry sergeant from a staunchly nationalist family.[2] José Cáceres walked out when Berta was five, after imposing years of what many family members called 'alcohol-fuelled misery' on them, and she had little contact with him while growing up. Berta was a sparkling little girl with thick curly hair and a wide smile. By the age of seven or eight she was a regular competitor on the local beauty pageant circuit, picking up prizes as the best-dressed Mayan princess and Señorita Maize. She liked to play football, choreograph dances and put on plays, showing a notable flair for organizing and bossing the other children. But she also grew up running in and out of secretive, politically charged meetings, and from a young age was spellbound by the fiery debates centred on injustices in her corner of the world. By then, in the early to mid-1980s, Austra was involved in fledgling rights groups like the women's collective, Movimiento de Mujeres por la Paz 'Visitación Padilla',[3] and helping to organize against the US-backed death squads operating across Central America. Thanks to Austra's dedication as a community midwife, Berta also saw first hand the miserable conditions endured by neglected hill communities.

Aged twelve or thirteen, she would walk miles with her mother to reach pregnant women in isolated rural cantons with no electricity or running water. Berta assisted: she would fetch hot water and towels, hold candles for light, and sometimes even cut the umbilical cord. Many women spent hours each day collecting clean water and firewood as well as working in the fields and raising children, with no access to contraception or antenatal care, and no escape from violent partners. The grim plight of rural women left its mark on both mother and daughter. Later, Berta came to understand these harsh realities as a local consequence of global rules, a vision which would define her.

Sometimes they travelled to the Colomoncagua refugee camp, forty miles south of La Esperanza, to help pregnant Salvadoran civil war refugees living in concentration camp conditions. These mother–daughter medical missions provided good cover, allowing them to deliver food and medicines, and then sneak out messages for Salvadoran rebel commanders lying low at the family home. The first refugee camps in Honduras opened in early 1981, just as the US (with the aid of military dictatorships) started rolling out the counterinsurgency doctrine, in what Ronald Reagan called 'drawing the line' in Central America.[4] From this point forward, any Honduran suspected of sympathizing with neighbouring communist revolutionaries risked being murdered or disappeared by US-trained elite soldiers. This disposition to fight American enemies was established as a core characteristic of Honduran military ethos.

It's worth noting that anti-communist fervour was not a Cold War invention. In the first half of the twentieth century, Central America's elite landowning families – who enjoyed absolute economic and political power in their regional fiefdoms – were more than comfortable branding popular uprisings as communist threats. Any sniff of a political, social or labour movement demanding even modest reforms to tackle the stark inequalities was crushed, often brutally, to protect the interests of these elites.

In neighbouring El Salvador, the 1932 peasant uprising was ruthlessly quelled, leaving around 30,000 mainly indigenous Pipil people dead.[5] In Honduras, the 1975 Los Horcones massacre in rebellious Olancho was one of the worst to be documented. By then, the north coast had been devastated by Hurricane Fifi,[6] and campesinos on the brink of starvation squatted on unused arable land in the hope of forcing agrarian reforms. The crackdown was prompt. At least fourteen campesinos, sympathetic clergy and students were rounded up, tortured and killed by soldiers and armed guards on the orders of local landlords unwilling to relinquish a single plot. The dismembered bodies were found buried on land belonging to local rancher José Manuel Zelaya Ordóñez,[7] father of the future (subsequently deposed) president, Mel Zelaya Rosales. Thus when the US entered into full-fledged Cold War paranoia, the anti-communist brigade found it easy to sell its counterinsurgency doctrine to Central American elites who were already versed in dirty war tactics, albeit at a more amateur level. The doctrine identified certain social actors – student and peasant leaders, journalists, union organizers and liberation theology priests – as part of the ideological enemy, equating them with violent guerrillas. With this enemy, normal rules of engagement didn't apply, and the US, with its psychological warfare handbooks,[8] torture manuals and death squads, turned Central American armies into well-organized killing machines trained to detect and destroy anyone suspected of even thinking about insurgency.

Sovereignty for Sale

Anti-communist rhetoric wasn't new, nor was the US peddling influence in Honduras. In fact, while many countries like to boast of a special relationship with the US, Honduras actually has one. Honduras was always connected to international markets via American capital – initially through mining, and then, most famously, through banana exports.[9] A 'banana republic' is among the worst examples of capitalist hegemony: a country run like a private business for the exclusive profit of corporations and local ruling elites. The term was coined by the American satirist O. Henry in 1901 to describe the corruption and exploitation imposed by the United Fruit Company, now called Chiquita, on Central America. The company relied upon a culture of bribery, a subjugated workforce and smarts to exploit these lands for obscene profits. Under the leadership of Samuel Zemurray, dubbed 'Sam the Banana Man', by the 1920s United Fruit controlled 650,000 acres of the most fertile plains in Honduras, almost one-quarter of all arable land in the country, as well as major roads, railways and ports. Here the company was known as El Pulpo, the octopus, for its far-reaching tentacles permeating every aspect of life from labour rights to infrastructure to politics. 'In Honduras, a mule costs more than a member of parliament,' Zemurray famously once said.

In the hot and humid northern city of El Progreso, a wonderful black and white framed photograph of the 1954 *huelga de bananeros*, or banana workers' strike, hangs above Jesuit priest Padre Melo's desk. Taken a stone's throw away on the main road known as the Boulevard, it shows hundreds of defiant-looking men and women standing together, like an impenetrable human wall. After decades of subjugation, a flourishing campesino movement decided to fight back against slave-like conditions and brought the industry to a standstill, in what was the first serious challenge to the 'special relationship' and US profits. The campesino uprising was spuriously blamed on agitators from Guatemala, and plans were hatched to tackle both problems using the 1954 Military Assistance Agreement, which authorized the US to treat Honduras as a military satellite.

The US used its new outpost to train and arm mercenaries against Guatemala's first democratically elected president, Jacobo Árbenz Guzmán. United Fruit had lobbied hard for the CIA-backed 1954 military coup,[10] after Árbenz proposed taking *some* unfarmed land from multinationals to redistribute to landless peasants. The violent intervention paved the way for a bloody thirty-six-year civil war. The 1954 bilateral military agreement was a watershed geopolitical moment for the whole region, and Honduras has hosted American bases, forces and weapons ever since.

As for the campesino revolt which promised so much it was tamed by a series of modest reforms including a new labour rights code, social security benefits, and false promises of land redistribution. Some organizers were jailed, others co-opted; the most stubborn were disappeared or killed in local crackdowns such as the Los Horcones massacre. In the words of Padre Melo, 'at that time when serious left-wing political and guerrilla groups were developing in neighbouring countries, in Honduras they were being co-opted and the insurgency was cleverly transformed into a benign popular movement pacified with a few gains.'[11] The fruit companies continued to meddle in Honduran affairs to lower costs and maximize shareholder profits. For example, in 1972 United Fruit, by then renamed United Brands, bankrolled its friend, dictator General Oswaldo López Arellano to power, again illustrating how US capital dominated the most lucrative markets by owning politicians.[12] It was a special relationship that demanded docile political lapdogs, not business partners, which partly explains why in Honduras a modern-day oligarchy took so long to emerge.

The End Justifies the Means

In Nicaragua, the Sandinista victory against the US-backed Anastasio Somoza dictatorship in 1979 caused blind panic in the US. Cuba was regarded as a humiliation, but at least it was an island, where socialist uprising could be isolated. Nicaragua on the other hand was on the same land mass, just a few hundred miles from the Panama Canal. So when Ronald Reagan was elected in 1981 on an anti-communism mandate, the US turned its number one geopolitical partner into a major Cold War proxy battleground. The big guns – the spooks, special forces and top ally Ambassador John Negroponte – were deployed to Honduras with a clear mission: do whatever it takes to stop the communist rot.

British-born Negroponte, a zealous anti-communist action figure who cut his diplomatic teeth in Vietnam under Henry Kissinger, served in Honduras during its dirtiest years. This was no unlucky coincidence. The Cold War zealot played down, in fact didn't mention, the huge spike in human rights violations – targeted arbitrary arrests, torture, the forced disappearances, and murder of suspected dissidents and refugees – in his diplomatic cables. During his 1981–85 tenure, military aid rocketed from $4m to $77.4m a year, a pretty straightforward cash-for-turf deal in which the US gained free rein over Honduran territory in exchange for dollars, training in torture-based interrogation methods, and silence.[13] This patronage created a loyal force hooked on American money, equipment, training and ideology: cheaply-bought loyalty which the US would count on again and again.

Negroponte was a cardinal figure in the Contra war, coordinating support for the anti-Sandinista mercenaries who were trained, armed and commanded from clandestine bases. But the US role was much more than merely supportive. According to covert ops veteran Mario Reyes (a Mexican-born soldier posted to Honduras during the Contra war), 'We conducted secret night-time missions to take out targeted Sandinistas on Nicaraguan territory; the killings were blamed on the Contras, that was the point, but it was us, and the Russians knew it was us.'

Reagan spent a billion or so dollars backing the Contras, whom he referred to as the 'moral equivalent of the founding fathers'. Some of that money came from CIA-backed drug trafficking which flooded poor neighbourhoods with cocaine, especially African-American neighbourhoods, and helped dampen post-civil rights social revolts. In the end, CIA-traded cocaine muzzled two impoverished communities thousands of miles apart, and fuelled the burgeoning international drug trade.

Another funding stream was illegal arms sales. Negroponte oversaw the approval of a new military treaty which authorized US use of the Palmerola Air Base, sixty miles north-west of Tegucigalpa. From here, Marine Lieutenant Colonel Oliver North ran the Iran-Contra operation – a clandestine effort to circumvent US law by selling weapons to Iran.[14] A key ally for this operation was Juan Matta Ballesteros, the original Honduran drug capo. More about him later. What else did Honduras get in return? It was a see-no-evil approach, but Negroponte knew perfectly well what horrors the military were perpetrating on civilians. He and his superiors positively applauded the elimination of so-called subversives. This is the essence of the counterinsurgency doctrine: the end justifies the means.

Michael McClintock is tall, with a soft Ohio accent and a long, thinning grey ponytail. He was Amnesty International's Latin American researcher during the Cold War years and became a renowned scholar on special forces and counterinsurgency doctrine. He witnessed the before and after effect first hand in Honduras. 'With the arrival of Negroponte,' he told me, 'there was a sudden and huge injection of American dollars and personnel, and within a year or two the military had identified and got rid of social leaders and incipient guerrilla groups. They literally wiped them out, clearing the decks to make Honduras an American aircraft carrier for Central America.

'It was a day-and-night change. The system changed from one of a sloppy rule of law, where powerful people get away with murder, to an organized ideological audit – a census of who's thinking bad thoughts and then going after them. It had a hugely corrupting influence on the armed forces and weak public institutions. Then add poverty and supercharge it with cocaine, and you understand why people flee,' he added.

The most prolific state-sponsored killing machine was

without doubt Battalion 3-16, which McClintock describes as America's 'most glowing innovation' in Honduras. It was created and commanded by General Gustavo Álvarez, a man the US could do business with.[15] Officially it was an intelligence unit, but it also stalked, kidnapped, tortured and disappeared scores of suspected subversives. Its operatives were trained in counterinsurgency surveillance and interrogation techniques by the CIA in secret locations in the US, and at home by Argentine torture specialists on US-controlled army bases.[16] In truth, the dirty war casualties in Honduras pale in comparison to its civil war-ravaged neighbours. Officially, 184 people were disappeared during the 1980s, though the exact number of people tortured and executed remains unknown, according to the Committee of Relatives of the Disappeared in Honduras (Spanish acronym COFADEH); for years, decomposed bodies were dug up on isolated riverbanks or in citrus groves. The 1981 forced disappearance of Ángel Manfredo Velásquez Rodríguez was the first such case ruled on by an international tribunal. The university student vanished after being interrogated and tortured at a police station and 1st Battalion military base by the DNI and G-2 (intelligence wing). The Honduran government denied any knowledge or involvement, told the Inter-American Court of Human Rights (IACrtHR) that he'd gone off with Salvadoran guerrillas, and refused to hear the family's case in domestic courts. The case changed international law, and forced disappearances were designated a crime without statute of limitations.[17]

Special Forces: 'Whatever, Whenever and Wherever'

To understand counterinsurgency, it is necessary to understand the role of special forces – an elite corps created by the

US in the 1950s to combat the occupying forces in Western Europe, using unconventional warfare. Under John F. Kennedy their numbers and role expanded to include preemptive strikes and terror tactics against the international menace that was communism. The time to act was now, according to the field manuals, in order to neutralize popular leaders *before* they became violently militant. In Honduras the Special Forces were created in 1979, a few months after the Sandinista victory, and were touted as an urban antisubversive ground force to liquidate guerrilla groups.

What's so special about the Special Forces? Special means irregular, super-soldiers trained to bend the rules and operate outside normal parameters because, they are told, the end justifies the means. When there are no limits, killing is the ultimate way to neutralize a threat. This threat might be real, like an armed guerrilla fighter, or imagined, like the children of campesinos slaughtered lest they grow into guerrillas. But before this ultimate penalty, a range of tried and tested techniques from the counterinsurgency spectrum – smear campaigns, blackmail, bribery, threats against loved ones, jail, torture and disappearance – can be deployed to neutralize the target. Informants, infiltrators and surveillance are key tools to gathering intelligence to divide, dominate and conquer communities. That's why to understand counterinsurgency, you need to understand Special Forces and military intelligence. Both are secret because both bend the law, McClintock told me.

US-backed special forces perpetrated some of the worst atrocities and most emblematic executions in the region, including the assassinations of Archbishop Óscar Romero and Bishop Juan Gerardi.[18] The crème de la crème from each country were sent for training to the School of the Americas (SOA) in Georgia, and its satellite centre in Panama. In Honduras, at least nineteen members of

Battalion 3-16 graduated from the infamous Fort Benning military school.[19] A much larger number were trained at home at the US regional training centre (Centro Regional Entrenamiento Militar, CREM), close to the Caribbean port city of Trujillo in the Bajo Aguán. 'The Americans trained the region's elite death squads at the CREM,' said Padre Melo, who in the early 1980s was posted at a church near the base. 'I would be stopped on my motorbike by American soldiers demanding to see my ID – they were authorized to do that!'

After the Cold War ended, these repressive security structures were not dismantled. Instead, they morphed into powerful criminal networks linked to corruption and the trafficking of arms and drugs, with clandestine parallel security structures that as part of their remit would target social justice activists labelled anti-development or terrorists. Modern enemies for modern times.

The implementation of US national security policies through the counterinsurgency doctrine marked a watershed in Honduras, and played a major role in Berta's life and death. In the months after the April 2013 community meeting at El Roble, under the eponymous old oak tree, a systematic campaign to crush opposition to the Agua Zarca dam was rolled out, using a classic sliding scale of counterinsurgency tactics: slurs, repression, inducements, infiltrators, informants, criminalization. A Guatemalan lawyer, with years of experience investigating civil war crimes, told me that Berta's murder bore the hallmarks of a military intelligence-backed special operation. That's why to understand who she was and why she was murdered, you have to understand the past.

The Corporate Campaign against the Agua Zarca Dam Opponents

The military background of senior DESA managers frightened Berta. Bustillo was openly aggressive towards her and community leaders, but it was David Castillo's intelligence past that troubled her most.

Years later, in text messages uncovered during the discovery phase of the murder trial, DESA's financial manager, Daniel Atala Midence, is shown using his political influence to press false charges against COPINH leaders, whom he referred to as criminals and even murderers. The texts also show how he authorized regular cash payments to informants in the community, including members of COPINH, who spied on Berta and the organization before reporting back to Bustillo and Rodríguez. It's a business practice that the company felt was justified in order to protect their investment from protests that delayed construction. Atala ran the day-to-day business with David Castillo, who offered Berta incentives such as money for local projects if she would support the dam and end hostilities between the company and the community.

Rebel with a Cause

By 1983, the twelve-year-old Berta was rebellious and outspoken, according to Ivy Luz Orellana who met her on their first day in 7th grade. 'She was very studious, learned quickly and was a natural leader who hated following pointless rules and would speak out against unfairness,' said Ivy, who shared with me a splendid collection of school photos that show a youthfully frivolous side of Berta. In one, Berta is fifteen and strutting along some sort of pageant catwalk wearing a fancy white dress, make-up and kitten heels, beaming happily. The picture appeared in the local paper.

By then she'd met her future husband, Salvador Zúñiga, a student activist six years older who was regularly invited by Doña Austra to the family home. Zúñiga had co-founded the radical Patriotic Student Organization of Lempira (Organización Patriótica Estudiantil de Lempira – OPEL), whose main objective was to purge Honduras of foreign armies. This made Salvador a target, and in 1984 rumours circulated that he was on a military hit list. With friends and colleagues already dead or disappeared, the nineteen-year-old crossed the border into El Salvador where he helped move the sick and injured to relative safety in Honduras.

After middle school, Berta, like most of her siblings, trained as a primary school teacher at the La Esperanza *normal*, mainly because it was the only free secondary education available. She started the three-year training course in 1986, aged fifteen, and immediately joined OPEL. When the radical student group's president was killed, Berta was elected to succeed him. In one of her first acts as president, she organized strikes to protest the unfair exclusion of a student, which saved him and got the teacher behind it thrown out. 'By the time we entered the *normal*, Berta's ideals were very clear: she was a leader and wanted to be free, do other things, rather than get married and have kids,' said her old schoolfriend Ivy.

This didn't stop Berta having fun, and her friends remember her as witty, outgoing and happy to break the rules. Ivy recalls that 'Berta was beautiful and had lots of boyfriends . . . She loved to dance, we were great dancers, but our mothers were strict so we'd sneak off to the Paraíso disco in the afternoons. We danced to merengue and 80s American pop music like Michael Jackson, songs in English we didn't even understand.

Berta was popular, happy and loved life, and that never changed in the thirty-plus years we were friends, even when things got so difficult at the end.' In later years, Berta would jokingly call old schoolmates, like Ivy, who became National Party voters, *capitalistas de mierda* (fucking capitalists). She never lost her playfulness, nor avoided people with opposing views.

Outside the *normal*, Berta got serious with like-minded new friends. Like her brother Carlos and his friends a decade earlier, the youngsters met in secret to read banned books on the Cuban revolution and Marxism, debating revolutionary ideas and real-world tactics to help comrades at home and in neighbouring countries. It was a dangerous time to be a revolutionary, and Berta kept this world from her school chums, who had no idea that she started dating Salvador Zúñiga in 1988, the last year of teacher training. She was seventeen, he was twenty-three, and by this time fully enmeshed in the Salvadoran war effort, supporting units across the tiny country with information analysis, logistics, intelligence and counter-intelligence gathering.

Berta couldn't get enough of his stories, and was impatient to be involved. 'Every time I came home I brought her revolutionary texts which we discussed, but we also exchanged poems and romantic novels. She wanted to come with me to El Salvador, that was the plan, that we'd go together after she graduated from the *normal* . . . then she got pregnant.'

Zúñiga planned to return to El Salvador for the last rebel offensive, but tried to dissuade Berta from coming with him. 'War isn't romantic, it's cruel, and I didn't want Berta to come, but she was insistent.' Doña Austra, who knew nothing about her youngest daughter's war ambitions, was at the same time trying to ship Berta overseas to have the baby, in order to avoid a town scandal. Berta refused, and the young lovers plotted behind her back.

Olivia Marcela Zúñiga Cáceres was born on 28 June 1989. She looked just like her mother. Three weeks later Berta said goodbye to Austra, telling her that she was taking baby Olivia to visit her brother Carlos in Canada. Instead the young parents left the newborn with Zúñiga's sister, who lived in nearby Siguatepeque, and went to join the guerrillas. It would be several months before they held Olivia again. The time Berta spent in El Salvador shaped the rest of her life.

Berta was eighteen years old and still weak from giving birth when she joined the war effort with the National Resistance – one of four guerrilla groups in the coalition that formed the Farabundo Martí National Liberation Front (FMLN). Here, her nom de guerre was Laura or Laurita. Life on the front line was tough. The unit was constantly on the move, and the incursions were rugged and dangerous. The young militants were assigned to logistics and reconnaissance missions – mostly supportive, non-combatant roles. They monitored the radio and put together communiqués for the leadership on what the State Department, Pentagon, European governments, BBC and international groups like Amnesty International were opining about the conflict now in its tenth year. Sometimes they went on separate missions to different parts of the country.

'From the very first sortie, she was intrepid and determined, even going ahead with the exploration unit without me. Berta never cried, she was calm, strong and fearless even when our unit came under attack. She ate and slept when she could, but showed great discipline even though she hadn't been trained,' Salvador said.

Vidalina Morales, a local guerrilla, remembered that Berta seemed shy in Salvador's presence, and that he at times ridiculed her in front of comrades. But she never shied away from any physical or psychological challenge, and positively bristled if anyone suggested taking it easy.

Antonio Montes, nom de guerre Chico, was a twenty-nine-year-old combatant when Berta and Salvador joined his unit on the imposing Guazapa Mountain in Suchitoto, from where the guerrillas launched the last offensive on the capital San Salvador in November 1989. Berta was part of the health brigade, drawing on her childhood experiences with her mother to help treat wounded combatants as they advanced towards the capital. Back at camp after the nine-day offensive, Berta organized classes for the children and taught literacy to adults in the guerrilla-controlled areas, which tried to retain a sense of normality despite being under constant threat of attack. Her commitment to the Salvadoran cause impressed Chico.

'Berta witnessed terrible atrocities, she saw the consequences of war on unarmed civilians and was visibly moved by the suffering. But she was a restless young woman, with a hardworking spirit and willingness to contribute to all sorts of activities with people trying keep their lives going in complex conflict zones. It's clear that these experiences marked the rest of her life.'

In late 1989, as Berta and Salvador prepared for the final offensive, a disarmament deal to end the Contra War in Nicaragua was signed in Honduras. The Tela Accord essentially marked the beginning of the end of the Cold War.

That same year, the once feared general Gustavo Álvarez was killed, prompting Carlos, Berta's big brother, to return home after more than a decade abroad.[20] In 1989, a few days after Álvarez was killed, human rights defender and physician Dr Juan Almendarez was in Bolivia at an anti-tobacco conference when he got word that his name was circulating on a military hit list. After Ambassador Negroponte had him sacked as university rector in 1982, Dr Almendarez had frequently been followed, photographed and harassed, so it came as no surprise. Before boarding the flight home, he told a friend: 'If I don't make it home, tell the world it was the military.' This probably saved his life. Arriving in Honduras, Dr Almendarez was held at gunpoint in an airport taxi by agents from the Argentine Anti-communist Alliance (AAA), School of the Americas graduates operating in cells across Central America. He was taken to the DNI's infamous torture centre in Tegucigalpa for interrogation. 'The main interrogator knew every move I'd made for years, and named several *compañeros* who'd been disappeared and murdered ..."How shall we kill you?" he asked me. "Peel your skin off, cut you in pieces, use a big hammer, or electric shocks, which would you prefer?"' Another interrogator demanded to know who killed General Álvarez. 'I told him that it was probably the CIA, which is what I believed.'[21]

Berta and Salvador returned in February 1990. Berta, almost nineteen, was pregnant with their second child and happy to be reunited with baby Olivia. But the couple remained committed to the cause and would secretly go in and out of the country with high-ranking fighters like Commander Fermán Cienfuegos, whom they escorted between Nicaragua and El Salvador, often via Doña Austra's safe house.

Bertita Isabel Zúñiga Cáceres was delivered at home in La Esperanza by her grandmother on 24 September 1990. But even then, the couple didn't end their militancy. They went back several times, sometimes with both infants who served as the perfect camouflage to smuggle Salvadoran fighters across the border. Once, when Olivia was eighteen months old and just learning to talk, she called out 'Pompa, pompa!' to the soldiers on the border, confusing them with friendly guerrillas on the other side whom she knew as *compas* (short for *compañeros*).

Enough Bloodshed

In El Salvador, 80,000 people died, 1 million were displaced and 8,000 disappeared over twelve years of brutal conflict. In Guatemala, more than 200,000 mostly poor indigenous campesinos were killed in the thirty-six-year war, 93 per cent of them by US-backed forces.[22] The decade-long Contra war in Nicaragua cost 50,000 lives. But no matter how many US tax dollars were funnelled to military dictatorship after military dictatorship, no matter how many weapons and planes America sent, there wasn't a single battlefield victory. Every peace deal, however flawed, was signed thanks to dialogue and negotiations off the battlefield, almost certainly greased by economic interests. Berta and Salvador came home certain of one thing: armed struggle was not the way forward. 'We saw with our own eyes how war generates abuses on each side, and that the majority who died were young, poor men and women who took up arms because they were hungry or forcibly recruited, not because of ideology,' said Salvador. 'Times were changing, and we came home convinced of the need to launch an unarmed social movement. Whatever we did in Honduras, it would be without guns.'

2

The Indigenous Awakening

La Esperanza, 1 January 1994

Berta is perched on the edge of the sofa, glued to the tiny television. It's early and her husband Salvador Zúñiga is still asleep. The children, Olivia, Bertita and Laura, all under the age of five, are busy playing as Berta watches extraordinary events unfold in Chiapas, southern Mexico. This was the day the North American Free Trade Agreement (NAFTA) between Mexico, Canada and the US came into effect.

It was also the day of the Zapatista uprising. Wearing a black ski mask and army fatigues, Rafael Sebastián Guillén Vicente, soon to be known as 'Sub-comandante Marcos' and the public face of the indigenous insurrection, declared war on the Mexican government on live television. 'We, the Zapatistas, say that neo-liberal globalization is a world war, a war being waged by capitalism for global domination,' Marcos said in a statement of intent, as 3,000 armed guerrillas took control of towns from the mountainous highlands to the tropical rainforests across Chiapas. 'That is why we are joining together to build a resistance struggle against neo-liberalism and for humanity,' he exclaimed. A leader was born.

'Salvador, wake up! You have to see this, indigenous people are revolting in Mexico,' Berta urged her husband, trembling with excitement. 'This is it. This is what we've been missing. We need to mobilize *los pueblos indígenas*, go on the offensive and demand our rights!' The events in Mexico were a light-bulb moment for the twenty-four-year-old. Another leader was born.

The newly-weds' small house on the outskirts of La Esperanza was soon filled with members of COPINH, the organization they had founded in March 1993. They released a public statement in solidarity with the Zapatistas and Marcos's demand for work, land, housing, food, health, education, independence, liberty, democracy, justice and peace.

COPINH was founded to revive Lenca fortunes in Honduras. It was, the couple believed, the right political moment to be talking about human rights, indigenous rights and demilitarization in the same breath. In 1992 (the year peace accords ending the civil war were signed in El Salvador) Rigoberta Menchú, a Guatemalan K'iche' Maya feminist leader, was awarded the Nobel Peace Prize, while the UN declared 1993 the first International Year of the World's Indigenous Peoples.

The Zapatista uprising gave COPINH confidence, but, unlike the Zapatistas, COPINH was not about to engage in armed struggle. Berta and Salvador had returned from El Salvador weary of bloodshed. In the midst of its civil war, they had debated class, gender, socialism, and even the limits of armed struggle with guerrilla commanders such as Fermán Cienfuegos. The couple saw dirt-poor campesinos driven towards the guerrilla movement by hunger, not ideology, and were baffled by claims that El Salvador had no more natives while fighting alongside men and women who lamented their sacred lands. Berta and Salvador came home tired of war but

The Indigenous Awakening

excited by the democratic possibilities in Central America after decades of military rule, death squads and social repression. Still, the Zapatista discourse helped the fledgling group grasp how indigenous rights went hand in hand with the protection of land, forests and rivers.[1] Safeguarding indigenous communities meant defending their territories. Soon after COPINH unveiled a strategy of direct action by organizing roadblocks, sit-ins and continuous protests to stop illegal logging in the Lenca community of Yamaranguila, a few miles west of La Esperanza. They were loud, stubborn and successful, making instant enemies of local landowners but eventually forcing out over thirty logging projects from ancestral forests across three departments. Berta and Salvador understood that indigenous rights were human rights. However, for the state and most other Hondurans in 1994, indigenous people didn't exist. The pre-Hispanic communities were considered living fossils, the stuff of history and folklore, not an ancestral community with rights. In response, COPINH hit upon a simple idea that turned out to be a stroke of genius.

The Pilgrim Marches

In June 1994, thousands of Lencas descended from the mountains in western Honduras and marched on the capital Tegucigalpa, to present the Liberal government of Carlos Roberto Reina Idiáquez with a list of demands including schools, clinics, better roads and, most importantly, recuperation and protection of ancestral territory. Scores of men, women and children from other indigenous communities – Maya, Chorti, Misquitu, Tolupan, Tawahka and Pech – joined the peregrination along the way. From the north coast came the colourfully dressed, drumming Garifunas: Afro-Hondurans who descend from West and Central African, Caribbean, European and Arawak people exiled to Central America by the British after a slave revolt in the late eighteenth century. Honduras had never seen anything like it. Curious crowds from the mixed Spanish and indigenous mestizo majority came to help the marchers with food, clothes and bedding during the six days it took to walk over 200 km. The pilgrims were even warmly greeted in the capital, where *indio* was a common racist term for those with suspected indigenous roots who mainly worked in low-paid jobs. Nobody expected this. Berta and the Lencas marched under a giant banner celebrating a great chieftain: '*Lempira viene con nosotros de los confines de la historia*' (Lempira comes with us from the confines of history).

When the Spanish invaded in 1524, the Lencas were the largest ethnic group in number and territory, and it was Lempira who united 200 tribes in battle against the invaders. After Lempira was killed in 1537,the Lenca believed a mystical woman would rescue them and restore the defeated nation, or so the myth went.[2] In front of huge crowds and TV cameras, Berta and Salvador impressed with their rousing speeches. So did Pascuala Vásquez, a petite Lenca elder known to everyone as Pascualita. 'We're not here because we love the capital city where there are bridges but no rivers, we're here because we have many needs in the communities, and we have rights, and we demand that the government sits down with us and listens,' she said. The energy and purpose conveyed by this wizened woman with her clarion voice earned her the nickname *primera dama*, first lady. It was the start of something, like a coming-out parade, which promoted the indigenous people of Honduras from fossils to citizens.

Diverse indigenous communities joined forces to create a national movement demanding recognition and rights through hunger strikes, roadblocks and several more pilgrimages – in turn emboldening even bigger multitudes from isolated mountain and coastal villages to march on the capital. In this jubilant atmosphere, Berta connected the dots from local to global.

One Garifuna leader, Miriam Miranda,[3] recalls Berta pausing the march to paint anti-imperial murals on the walls of the US airbase, Palmerola.[4] Militarization and repression, Berta explained as she wielded her paintbrush, go hand in hand with the neo-liberalism pushed by President Reina's predecessor, Rafael Leonardo Callejas, because it is an economic and political model which must destroy some of us in order to thrive.[5] For the first few years, victories came thick and fast. The most important was the ratification of the 1989 Indigenous and Tribal Peoples Convention of the International Labour Organization, known as ILO 169, a binding accord guaranteeing the right to self-determination. Honduras signed up in 1995, in part thanks to pressure by Liberal congresswoman Doña Austra who promoted indigenous and women's rights demanded by COPINH, OFRANEH and others, which Reina's more progressive government was open to. It was the first time Honduras was legally recognized to be a multicultural, multi-ethnic, multi-lingual society.

San Francisco de Opalaca, the birthplace of Pascualita, was declared an indigenous municipality – a landmark postcolonial triumph. A specialist prosecutor for indigenous issues was created to tackle crimes such as violating the right of indigenous communities under ILO 169 to free, prior and informed consultations for projects which could impact on their land, culture or way of life.[6] ILO 169 played a crucial role in the recuperation of small but significant territories lost after colonization: over the next few years, COPINH helped more than 200 Lenca communities acquire land titles across five departments. The treaty was the precursor to the UN

Declaration on the Rights of Indigenous Peoples which Honduras adopted in 2007. Both international tools deal with the mandatory rights of indigenous peoples to their cultural and spiritual identity, habitat, food, water, self-government, control over territories and natural assets, respect and inclusion. Of course, these instruments didn't put an end to the violation of ancestral and community land rights. But they set the legal battleground for Agua Zarca and hundreds of other projects sanctioned for indigenous territories with blatant disregard for ILO 169.

Old Tactics Die Hard

The new indigenous movement injected energy and optimism into the country's flagging social movement, sociologist Eugenio Sosa told me over coffee in Tegucigalpa. In the mid-1990s, banana workers' and campesino unions were in crisis, having grown rather too cosy with the government and the United States after the 1954 strike. Meanwhile, new exploitative industries such as the *maquilas* or assembly factories strongly discouraged unionization;[7] student and socialist groups had been decimated in the dirty war, leaving only the teachers and fledgling human rights groups battling to find the disappeared, demilitarize the country and promote women's rights. The indigenous movement with its dynamic leadership worried the ruling elites – and Uncle Sam. Despite no sniff of armed insurgency, rumours spread that Honduras could become the next Chiapas, and the response was predictable. More counterinsurgency – but this time with a softer face, the so-called battle for hearts and minds.

World Vision, the American evangelical aid charity with an anti-communist vocation, appeared in neglected Lenca communities alongside USAID, offering maize, medicines and housing. US soldiers helped construct schools and hospitals. 'It was a clear reaction to the uprising by indigenous people in a strategically important zone for the US,' said Salvador Zúñiga. 'There was constant scaremongering about armed insurgency, but the real fear was that people were starting to understand and demand their rights, and COPINH was achieving victories through unarmed mobilizations.'

Global to Local

The hard-won government pledges on ancestral land rights were at odds with aggressive development programmes being pushed across Latin America by international financiers like the World Bank, International Monetary Fund (IMF) and US Treasury. Honduras, like many other countries, was pressured to introduce market-based land reforms, which included allowing the sale and mortgage of *ejido* (collectively owned) land for the first time. This, it was claimed, would unlock the wealth of the poor as the capital raised could be invested to make the land more productive. This economic thinking was part of the Washington Consensus – a set of free-market policies including free trade, floating exchange rates, deregulation and privatization of state enterprises like roads, health and education.

President Rafael Callejas promoted programmes to break up collective land rights of indigenous and campesino communities in favour of multinational conglomerates. This is what ignited the modern-day land conflicts in Honduras, by pitting rural communities opposed to environmentally destructive projects (like the Agua Zarca and Los Encinos dams in Lenca territory, the Jilamito and Pajuiles dams in the northern region of Atlántida, and African palm plantations in the Bajo Aguán) against the country's elites and international financiers invested in so-called green energy projects. Although Berta would be mostly remembered as an environmentalist who defended rivers, she was much more than that, because she always understood local struggles in political and geopolitical terms. Marvin Barahona, a modern historian at the National School of Fine Arts in Tegucigalpa, said that the introduction of neo-liberal policies in Honduras made the environment a double-edged sword. 'For Berta, the environment became an instrument of struggle, while for the government and international investors it represented a development policy with profit potential.'

Spiritual Awakening

Berta was raised in a staunch Catholic churchgoing family, her husband Salvador as an Evangelical Christian. Back in the 1960s and 70s most people were either ignorant or ashamed of any indigenous heritage, after centuries of 'civilization' policies imposed by the state and Church which had robbed native peoples of their language, customs, religion and collective pride. Yet, both Cáceres and Zúñiga proudly identified as Lencas, even though their parents didn't.

Berta conducted spiritual Lenca ceremonies with her children, and encouraged them to be critical of organized religion, though she never completely rejected Christianity – meeting Pope Francis at the Vatican in October 2014.[8] She admired a progressive Jesus much as she did the murdered Salvadoran prelate, Monseñor Óscar Romero, but was also inspired by the spirituality of First Nation and Native American tribes, and Garifuna and Mayan customs.

COPINH's pioneering struggle centred on rescuing Lenca identity, customs and traditions. Pascualita, the little old woman who spoke at the march on Tegucigalpa, was a key figure in this aspiration and would become COPINH's spiritual leader. An oral historian and Lenca legend in her own right, she is instantly recognizable by the bright red clothes that she wears to ward off evil spirits, along with an oversized woolly hat to ward off the chilly La Esperanza wind.

Born in 1952, Pascualita was brought up a Catholic Lenca – part of a churchgoing family with strong indigenous traditions. At their core is a spiritual connection with Mother Earth nurtured through the *compostura* – smoke ceremonies with offerings such as cacao, candles, firecrackers and the ancient maize-based liquor chicha, banned by colonial powers because they couldn't tax it. 'I taught Berta and the communities we visited the *compostura*, the river and angel blessings I learned from my grandparents, but nothing was written down,' said Pascualita. 'From the beginning, it was a political *and* a spiritual fight.'

In the early 1990s these ceremonies were still practised in many communities, but often in secrecy. Berta encouraged communities to revive ancient customs openly and with pride. Today, every COPINH event starts with a smoke ceremony. If you visit La Esperanza, Pascualita is always on call to explain Lenca traditions and COPINH's role in their rescue.

For Berta, ancestral spirituality and how these spirits bridge the past and the present were fundamental. She helped recover the memory of Lempira as a courageous hero, a symbol of resistance, not just another vanquished native leader. Some would argue that Berta's greatest legacy is the rehabilitation of Lenca culture. It was no coincidence that outside the courthouse, after the first arrests for Berta's murder, people were chanting: '¿*Quienes somos? ¡Venimos de*

Lempira!' (Who are we? We come from Lempira!) Pascualita was there.

Berta and Salvador often visited remote Lenca communities at weekends with the children or *cachorros,* cubs, as she called them. Just like her own experience of helping Austra, her mother, deliver babies when she was a girl, these excursions on foot and horseback exposed the four children to terrible discomfort and beautiful natural wealth. And they loved it.

'They took the four of us everywhere like suitcases, no matter how bad the conditions. We'd tuck our pyjamas into our socks so we didn't get bitten by bed bugs and mosquitoes,' recalls Olivia, the eldest. 'We were brought up to feel proud of our Lenca culture, and strong enough not to care when the other children and teachers called us *indios*.'

Berta hadn't intended to have children so close together, in fact she used to tell her girlfriends at school that she would never get married at all – but then she met Salvador. Four children within six years wasn't easy. In a classic good cop, bad cop scenario, Berta was the disciplinarian, whereas Salvador was more playful. He was a homebody, and became the national figurehead of COPINH, while Berta constantly travelled, forging alliances across the world. Money was tight, and at times they relied upon food packages from Doña Austra. Behind her back, some relatives called Berta a bad mother who cared more about the *indios* than her own children. This hurt.

Berta wasn't like most other mothers in La Esperanza. She hated domestic chores; she wouldn't let the children watch Cartoon Network or spend hours on PlayStation, like some of their cousins. Instead she brought them microscopes, telescopes and dark-skinned dolls from her travels. At night she would sit the four squabbling children in a circle, to talk through their gripes, or to dance or learn about plants and nature. 'All my fun memories are with my dad, but these nightly sessions were very intimate, she would try to open our minds by teaching us right and wrong through spirituality,' said Bertita. 'It was hard for her when we were little, but she definitely enjoyed us and motherhood much more as we got older.'

'At home we were little devils,' said Olivia, laughing as she recalled leading a sibling protest armed with homemade placards opposing some parental diktat. Physically, Olivia is the most like her mum. She too is stubborn, charming, rebellious and a persuasive public speaker. Their relationship, however, wasn't a smooth one, perhaps because they were too similar, perhaps rooted in unresolved grievances. Their relationship was a work in progress when Berta was murdered.[9]

Miriam Miranda: Closer Than Sisters

Those who took part in the pilgrim marches of 1994 and 1995 say they were characterized by energy, solidarity, and genuine hopes for a more just and inclusive Honduras. It was during those heady times that an unbreakable bond was forged between Berta and the Garifuna leader Miriam Miranda. As two clever, strong, courageous women, they grew closer than sisters, becoming co-conspirators in every sense of the word. If Berta was in trouble, Miriam was the first person she called, and vice versa. Both were threatened, put on hit lists and hated by the political, economic and military elites whom they fought fiercely with words. Similarly, their organizations bonded like non-identical twins.

I interviewed Miriam in Vallecito,[10] a 1,200-hectare (3,000-acre) parcel of ancestral land in the municipality of Limón on the north-east coast, that was reclaimed by OFRANEH in

2012 after illegally being given away by the government. The Garifunas have a patchwork of ancestral titles dating back to colonial times across this zone, but these days a combination of rising sea levels and relentless land grabs have made Vallecito an isolated oasis.

In these parts, palm oil magnates obtained scores of land titles thanks to a market-based modernization plan which allowed new claims for unused, untitled land from the National Agrarian Institute (INA). Ignoring the ancestral land claims by the Garifunas, the INA handed out new titles to new 'settlers' who promptly sold them to the palm oil magnates. In this area alone, the Garifuna communities went from owning 20,000 hectares to 400 within a decade.

Out of options, the Garifunas obtained Vallecito in the same way as the unscrupulous palm barons, forced to make a claim for land that belonged to their ancestors. That didn't stop Miguel Facussé, the most powerful palm oil tycoon in Central America, from planting palms there anyway. But, in a rare example of justice, Facussé was forced to return the 100 hectares after a Supreme Court ruling in 1999. Not long after that ruling, a local strongman turned drug trafficker took over Vallecito by force and built himself a mansion, complete with landing strips and a small dock to unload cocaine.

Aurelia Arzú, nicknamed La Patrona for having coached a male football team, was among 150 Garifunas who took back Vallecito in 2012. Back then, the still nights were frequently interrupted by the sound of motorized *lanchas* (canoe-like small boats) and small planes apparently descending towards Facussé's sprawling Farallones ranch. These days, they hear only lanchas, which makes sense, as US drug intelligence indicates that most cocaine now arrives by sea.

In Vallecito the Garifuna dream is simple: build a safe community and revive traditional gastronomy. Plant yams, yuca and acres of coconut palms, open a coconut oil processing plant, and one day buy lanchas to go out fishing in the Caribbean waters beyond the plantation. But Berta and Miriam understood that struggles never really end where there's money to be made. The area is blessed with minerals, oil, unspoilt beaches and fertile land, which doubtless explains why Vallecito was earmarked as a potential site for a 'model city' – a custom-made community with its own police force, laws, government and tax system designed to attract foreign investors by offering absolute control with no risks. The model city plan is so radical a neo-liberal experiment that even Berta and Miriam were shocked.

Miriam was seven years older than Berta and raised in banana plantations where she witnessed the harsh conditions especially for women, who she also saw suffered most in the shanty towns around the capital Tegucigalpa when she visited with Visitación Padilla in the 1980s. 'These experiences woke me up, and I started speaking out about the Yankee invasion and militarization.' No wonder she and Berta bonded.

Berta loved coming to Vallecito, enchanted by the Garifuna rituals with their smoke, drums, herb-infused liquor and dancing. By all accounts she wasn't a great dancer, but that didn't stop her joining in.

'We were sisters, friends, colleagues. We were together in every important moment,' Miriam said, describing a scary incident when she was beaten and detained by police and Berta was the first to call.[11] Then, a few years later in Vallecito, Miriam had to flee into the hills after she and other Garifuna activists tried to stop the narcos from building a landing strip on the reclaimed land. Berta was the first to arrive.

Miriam recalls Berta being deeply hurt by accusations that she was a bad mother: 'As women, it's much harder for us to take on leadership and political roles, we're not allowed to show any weakness in such a patriarchal system.

'She was criticized for neglecting her children, for choosing *la lucha*, the struggle, over motherhood. Berta loved her children, but she loved this country, too. She refused to accept that there must be poor people so there can be rich people, not when Honduras has so much potential and enough resources for all of us to live well.'

3

The Neo-liberal Experiment

Quebec City, April 2001

Every head of state from the Americas, except Fidel Castro, was in Quebec City for negotiations on the Free Trade Area of the Americas, a proposed duty-free zone stretching from Canada to Chile, excluding Cuba. Although it was lauded as revolutionary by big business, many believed the neo-liberal FTAA (ALCA in Spanish) would only intensify poverty and inequality across the region and threaten the survival of rural and indigenous communities. It was a crisp spring day and Berta was there wrapped up, pumped and ready to resist on behalf of the Lencas.

Tens of thousands of spirited protesters armed with drums, flutes, confetti and canny banners had descended on the picturesque French colonial city in eastern Canada, determined to force the continent's leaders to pay attention. Amid the colourful crowd were indigenous leaders, environmental groups, trade unions, students, fringe political parties and anti-poverty campaigners, all ready for open debate and direct action. A giant catapult was being winched up to launch teddy bears towards the summit site, in contrast to the secretive negotiations taking place inside.

Berta was with the Mexican environmentalist Gustavo Castro. They had travelled to Quebec up the east coast as part of a speaking tour organized by Rights Action,[1] a not-for-profit group investigating the impact of North American trade, economic and security policies in Central America. 'Berta's family history and early experiences fostered a clear local-to-global perspective,' said Rights Action's Grahame Russell. 'She understood that free trade agreements were just the latest repackaged tool of repression, a new twist on the same exploitative economic model imposed on Central America for hundreds of years.' Berta told audiences in Toronto and Montreal: 'Free trade deals are legal tools to impose a model that advocates taking control over the planet's natural resources for profit.' She went on: 'I don't accept a system that must destroy some in order to thrive. Cutting down forests our ancestors protected for centuries cannot be called development . . . we need to fight this oppressive political and economic model together. This is *our* problem.'

Details were already emerging about the Plan Panama Puebla (PPP), a US-inspired Mexican brainchild, soon to be launched as the missing development piece of the neo-liberal jigsaw puzzle. It was extolled as the mother of all development projects, tackling poverty by opening up the 'backward' Mesoamerican region to the global market. The two central pillars of PPP were transport infrastructure – a network of highways, dry canals and ports to speed up the movement of freely traded products – and energy liberalization: specifically, an increased capacity to generate energy by constructing dozens of dams and gas and oil pipelines, and then transport it further and faster by connecting the region's energy grids from North America to Colombia (a sort of NAFTA–CAFTA energy grid).

The multibillion-dollar, mainly publicly funded, project promoted and depended on a momentous shift of the region's economy, from small-scale farming to agro-industry and manufacturing, and expanding private control over natural resources. It included the Mesoamerican Biological Corridor which sounds like a good thing – a mammoth protected nature reserve – but in reality involved patenting the genetic codes of plants and animals in the second biggest bank of bio-genetic resources in the world. Why? To provide essential raw material for biotechnologies that could revolutionize medicines and food production, but without sharing economic benefits with local people. You could call it corporate bio-piracy.

PPP enthusiasts such as the Mexican president, Vicente Fox, considered this the only way to lift rural communities out of entrenched poverty.[2] However, the Zapatistas and the Convergence of Movements of the Peoples of the Americas (COMPA) – the fledgling regional coalition where Berta and Gustavo first met – saw PPP as a poverty plan masquerading as development, which would force thousands of rural families to migrate to overcrowded cities or north to the US. Auctioning off rivers, seabeds, fertile plains and forests to the private sector threatened to raze or prohibit access to vast swathes of the ancestral land and natural resources that define the economic, social and cultural survival of countless rural and indigenous peoples. Looking back, nowhere has this played out more flagrantly than in the Isthmus of Tehuantepec, a narrow, richly biodiverse strip of Mexican territory connecting the Pacific and Atlantic oceans, which is home to Huave, Mixe, Zapotec, Zoque and Chontal communities. Its abundance of natural resources – oil, timber, rivers and minerals (silver, copper, iron, crystalline graphite, coal, gypsum and travertine) – has favoured scores of mining, infrastructure and energy projects including oil refineries, electricity substations, dams and massive wind farms. Communities complain that many of these megaprojects provide inadequate information, consultation and compensation, fuelling social opposition, military repression, environmental damage, evictions and forced migration.[3] In Honduras, Berta warned back in 2001 that PPP would be a death sentence for the Lenca people, and the Agua Zarca dam turned out to be a perfect example of this.

Berta was right: it was the PPP that killed her, according to Annie Bird.

At the anti-capitalist gathering in downtown Quebec City, people had had enough of talking. It was time for direct action. But the summit organizers were determined to shield political leaders from the deafening crowds branded as anarchists by Canadian intelligence. A three-metre-high concrete and wire partition was erected around Parliament Hill as a first line of defence. Hundreds of riot cops unleashed a wave of brutality the protesters weren't prepared for. Tear gas engulfed the city in dense, eye-stinging smoke. So much of it was fired that it seeped into the summit hall, forcing delegates to take cover. Berta and Gustavo stood in front of parliament facing the impenetrable chain of riot cops, among protesters drumming and singing. It struck Berta that the demonstration was too far back. '¡*Hermano!* Let's get closer. *Vamos*,' she shouted, grinning at Gustavo, grabbing one end of the blue and white Honduran flag. Gustavo seized the other end and they rushed forward into a cold jet of water from a cannon behind police lines. They were pushed back and soaked, the flag went flying. But Berta jumped up and yelled, 'Let's go again.' This time, blinding tear gas forced the pair back. But they surged forward again and again, recalled Gustavo. 'That was Berta. Always tenacious and always willing to put herself in the middle of every act of resistance. She never lost that energy.'

~

The Neo-liberal Experiment

COPINH, founded as a grassroots organization, managed to stay true to its roots partly because Berta was never power-hungry. Whenever possible, everywhere she went, busloads of COPINH members went with her, meaning she and the organization evolved together. At one anti-FTAA meeting in Cuba, Gustavo and Berta were invited as speakers and put up in a fancy Havana hotel. Berta preferred the cheaper digs with the rest of the COPINH faction. 'COPINH was never a closed shop,' recalls Alba Marconi, who worked alongside Berta for over a decade. 'For Berta, sharing ideas and experiences was fundamental to ensure COPINH was a true grassroots organization where the power and energy came from its base.'

Berta's early years were filled with Cold War drama and meeting the guerrillas seeking sanctuary at her family home. She grew up looking beyond borders, and in COPINH connected the dots between far-flung boardrooms and parliaments and everyday struggles in Lenca communities. Berta wasn't an avid reader or particularly academic: bearing four children at a young age and launching a new organization made university impossible, and her children agree that studying wasn't her thing. But she was an avid learner, an insatiable sponge, who evolved through experiences and through the people she met and debated with late into the night. Her ability to cite community struggles in Kurdistan, Brazil, Guatemala or Canada to explain big issues like capitalism, militarization and patriarchy was impressive. 'I always remember Berta,' said Gustavo, 'with an open notebook under her arm and a pen in her hand, taking constant notes, absorbing everything, and encouraging COPINH colleagues to learn and grow alongside her.'

Convergence of Movements of the Peoples of the Americas (COMPA)

Berta first met Gustavo Castro in 2000, at a three-day event in San Cristóbal de las Casas, a colonial city in the Mexican state of Chiapas (site of the Zapatista uprising that six years earlier had inspired COPINH). It was a ground-breaking confluence of diverse movements from across the Americas and Caribbean, with the aim of formulating a unified political strategy. No easy task, but COMPA united as an anti-capitalist coalition at a time when identifying as such still carried the risk of being branded as communist.[4] Berta, then twenty-nine, was assigned a high-profile role alongside Gustavo to draft the coalition's message of intent. The six agreed objectives were struggle *for* gender equality, indigenous rights and sustainable rural development, and *against* the FTAA, militarization, and external debt and structural adjustment policies imposed by international banks under the Washington Consensus.

Berta demonstrated intelligence, sharp analysis and political know-how beyond her years, alongside an indomitable 'yes we can' attitude. 'Berta helped make Honduras visible,' said Gustavo. 'Until then, its social movements, political struggles and resistance were largely unknown to the rest of the region.'

COMPA served as a bridge connecting communities across the continent during six intense years of resistance. The collective produced educational radio soaps, worksheets, books, and videos about PPP, biodiversity and free trade which Berta took back to her base in Honduras. COPINH travelled to Guatemala, where Canadian mines were already polluting water sources and displacing communities; Guatemalans gave workshops in La Esperanza on genetic modification and crop diversity. This fluid exchange of ideas and experiences across borders was pioneering. Over time, the central themes evolved through spin-offs such as the COMPA women's collective where gender equality developed into a broader anti-patriarchal model that Berta sought to integrate into COPINH.

Berta and Salvador separated around 2000, but continued to lead the organization together. In its second decade, COPINH's national profile declined as the indigenous struggle consolidated on the back of important wins. But its international profile grew as it evolved into an organization whose struggle identified with the anti-globalization movement opposed to the neo-liberal economic model. Berta's involvement in COMPA helped her develop a deeper, more structural understanding of the role of international financial institutions and free trade agreements in local land struggles, forced migration, biodiversity and natural resources. COMPA's six original objectives remained central to Berta's struggle to the end.

It's Always about Land

Every conflict in Latin America is, at its heart, about land. Why? Because the distribution of land is directly linked to the distribution of wealth. In Honduras, both are scandalously unequal. This is the most unequal country in Latin America,[5] with the most regressive tax system, and the gap between the richest few and the poor majority keeps growing. Over two-thirds of the population live in poverty.[6] While big cities are marked by gang violence and precarious employment and living conditions, the great majority of the poor are landless peasant farmers and indigenous or Afro-descendant Garifuna and Miskitu peoples. The most arable plains are in the hands of a few: approximately 70 per cent of farmers hold only 10 per cent of land in small plots, while 1 per cent of farmers hold 25 per cent in massive estates.[7] Redressing land inequalities was a central issue for Berta and COPINH, and that meant taking on the country's elites.

The Elites

Las élites, las familias, la oligarquía, los turcos ... catch-all terms used interchangeably for the small group of transnational families whose vast wealth and political power allow them to influence, some would say dictate, public policies to benefit their economic interests. The origin and trajectory of the Honduran elite are unique in the region. These ten or so families played only a supporting role during the first half of the twentieth century, when Honduras was subservient to US capital and geopolitical objectives. Back then, local landowning elites – who got rich and powerful primarily from timber, cattle, cotton and sugar plantations, and mining – were still the biggest *cojones* in town, yet they were in fact the poorest and politically weakest rural elites in Central America. So, in the 1990s, unlike their peers in Guatemala and El Salvador, Honduran landowners found themselves outwitted and unable to evolve fast enough to take advantage of globalization and international capital. Instead, waiting in the wings was the incipient bourgeoisie, composed largely of Christian Palestinians (mostly from Bethlehem) and eastern European Jews.

The ethnic mix of this elite class – most with surnames like Kattán, Canahuati, Násser, Kafati, Atala, Larach and Facussé – is the result of the liberal migration policies of the late nineteenth century. With the Ottoman Empire in decline, there was a wave of migration of Christian Palestinians to Central America, and a handful of families settled in Honduras during the 1870s and 1880s,[8] when the liberal government was trying to attract immigrants with knowledge of modern agricultural techniques to jump-start the economy. Most came via Turkey, where they sought refuge first with Turkish passports, hence the umbrella term *'turcos'* for them all. But the new arrivals rejected generous farming incentives in favour of commerce, to slowly establish themselves as the new merchant class. Initially, they jostled for market position in the shadow of Americans who controlled trade through general stores stocked with cheap merchandise arriving on empty banana cargo ships. But the Arabs brought knowledge of external markets lacking among local landowners, and quickly applied commercial rules (buy cheap, sell dear) to the import-export market.[9] The traders accumulated wealth independent of politics, until the late 1980s and early 1990s when structural adjustment policies – free-market privatization programmes favouring big business – were imposed by international financiers to guarantee loans and debt payments (aka the Washington Consensus). This sparked a massive transfer of state wealth to the private sector, and opened up unparalleled access to global markets, credit and political power for the transnational merchant elites. Soon they were acting not unlike the banana companies, running Honduras like a collection of private fiefdoms and 'counselling' presidents, ambassadors and the military.

The main gold-rush industries to emerge were manufacturing in the maquilas, African palm oil for biofuels and processed food, and coastal tourism. Then, armed with their new capacity to amass capital, the elites smartly diversified, opening banks, newspapers and meat processing plants, as well as investing heavily in energy projects and mines. The locally prominent landowners didn't miss out entirely on the benefits of globalization: by positioning themselves as the bridge between international investors and new transnational elites, they became the boots on the ground, so to speak, in both business and politics.[10] This economic and power shift happened hot on the heels of the US-backed counterinsurgency war which alleged military and business interests determined to protect the status quo. The most formidable manifestation of this symbiotic relationship was the anti-communist, some say fascist, Association for the Progress of Honduras (APROH), founded in 1983. This club, joined by most major Honduran industrialists, promoted deregulation, free trade and a ruthless response to social movements demanding better wages and conditions. APROH's founding president was General Gustavo Álvarez Martínez, commander of Battalion 3-16.

Since then, the rural poverty generated by land inequality has been compounded by climate change and natural disasters like Hurricane Mitch in 1998; rising food prices; systematic land grabs by agribusiness and tourism developers; and shocking levels of violence perpetrated by state security services and private militias contracted by organized criminal gangs, corrupt politicians and seemingly reputable businesses, at times all working together.

Paradoxically, it was this complex set of harsh conditions which sparked new grassroots social and political movements like COPINH and campesino collectives challenging land distribution in the Bajo Aguán. This pitted the campesinos against feudal king and political heavyweight Miguel Facussé Barjum.

Facussé trained as an aeronautical engineer in Indiana, in the American Midwest, and started his career by converting war planes into commercial carriers, but he built his fortune and notoriety through Dinant Chemicals.[11] In the 1980s, during the Contra years, he served as chief economic adviser to the Liberal president Roberto Suazo Córdova *and* vice-president of APROH;[12] he even endorsed selling off Honduras to foreign investors to resolve its fiscal woes. This was Facussé's breakthrough decade, a time when political connections and capitalist instinct helped him take lucrative advantage of a controversial debt restructuring programme.[13] This, and other economic policies blueprinted in the Facussé Memorandum,[14] acted as a springboard to convert the evolving merchant class into a cash-rich globally oriented agro-industrial bourgeoisie, perfectly positioned for foreign investors.

But Miguel Facussé was no political ideologue. He believed in making money, and that is what drew him to the fertile Bajo Aguán. The Bajo Aguán was dominated by banana plantations in the first half of the twentieth century, but the population and crop production nosedived in 1974 after Hurricane Fifi destroyed everything, including the railway, and the fruit moguls abandoned the region. Fifi accelerated major agrarian reforms designed by military dictator General López Arellano, who used public funds and post-hurricane international aid to rebuild the region and entice landless peasants to farm uncultivated plains in exchange for community land titles. The general became an unlikely campesino hero, sanctioning technical and financial support to more than 4,000 farming families organized into eighty-four cooperatives. It paid off: by the 1980s the lower Aguán valley was one of the most diverse crop regions in Honduras, known as the grain basket of Central America. But the glory days were short-lived thanks to the imposition of inedible, invasive African palms.

The lofty palm species was aggressively promoted from

the early 1990s by World Bank-funded modernization programmes.¹⁵ The palms were lauded as the ultimate cash crop which would finally lift peasant farmers out of poverty. Then the official line changed: campesinos were no longer capable of farming palms, because they were too tall and required machinery to extract the fruit and oil. Technical assistance and credit from the government plummeted just as global prices crashed, a devastating combination which asphyxiated the farmers. This wasn't down to Lady Luck: the plan was always to let the cooperatives fail, affirmed campesino leader Yoni Rivas. Waiting in the wings to pounce was Facussé.

Agrarian law prohibits collective or *ejidal* legal titles from being sold or mortgaged without permission from the National Agrarian Institute (INA). To circumvent this inconvenience, President Callejas approved a municipal law in 1993 which allowed local governments to sell land titles for a period of three months only.¹⁶ This they did via hundreds of small transactions benefiting a handful of powerful businessmen, who had woken up to the profit potential of exporting palm oil for biofuels and processed food. The sales were rushed through with total disregard for *ejidal* and ancestral land titles owned by Garifuna communities. How did they get the deeds? Some campesinos sold up for the money, but far more were duped or intimidated into signing over the land. The wannabe palm magnates made alliances with local politicians to convince cooperative leaders that there was no hope of competing with modernization, so best to sell up and move on. To deal with those who couldn't be convinced, the cooperatives were infiltrated and divided, and secret meetings known as *misas negras* (black masses) were convened under menacing military supervision. And if that failed, stubborn campesino leaders were tortured, abducted and killed, starting with the president and treasurer of the San Isidro cooperative in 1990. In other words, good old-fashioned corporate counterinsurgency. Thousands of campesino families were evicted: they went from being landowners to pawns on their own land – a starting gun for a protracted bloody struggle that has yet to end.[17] Facussé was the biggest beneficiary, gaining control over large swathes of Aguán and beyond for industrial palm oil production. The other major winners were the Salvadoran Reynaldo Canales and the Nicaraguan-born René Morales, whose legal affairs were handled by lawyer Roberto Pacheco Reyes, who later became the secretary of the Agua Zarca dam company, DESA. The three men rapidly acquired the majority of the cooperatives and began importing unregulated armed private security guards to work alongside the military to protect their interests. This toxic mix of ambition, political connections, bullish tactics and military alliances helped turned the Aguán into one of the deadliest parts of the country. The violence was fuelled by the West's drive for 'clean energy'. The big fat clean energy lie. But as always, it's about the land.

Then the coup happened, and the struggle got harder, faster and deadlier.

4

The Dream and the Coup

Toncontín Airport, Tegucigalpa: 5 July 2009

Berta stood arm in arm with Miriam Miranda among the crowd waiting that Sunday afternoon to welcome back Manuel 'Mel' Zelaya. It had been exactly a week since an elite military unit bundled the Honduran president onto a military plane bound for Costa Rica, after having kicked in the front door of his private residence in leafy Tres Caminos.[1] It was 6 a.m., and Zelaya was ordered to come downstairs holding his hands high, like a common criminal. 'Shoot me,' he dared them, still in his pyjamas, 'if your orders are to kill me.' Instead he was flown fifty miles north-west to the Palmerola military airport, which is also where the US war on drugs mission is headquartered. The deposed president stared out of the window at hundreds of battle-ready soldiers as the plane refuelled. The lights were out, the internet was down, radio and television sets stood silent, and church doors were closed.

Zelaya had been warned that a coup could be imminent, but he wouldn't believe it. 'You're living in the Jurassic period,' he told advisers. 'This is the twenty-first century, the world wouldn't allow it.' But he was wrong. Zelaya was ousted in an old-fashioned coup d'état plotted by a powerful cabal of ultra-right business, political, religious and military players. It was still dark when the plane left for Costa Rica.

A week later, Zelaya was heading back to Honduras after crisis talks with the UN and Latin American heads of state. Berta and Miriam were anxious. The Garifuna contingent were drumming loudly and the air was thick with ceremonial smoke; the atmosphere was charged.

Zelaya thought it safe to return, but the coup plotters had other ideas. Congress had produced a fake resignation letter hours after Zelaya was deposed. The Supreme Court issued a secret arrest warrant based on trumped-up charges and named Congress leader Roberto Micheletti as his replacement, while on television Cardinal Óscar Rodríguez warned that Zelaya's return could trigger a bloodbath.[2] Ironically, in a country so long ruled by military governments, the armed forces had been the last democratic pillar standing until the generals also flipped. After that, it was left to ordinary people to flood into the streets, demanding democracy be restored and Zelaya allowed to serve the final six months of his term. As tension built, security forces surrounded the airport.

Word spread that Zelaya's plane was approaching. A small section of the crowd ran past cordons towards the runway, where soldiers and army trucks were stationed to prevent the plane from touching down. Suddenly there were gunshots, followed by screams. Isis Obed Murillo Mencías, a nineteen-year-old grocery clerk, had been shot in the back of the head. He was the first victim of the coup.[3] Zelaya's wife, Xiomara Castro, was in the crowd and called the military chief, Romeo Vásquez Velásquez, pleading for the gunfire to stop. 'Are you going to shoot down Mel's plane?' she asked. 'No,' said Vásquez, 'he's not an enemy of

Honduras. This is a political crisis; your husband is my friend.' He explained he would not let the plane land because to do so would mean arresting Zelaya. 'I won't humiliate him and risk chaos,' he told Xiomara, and hung up. Sparing her husband's life was a modern twist on what was an old-school Latin American coup.

After the fatal gunfire, it was announced that a military curfew would start in an hour. Anyone on the streets after 6 p.m. would face arrest. Berta and Miranda watched Zelaya's plane swerve up and away and embraced each other tearfully. The last time they'd been together at Toncontín airport, it was to welcome Hugo Chávez, the Venezuelan president. A week, they say, is a long time in politics and now Berta wondered if she would still stand for the vice-presidency if Zelaya wasn't allowed back before the November elections.

'We cried because we knew what this meant,' Miriam told me years later. 'Until then, we could still hope democracy would be restored. But when the plane wasn't allowed to land, we knew the only option was resistance, which meant social movements would be repressed and leaders like us targeted. It was never about Mel or any political party, it was about fighting to restore the rule of law. We cried because at that moment we understood that it was going to be a long, hard struggle, and we were right. Berta is dead, and the struggle continues.'

Making Friends, Losing Friends

Mel Zelaya, wearing his trademark cowboy boots and white sombrero, was inaugurated on 27 January 2006 inside a packed-out national stadium, twenty-five years after the end of military rule. The fifty-three-year-old landowner had beaten National Party veteran Porfirio 'Pepe' Lobo Sosa by promising a new kind of Liberal government, centred on transparency and citizen participation. At the inauguration he announced an end to open pit mining, a new reforestation programme, help for small businesses, and energy reform to cut dependence on fossil fuels. The rousing speech left his grassroots supporters enthused, his rivals confounded, and the economic elites reassured by warm words from Carlos Flores Facussé, the business-friendly former president and political dealmaker. Zelaya thanked God, Cardinal Rodríguez, indigenous communities and the new president of Congress, Roberto Micheletti, before leaving feeling pretty pleased with himself.

Zelaya was still basking in the glow when US ambassador Charles Ford called to invite him to lunch at the embassy.[4] After a couple of hours of diplomatic chitchat in Spanish,[5] Ford gave Zelaya a sealed white envelope. 'He said not to open it until I got back to the Casa Presidencial,' Zelaya told me at the Libre HQ more than a decade later (it's a story I'd already heard, one he's often recounted over the years). According to Zelaya, the envelope contained a list of nine ministries, the important ones like defence, security, foreign affairs and finance, each alongside three names of potential ministers whom the US would find acceptable.[6] 'He gave me three options for each ministry, letting me pick one was the democratic part ... In Honduras, a recommendation by the US is a thinly veiled order.' I asked Zelaya what he had done with the list. 'I threw it away.' Whether fully or partly true, this incident was the beginning of the end of Zelaya's relationship with Ford.[7]

Two years later, Ford sent a notably hostile cable. 'Zelaya remains very much a rebellious teenager, anxious to show his lack of respect for authority figures ... There also exists a sinister Zelaya, surrounded by a few close advisers with ties to both Venezuela and Cuba and organized crime.' He continued,

> Unlike most other Honduran leaders in recent times, Zelaya's view of a trip to the big city means Tegucigalpa and not Miami or New Orleans ... I have found Zelaya's real views of the United States hidden not too very deeply below the surface. In a word, he is not a friend. His views are shaped not by ideology or personal ambitions but by an old-fashioned nationalism where he holds the United States accountable for Honduras' current state of poverty and dependency ... The last year and a half of the Zelaya Administration will be, in my view, extraordinarily difficult for our bilateral relationship ... Honduran institutions and friendly governments will need to be prepared to act privately and in public to help move Honduras forward.

Just over a year later, Zelaya was deposed. What had gone wrong?

The two most popular theories on the coup are that it was to prevent Zelaya from amending the constitution in order to stay in power, and that it was orchestrated by the US, who feared he was going rogue and could become the next Hugo Chávez. The truth is more straightforward: it was about protecting the wealth and privilege enjoyed by the country's elites. 'The coup reminded us that the Honduran oligarchy won't tolerate even minor reforms if these changes affect their profits,' said sociologist Eugenio Sosa.

Or, as the former finance minister Hugo Noé Pino put it: 'The economic elites claimed Honduras was moving towards twenty-first-century socialism, but Zelaya's fiscal policies were modest, never radical. What they actually feared was losing their absolute grip over the country, that a few state contracts and concessions could slip out of their hands.' This is perhaps what the US, too, feared most – losing its absolute influence over a country it had dominated economically and politically for over a century. And what could be worse than losing it to the number one enemy, Hugo Chávez?

But Zelaya's alleged transformation from capitalist landowner to socialist was unlikely, and untrue.[8] At best he shifted somewhat to the left, partly because a close circle of progressive advisers encouraged him to listen to and form alliances with civil society groups and Chávez, and partly because the US and its Honduran allies refused to concede on a single issue.

Oil

At the top of Zelaya's presidential to-do list was energy.[9] He convened a meeting with the Honduran who's who of oil requesting them to abandon or reduce the 'fuel formula', a shady tariff which enabled industrialists (distributors, importers, petrol station dealerships) to fix prices and overcharge the state by 4 or 5 Lempiras per gallon. No deal, we won't give up a penny, came the response. Soon after, Mel opened a bidding war and approached Chávez about buying cheap oil from Venezuela, which was already extending its net across Latin America through the Petrocaribe agreement.[10] Zelaya's search for cheaper oil started a political war. Ford warned Zelaya that the proposed deal with Chávez 'was changing the rules of the game' and could jeopardize a pending US aid package. Business leaders, those with oil interests and others, also warned against picking a fight with the US, the country's principal trading partner. But Zelaya is visceral and combative by nature, and his mind was made up. Soon after, in June 2006, Zelaya met with President George W. Bush. Bush presided over a two-hour meeting at the Oval Office, also attended by Vice-President Dick Cheney, Secretary of State Condoleezza Rice and Ambassador Ford. I've heard several versions regarding the exact words that were uttered at that meeting. Arístides Mejía, then defence minister, remembers it as follows: 'Look, Mr President,' said Bush, 'I know you've got an oil problem but listen to me, my family is in the oil business, so I know what I'm talking about, the market sets the price. Chávez can't give you a better price, he's just going to bring you problems.'

He went on about Chávez for ten minutes or so, according to Mejía, before finishing in Spanish with '*Cuidado con Chávez*' (Careful with Chávez). Mel responded smoothly: '*Mira, señor presidente*, a famous French philosopher once said that great men are measured by the problems they solve. But Chávez is a small problem, there's no need to spend so much time worrying about him.' Bush smiled and the tension was broken. 'Who's the French thinker you pulled out of the bag?' Mejía asked after the meeting. 'No idea, I made him up,' said Zelaya. Honduras joined Petrocaribe in December 2007.[11]

Zelaya's allies were more perturbed about joining Chávez's other regional trade project, ALBA.[12] He signed up anyway, with Chávez at his side, promising cheap oil for a hundred years and free tractors for campesinos to boost food production. Love him or hate him, Chávez had a flair for name-calling, and he took the opportunity to rub up the country's businessmen and media moguls, calling them *pitiyanquis*. The catchy insult made headlines, as did calling Cardinal Rodríguez a parrot of the empire. Yet despite the anti-US posturing and public displays of affection, Chávez and Zelaya were not especially close, personally or politically. 'Chávez was a military man who never took Mel seriously, saw him as a cowboy in politician's clothes,' said the academic Víctor Meza, Zelaya's interior minister. 'The relationship was pragmatic and opportunistic, never ideologically driven,' said economist Hugo Noé Pino. 'Both were populists and provocateurs, but that's where the similarity ends.'

Berta backed Zelaya's alliance with Petrocaribe and ALBA, and respected Chávez, though she was privately very critical of the imposition of energy and petrol projects on indigenous territories in Venezuela. 'My mum didn't blindly follow. She taught us never to idealize anyone, including her,' said daughter Bertita. Still, the Comandante Chávez was for a while Berta's online profile picture.

Energy

In 2006, ENEE, the national electricity company, was on the verge of bankruptcy after years of mismanagement, corruption and perverse contracts favouring a tiny handful of suppliers and distributors. Prices were high, defaults mounting, and blackouts long and frequent.[13] The energy matrix was dominated by oil- and coal-fired plants controlled by two of the country's richest industrialists: Fredy Násser, son-in-law of Miguel Facussé, and Schucry Kafie. They boasted lucrative contracts, negotiated in the early 1990s during a regional energy crisis, in which ENEE paid fixed prices and remained responsible for repairs and maintenance. The energy magnates were furious when these and other inflated contracts were sent to Congress for revision.[14] But ENEE was haemorrhaging money, so in 2007 Zelaya sent in the big guns, the defence and finance ministers, to stop the rot. (The finance aspect makes sense, but deploying the armed forces seems like a retrograde step in a fragile democracy.)[15] Mejía asked General Romeo Vásquez to put together a management team to run ENEE. Two of its members are important to Berta's story.

Julián Pacheco Tinoco, then a colonel and head of military protocol, was assigned to manage human resources at ENEE. An SOA-trained counterinsurgency and intelligence specialist, Pacheco went on to become security minister under Juan Orlando Hernández (president since 2014), with overall responsibility for policing COPINH protests against Agua Zarca and for providing protection to Berta,[16] as well as to hundreds of other threatened defenders and journalists – a position he held when she was killed. Pacheco was named in at least two separate US drug trafficking cases involving Los Cachiros, the criminal group which thrived in the department of Colón during his time as regional commander. He was also targeted in a US Drug Enforcement Administration (DEA) investigation, alongside Juan Orlando Hernández, into 'large-scale drug trafficking and money laundering activities relating to the importation of cocaine into the United States' dating back to 2013,[17] according to court documents unsealed in 2019. Pacheco has never been indicted and has denied any wrongdoing.

The other relevant character was Roberto David Castillo Mejía, a second lieutenant in the Intelligence and Counter-Intelligence Department, who in 2004 graduated from the prestigious US military academy West Point with a degree in electrical engineering. Castillo was assigned as head of operations at ENEE's Tegucigalpa electricity dispatch centre. He so impressed his employers that in January 2008, when the rest of the military intervention team left after having apparently rescued ENEE from collapse, he stayed on to work with the newly appointed director, Rixi Moncada.[18] Arístides Mejía said Moncada asked for Castillo to stay on; Moncada claimed it was the other way around. What's clear is that Castillo was looking for a way out of the army, reluctant to serve the full eight years agreed in return for the West Point subsidy. Castillo was formally hired in January 2008 as management control coordinator, a fancy title for technical expert. Over the next twenty months, until September 2009, Castillo improperly claimed salaries from both ENEE and the armed forces, profiting by 212,986 Lempiras (around $9,000), according to a government audit. He was also rebuked for selling office supplies and computer accessories from his company, Digital Communications SA,[19] to the armed forces at inflated prices in 2007 and 2008, and ordered to repay 270,568 Lempiras (around $11,000). The sales violated state contracting rules, and auditors were not fooled by his name having been removed from the company just before the sales. I spoke to an old army friend I'll call Adrián, another graduate officer who, like Castillo, felt uncomfortable in the military environment. Adrián claimed that Castillo offered him a 10 per cent cut if he helped secure similarly overpriced sales. 'I asked him why not just lower prices, win the contracts fairly, and not pay bribes, but he just laughed.'

In October 2007, David Castillo travelled to Brazil with ENEE to open negotiations with Constructora Norberto Odebrecht to finance and build two new mega dams, Los Llanitos and Jicatuyo, on the Ulúa River. This is the country's most important waterway, flowing 400 km north to the Caribbean and connecting to the Gualcarque in Río Blanco. The contract was signed in January 2009 by Moncada and Zelaya, and modified a year later, post-coup, at an ENEE board meeting attended by Castillo.

Odebrecht is a subsidiary of Odebrecht SA, the region's

largest construction conglomerate, which in 2016 admitted to spending hundreds of millions of dollars in corrupt payments to foreign political parties, campaign funds and politicians, in order to grease the wheels of public works projects such as gas pipelines, airport terminals and hydroelectric dams.[20] In the biggest corruption scandal ever uncovered in Latin America, executives eventually admitted paying bribes in over half the countries on the continent, as well as in Angola and Mozambique, among others, and in a leniency deal agreed to pay $2.6bn in fines to US, Swiss and Brazilian authorities. In Honduras, prosecutors announced in early 2018 that several officials, from three administrations (presidents Zelaya, Micheletti and Lobo), were under investigation for possible Odebrecht-linked corruption. By mid-2019, no charges had been brought, but the case remained open.

Berta first met Zelaya in the mid-1990s when he was director of the social development fund (FHIS), working closely with Doña Austra, La Esperanza's first female mayor at the time.[21] (Austra was a card-carrying Liberal until the coup, after which she stopped backing the party.) Berta's brother, Gustavo Cáceres, was minister for youth in Zelaya's government. I never asked Berta if she voted for Zelaya. Berta and Salvador advised him after the coup, but she was hardly a *Zelayista*.

Zelaya's negotiations with Brazil irked the energy and construction magnates, as well as community groups like Berta's COPINH and Miriam's OFRANEH who objected to yet more projects being imposed on indigenous and rural lands without free, prior and informed consent. In contrast, the working poor applauded Zelaya's decision to raise the minimum wage by 60 per cent, to $289 in urban areas, to cover the cost of the *canasta básica*, or basket of staple goods. But this move infuriated the business sector. Adolfo Facussé, the bullish business figurehead, accused the president of imposing communist policies in order to create economic chaos and justify tax increases. 'The private sector will resist,' he warned.

I myself first met Zelaya in mid-2017, at party headquarters in Tegucigalpa, where he was coordinating the campaign for the forthcoming elections. It was late, after 9 p.m., and he started the interview disconcertingly: 'Your blouse needs ironing,' he said, rubbing the ever so slightly creased fabric between his thumb and index finger. A typical example of everyday machismo in Honduras, or an attempt to put me off? Probably a bit of both.

Zelaya said that it was during his time as director of the FHIS that he realized that capitalism had turned the country's genuine landowners – the natives and Afro-Hondurans – into its poorest people. 'I dedicated my presidency to governing for the majority but not by taking away from the minority; they did very well in my time.'

Standing for Vice-President

In a deeply polarized society like Honduras, where everyone picks sides, Berta rejected party politics and regarded the country's two-party system as fundamentally corrupt. The transition from military rule to democracy had generated power- and wealth-sharing pacts between the two parties, or at least its uppermost cliques. In practice this meant that whoever won at the ballot box, politics continued to serve the interests of the country's economic elites. Why? Because campaign finances and political careers depend on the same powerful families, who, despite superficial differences, are bound together by the shared political project of making money.

In such a context, how did Berta find herself standing for vice-president? The best person to tell this story is Carlos H. Reyes, a burly, forthright man with an infectious laugh and shiny bald head, whom I interviewed over breakfast in his glorious back garden. Reyes, born in 1940, is the straight-talking leader of what's widely considered the country's most principled and belligerent union, STIBYS, representing the workers in beer and soft drinks factories. In 2009, Reyes was nominated by the Bloque Popular to stand for president, with Berta, Carlos Amaya (son of the revolutionary writer Ramon Amaya) and teacher Maribel Hernández as his running mates.[22] The objective was to break the bipartisan system and open up spaces to new leaders from outside what they regarded as the cesspit of party politics. The Bloque Popular took off in Tegucigalpa at the end of the 1990s as an attempt to halt the privatization juggernaut circling round public services like ENEE, egged on by the IMF and World Bank. Similar blocs or alliances between unions, campesino and indigenous groups, students and teachers sprang up across the country, organizing huge rallies which were frequently met with force.[23] Reyes recalled one particularly thuggish encounter back around August 2004, when thousands marched on Congress, blocking the four entrances into the capital. 'The army surrounded us, but Berta stood up to them face to face. That kid [*cipote*] never backed down, not once in the twenty years I knew her,' he said. Berta was reluctant to stand at first. Back then she wasn't as well known as Salvador Zúñiga, who was the face of COPINH at home while she focused on international work. She accepted the nomination after touring the country, consulting communities: it emerged that people wanted genuine representation, not empty campaign promises, and they wanted deep, genuine, lasting change. They believed Berta could help make that happen.[24]

The Cuarta Urna: Dictator or Democrat?

The first legislation Zelaya sent to Congress was a citizen participation law. This envisaged a Cuarta Urna, or fourth ballot box, at the November 2009 general elections, enabling voters to decide whether a National Constituent Assembly should be convened to amend the 1982 Constitution.[25] The Bloque Popular saw the Cuarta Urna as *the* opportunity for change. Here, finally, was the chance to create a constitution which recognized the country's diverse cultural and ethnic groupings, as in Ecuador and Bolivia. They believed this could open up democratic spaces for genuine community participation and the redistribution of power. It was the Cuarta Urna that convinced Berta that Zelaya was sincere about constructing a new, fairer, more equal Honduras through a social pact between the state and the mass of ordinary people.

But to the country's elites, who had no interest in sharing anything, the Cuarta Urna represented a ticking time bomb. As a sop to their concerns, a popular non-binding vote was scheduled for Sunday 28 June to determine whether or not the Urna would be introduced six months later, concurrent with the general elections.

However, with just over six months left of his term, Zelaya had no friends in high places, and the yes–no vote was ruled unconstitutional by the Supreme Court and outlawed by Congress a few days before it was scheduled. In response, Zelaya ordered army chief General Vásquez to provide logistical support to distribute the ballot boxes. He refused. Zelaya sacked him on Tuesday 24 June, which prompted the commanders and defence minister to resign in protest. A few hours later, troops descended from their barracks into cities across the country. Vásquez was soon reinstated by the Supreme Court justices, who ruled their decision could not be challenged. The electoral tribunal judges likewise declared the consultation illegal and, together with the Attorney General's Office, confiscated all the ballots and locked them inside the Hernán Acosta Mejía airbase. 'There's a coup under way,' Salvador Zúñiga warned Zelaya, but the president refused to believe it. Instead Zelaya led a group of supporters to the base and seized the confiscated ballots, ordering all hands on deck to ensure the materials were delivered and the vote went ahead. It was frenetic.

The first plan to get rid of Zelaya, hatched in Congress, involved mustering a political consensus to declare him mentally unfit for power. When US Ambassador Hugo Llorens cottoned on to this strategy,[26] he called Roberto Micheletti, Carlos Flores and other powerbrokers to make clear it was unconstitutional, and the US would not support it. 'Llorens tried to stop them, but they stopped returning his calls,' said Víctor Meza, the softly spoken former interior minister. 'Them' meant the economic elites, who in the weeks leading up to the Cuarta Urna were busy trying to raise money to finance the coup, and persuading high-ranking judges, politicians, prosecutors and the clergy to play their part in time for the grand finale.

While Micheletti was no coup mastermind,[27] he played an important role as president of Congress in aligning the right-wing section of the Liberal Party with the opposition Nationalists to execute it. The coup made him the most powerful man in Honduras for seven months, during which he defended it like a Cold War victory. Former president Carlos Flores, who helped Zelaya win the presidency, admits orchestrating a campaign against Zelaya in the run-up to the coup, and also a campaign to stop his return to the country, yet denies any direct involvement in the coup! A private jet belonging to his uncle Miguel Facussé was used to fly Zelaya's foreign minister Patricia Rodas out of the country on 28 June, though without his knowledge, Facussé claimed.

General Vásquez had refused to participate in the 'mentally unfit' plot – so what changed his mind?

I interviewed him at the end of 2018 at his gated mansion on the south-westerly edge of the capital.[28] It was here, Vásquez said, that he invited Zelaya, nine days before the coup, to explain his intentions and resolve the Cuarta Urna crisis. But Zelaya came accompanied by his so-called political rival Pepe Lobo, and the evening ended in stalemate. 'Mel said, "It's just a poll." Pepe said, "You want to stay in power." Mel said, "No, I just want change," and it went on like this.' According to Vásquez, Zelaya was more upset by the idea that his own vice-president, Elvin Santos,[29] could be the next ruler than by the looming constitutional crisis. It was just a poll, a non-binding poll, I reminded him. 'You say that, but this little poll had turned everyone against Mel: politicians, and not just the National Party, half of his own party, Church leaders, businessmen, everyone came to this house asking me to find a solution,' Vásquez told me. 'The *empresarios*, the business people, were scared of twenty-first-century socialism. They wanted me to solve the problem with a military coup and restore order to the country, but I said no, even after he sacked me, because I'm not ambitious and Mel was my friend. But when he insulted the armed forces during a television interview, that was too much, we were angry, and the Supreme Court saw an opportunity. Until then, they were all too scared to make a move.'

On Saturday 27 June the mansion was full of ambassadors, congressmen, functionaries, commanders, dealing with the crisis, according to Vásquez. At 11 p.m., sitting in the formal lounge on spotless cream sofas, Vásquez and his commanders made the decision.[30] 'I felt very bad, we were good friends, like brothers, but there was no other option to avoid a huge crisis, perhaps even civil war. It was only a poll, but it had set all the people against one another.' Any regrets? I asked at the end of the interview.

'The truth is, Mel wanted to stay in power. In 2008 Chávez told me, soldier to soldier ... and my intelligence sources in Venezuela confirmed it, that Chávez saw Honduras as the gateway to Central America for his Bolivarian political project.' Even if true, that doesn't mean Chávez would have got his way.

Uncle Sam

The soldiers deployed to execute the coup were from the 1st Battalion, with which US special forces were conducting a training operation. Zelaya had told me that he saw US soldiers milling about at Palmerola as the plane refuelled. Did the Pentagon know, and if so, were they in on it? I asked Vásquez. No, he said, they weren't. US military and diplomatic bigwigs were at a party that Saturday night, so had no idea about the final plans.

Víctor Meza, the former interior minister and public policy wonk, posed an interesting question when we spoke: 'What possible interest could the US have had in organizing a coup against a government with only six months left in power, when they were fighting wars in Iraq and Afghanistan? I don't think they organized it, but they certainly took advantage of it,' he concluded.

Shortly after Zelaya was marched out in his pyjamas, Barack Obama called the coup a coup. 'We believe that the coup was not legal and that President Zelaya remains the president of Honduras, the democratically elected president there,' he said. 'It would be a terrible precedent if we start moving backwards into the era in which we are seeing military coups as a means of political transition, rather than democratic election.'

His unequivocal condemnation buoyed social leaders like Berta and Carlos H. Reyes as they secretly gathered in safe houses to organize demos and talk strategy. The coup plotters grew nervous. Could the North American president possibly champion a Chávez lackey over *us*, their closest and most loyal allies in the region? The illusion didn't last long: an old-school military putsch to effect leadership change was exactly what happened. That is, Hillary Clinton happened.

'We do not think that this has evolved into a coup,' Clinton told reporters on 29 June 2009. This statement was designed, according to the official line, to prevent suspending US aid to needy Hondurans (US law bans aid to any country whose leader has been toppled by a military coup). 'If we were able to get to a ... status quo that returned to the rule of law and constitutional order within a relatively short period of time, I think that would be a good outcome,' Clinton added.

The plotters breathed a collective sigh of relief.

What Clinton really meant was a restoration of the status quo *ante*, the old order that existed *before* Zelaya upset the apple cart. She wanted him replaced with a president she liked better, as she explained in her memoir *Hard Choices*: 'We strategized on a plan to restore order in Honduras and ensure that free and fair elections could be held quickly and legitimately, which would render the question of Zelaya moot.'

Yet the US embassy was explicit in its definition of the event. In a July 2009 cable, entitled 'Open and shut: the case of the Honduran coup', Ambassador Llorens said that while Zelaya might have 'committed illegalities' and 'even violated the constitution', for his team there was 'no doubt that the military, Supreme Court and Congress conspired on June 28 in what constituted an illegal and unconstitutional coup against the executive branch ... Micheletti's ascendance as "interim president" was totally illegitimate.'

Despite Llorens's immediate and unequivocal assessment, the State Department was only interested in two things: negotiations and new elections. The coup vanished from the discourse.

Meza thinks the flip was most likely the result of hardball lobbying and scaremongering by ultra-right Honduran political and business leaders, ex-ambassador Ford, oil companies and other transnationals unhappy with Zelaya's reforms, along with the Cold War neocons operating around the Pentagon and State Department. Former Bush adviser Roger Noriega was hired by the coup plotters to impart his world view that Honduras was 'ground zero' with regard to the spread of Chavista authoritarianism under the façade of democracy. In *Hard Choices*, Clinton writes that Micheletti and the Supreme Court claimed to be protecting Honduran democracy against an unlawful power grab by Zelaya, who aspired to become another Chávez or Castro: 'Certainly the region did not need another dictator, and many knew Zelaya well enough to believe the charges against him.'

The coup against Zelaya was framed as a victory against Chávez, with lavish help from Honduran media tycoons.

No matter what you think of Zelaya and the size of his ego, facts are facts. The Cuarta Urna consultation was a nonbinding vote which Congress could have vetoed, and the Supreme Court could have nullified. Zelaya could not have clung to power in 2009. He may have fancied bidding for a second term in the 2013 elections, and Chávez may have been advising or even using him. But to claim that Zelaya planned to rewrite the constitution in order to cling to power and forge forward with a Bolivarian revolution – as Clinton does in her memoirs – is hogwash. The plotters know it, and they knew it then. So did US officials, who must also have known that the chosen path would fracture a fragile democracy and usher in the pro-American, right-wing, anti-democratic National Party.[31] This looks like a classic case of selective democracy. I've been told that privately Clinton was furious about the coup, yet nothing she said publicly gave that impression.[33]

The dawn coup against Zelaya was the first in Central America since the end of the Cold War. Now, almost a decade later, a few weeks in Honduras can take you right back to those bad old days. 'US policies after the coup ignored us, the Honduran people, and in effect legitimized an illegal takeover,' concluded Bertita, Berta's second child. 'Since then, we've lived with the militarization of our society, serious violence and the criminalization of social protest. My mum wanted to build a better Honduras, but that hope died with the coup.'

5

The Aftermath

The public response came as a surprise to the coup plotters. Tens of thousands of people, including many who didn't like Zelaya or hadn't voted for him, occupied streets, marched on Congress, and manned roadblocks every single day for six months, demanding the return of democracy.

Berta's daughters were in the thick of it, disobeying strict orders from their parents to stay away from trouble. Bertita, who was nineteen and at home on holiday from university in Cuba, recalls how she argued with her parents: 'You've lived your lives, you were guerrillas, this is our time, we want to fight the coup!' At one point, Berta parked Bertita and older sister Olivia in a Tegucigalpa hotel to try to keep them away from the tanks and tear gas. It didn't work. Berta called Olivia as soldiers were storming the university campus: 'Where are you? I can see you on live television, *cabrona*, wait till I get home!'

The Bloque Popular morphed into a broader coalition of grassroots groups, political parties, unions and outraged millennials called the Popular National Resistance Front (El Frente for short). It was the country's most unified and energetic popular crusade in modern times. 'We were on the streets every day,' said union leader Carlos H. Reyes. 'It was the only way to stay alive, that was our only security.' He showed me his partially disabled right hand, the result of a heavy fall after a cop kicked his leg to prevent him helping a teacher who was being beaten up by security forces.

Zelaya made three attempts to re-enter the country. The first was by plane, the day Isis Obed was killed. The second was an overland trek from Nicaragua at the end of July 2009, which Clinton described as 'reckless'. Salvador Zúñiga and Sotero Chavarría, the COPINH leader who had served as an infantry soldier in the 1980s, led several hundred into Nicaragua to escort Zelaya.[1] It took eight days and nights, walking over mountains in silence as military aircraft flew overhead. 'Most groups got caught and sent back, but we ran our system like a military op,' said Sotero. With all this radical fervour, it seems odd there was no armed uprising against the coup. One was certainly contemplated. Several people I interviewed heard the idea discussed in Nicaragua, and the CIA was aware of old-school radicals being trained at the border. I also understand that Hugo Chávez and his foreign minister, Nicolás Maduro, favoured using military force to reinstate Zelaya. Zelaya himself, however, spoke out against an armed civilian uprising – though some said he simply lost his nerve when it came to deploying armed force, so he was driven back from the border. That was the second failed attempt.

Zelaya finally got back into the country, but only as far as the sanctuary of the Brazilian embassy in Tegucigalpa, where he remained cooped up with his family for three months. Sensible, said some; cowardly, said others, who reckoned that photos of a democratically elected president behind bars could have been the media counter-coup Zelaya needed.

During this period, the Brazilian embassy became a focal

point for protests. Just after sunrise on 22 September, Berta's sister, Agustina Flores, a teacher and union activist, was getting a coffee when things turned ugly. 'The police and soldiers fired rubber and live bullets, and were beating women and the elderly. One grenade exploded near me; after that I blacked out,' she recalled. After coming to, Flores was surrounded by police officers who punched and clubbed her all over before taking her and hundreds of others to the national stadium, used as a makeshift detention centre. Berta later visited her battered sister in jail, where she was held for seven days accused of a crime against the state.[2] The protests continued undeterred and the crackdown became increasingly brutal, said Karen Spring of the Honduras Solidarity Network who was present. 'People were beaten, tortured, disappeared, jailed illegally. There were no conditions for free and fair elections; there was no peaceful transition.'

'I did everything I could to avoid fatalities,' General Vásquez told me. He claimed that some protesters provoked the soldiers in order to film their reaction, and send the footage to the world.

Soon after, talk of a hit list emerged, with Berta, Carlos H. Reyes, Padre Melo and Miriam Miranda among the civil society leaders rumoured to be on it.

The mass protests helped launch a gravy train for the security services as the armed forces were given unrestrained access to the public purse and made themselves indispensable by repressing protesters and militarizing the streets. This gravy train has yet to stop chugging.[3]

Berta was part of the Frente's leadership team, and being a gifted orator she emerged as an important political voice after the coup, especially on the international circuit. In an interview with the Cuban magazine *La Jiribilla*, some three months after the coup, Berta predicted that state repression would intensify in light of the unprecedented public outcry: 'The power in Honduras, the power of the dictatorial regime, is held by the army. Romeo Vásquez Velásquez. And, of course, by the corporate coup plotters ... and the transnationals, without whom the *golpistas* could not hold on. It has been important for the struggle that the people understand that these transnationals too are responsible for the coup. The gringos are involved, and the Honduran people know it.'

Berta was a political fox, says Jesuit Padre Melo. 'She was a smart strategist who knew how to talk to people in power in order to get what was important for COPINH's grassroots base.' At the same time, her strong political leadership threatened the status quo: 'Berta was unacceptable to the elites whose power she challenged.'

The coup buried the political dream of democracy. Roberto Micheletti's de facto government presided over the November elections, which were boycotted by the independent candidates, most of Zelaya's splintered Liberal Party, and half the electorate, and denounced by most international observers (apart from a Republican Party delegation). 'The US wanted to use the elections to clean up and cover up the coup, and we refused to be part of that fraud,' said Carlos H. Reyes. In his inaugural speech on 27 January 2010, the new president, Pepe Lobo Sosa, made a point of thanking Hillary Clinton.

Lobo's flawed election was a huge setback for the fledgling social movement. 'Berta was a hopeful realist,' said her old friend Gustavo Castro. 'She never censored the truth, but always believed in change. But after months of resisting the coup, when Lobo was inaugurated despite everything, she felt weary.'

Berta went back to the streets to fight against the inevitable, but democracy was lost, the dream over.

The Great Nature Sell-Off

The coup unleashed a tsunami of environmentally destructive 'development' projects as the new regime set about seizing control of resource-rich territories. Land grabs across the country's fertile valleys to farm biofuel cash crops like African palms and sugar cane started in the 1990s. But after the coup, eyes also turned to minerals and renewable energy sources.[4] In August 2009, Micheletti's interim government passed a law allowing the country's water resources to be privatized. Then, a few days before Pepe Lobo's inauguration, a long-standing ban on commercial projects in protected water reserves was overturned, paving the way for a massive river auction. 'We didn't oppose it because we didn't know about it, there was no debate, no news,' said Donald Hernández from the environmental group CEHPRODEC (Honduran Centre for the Promotion of Community Development).

Honduras has an inglorious record of shoving through controversial laws – the high-impact kind that require careful debate and analysis – when people are least likely to notice.[5] Juan Orlando Hernández liked burning the midnight oil when he was president of Congress:[6] at one late-night session in September 2010, he sanctioned forty hydroelectric dams without debate, consultation or adequate environmental impact studies. In the eight years following the coup, 197 mining concessions were registered, compared to 64 over the eight previous years, fuelling even more demand for cheap energy. 'After the coup, you got the impression that the Honduran elites were willing to facilitate the almost total destruction of the country to increase their wealth,' said historian Marvin Barahona. This was done by imposition, not consultation. It's how Agua Zarca was born.

Open for Business

The economy tanked after the coup as sanctions on trade, loans and aid packages were temporarily imposed by international banks and governments.[7] The big plan to kickstart the economy was unveiled in May 2011, before dignitaries from fifty-five countries attending the 'Honduras is open for business' forum in San Pedro Sula. It was an auction of sorts, in which Lobo and Hernández guaranteed investors low interest rates and generous tax breaks. In a statement, the Council of Hemispheric Affairs concluded: 'The largest benefits will be directed towards a handful of domestic investors who can invest more than $1 million, along with foreigners whose daily lives will remain unaffected if the plan fails to live up to its expectations.'

Less than two years after the coup, the economic forum signalled a 360-degree wholesale diplomatic turnaround. How had this come about? There were three steps. One, Micheletti removed the legislative padlocks as the international community condemned the coup. Two, Lobo declared Honduras 'open for business' and the international community forgot about the coup. Three, Congress approved a series of laws, concessions and contracts by taking advantage of the party's majority,[8] won thanks to the election boycott, which persuaded international banks and businesses to make the most of the coup. It was a well-planned series of manoeuvres executed with minimum grace and maximum impact. It was business as usual.[9]

Berta received a leaked list of rivers, including the Gualcarque, to be secretly 'sold off' by Congress, which approved dozens of hydroelectric dam concessions without debate or consultation in a handful of sittings. With no representation in Congress, direct action was the only option. On

26 July 2011, she led COPINH in a vociferous march on the presidential palace bearing a list of demands, including long-promised land titles for Lenca communities, new classrooms and sports fields, cancellation of the REDD carbon-credit scheme she called 'forest capitalism', details on mining projects solicited and sanctioned in Lenca areas, and the suspension of several dam projects, including Agua Zarca. Two days later, Pepe Lobo, nine ministers and Berta signed a memorandum of understanding which affirmed the state's duty to comply with international conventions protecting the rights of indigenous and Afro-descendant peoples. Specifically, Lobo et al. agreed that no dams, environmental licences or other high-impact projects on Lenca territory would be authorized without prior, informed and free consultations.[10] Those promises were overwhelmingly broken, and not even the highest court in the land could stop the neoliberal juggernaut.

The Judicial Coup

In October 2012, the government's flagship model cities policy was ruled unconstitutional by a four-to-one majority in the Constitutional Court, on the grounds that it involved transferring national territory to foreign hands. As the vote wasn't unanimous, the case should have gone to the full fifteen-judge panel. Instead, the four judges were dismissed in an infamous midnight night session chaired by Hernández,[11] and four friendly justices were appointed the next day. An ever-so-slightly revamped model cities law was approved by the new judges the following year. The one dissenting judge from the original four, Óscar Chinchilla, was made attorney general after Hernández became president in 2013, despite scoring below other candidates. (Chinchilla proved loyal, and five years later was appointed for a second term despite not undergoing the legally required vetting process.) This judicial clear-out was extraordinary, especially given that the Supreme Court was no bastion of legal independence. It played a key role in giving the coup a fake sheen of legality, and sacked another four judges who challenged that legality.[12] But in the post-putsch landscape, any dissent was quashed. Guillermo López Lone, one of the judges sacked for denouncing the coup, told me: 'The coup marked a before and after in the country. At first, I thought it was a move against Mel, but actually it was a political decision to expand the economic model and the roll-out of extractive industries which his reforms threatened. Congress plotted the coup, and then approved the concessions. Anyone threatening the model had to be sent a message. Berta was a threat to the model.'

Desarrollos Energéticos SA: Agua Zarca

The opaque way of doing government in Honduras makes tracing concessions and contracts hugely challenging. Tracking who's behind each company is even tougher, as public records are incomplete, not centralized or fully digital. Secrecy is king in Honduras, transparency the court jester.

Agua Zarca is a rare case on which, thanks to Berta's doggedness while she was alive and investigations since her death, we have substantial information. This one project helps us understand the winners and losers of the natural resources sell-off, and, by following the permits and the money, we can get closer to the interests behind the dam. This brings us nearer to those who had most to gain from her death.

In 2019, David Castillo was among sixteen people indicted on corruption charges, including fraud and using false documents linked to the dam. In this case, known as the Gualcarque Fraud, prosecutors alleged that Castillo used proxies to create DESA in order to avoid being named as the owner, meanwhile negotiating permits and lucrative energy contracts with the national energy company (ENEE), which he worked for at the time. Carolina Castillo, DESA's legal representative and former ENEE employee, was also indicted; both deny any wrongdoing.

It's worth recaptulating. DESA was created on 20 May 2009, solely to execute the Agua Zarca dam project.[13] On 28 June, the day of the coup, the army raided ENEE headquarters, removing files and computers from director Rixi Moncada's office. David Castillo continued at ENEE until early 2012, with access to contracts and long-term studies assessing the suitability of rivers, including the Gualcarque, for hydroelectric dams.[14] DESA submitted its feasibility study for the Gualcarque River only twenty-four hours and five minutes after the environmental authorities granted ENEE permission to undertake the study.[15] Rivers are typically studied for at least three years to establish whether there is adequate flow to generate power even during the dry season. How did DESA obtain the data so fast? Both David Castillo and Carolina Castillo (no known relation) had access to the study, which was most likely misappropriated from ENEE, prosecutors alleged in court.[16] On 22 January 2010, during the final days of Micheletti's rule, DESA was granted an operating contract – the permit needed to generate and supply energy – and permission to use national water by the ministry for national resources and environment (SERNA) without having conducted the legally required environmental impact study.

At a board meeting on 2 June 2010, ENEE signed contracts

with eight renewable energy companies, including DESA. Castillo was present representing ENEE; his name did not appear on DESA's company files. The contract was approved by Congress in December 2010. In its first year, DESA, a company with no track record in anything, obtained permits from SERNA, a sales contract with ENEE and Congress's seal of approval.

The environmental licence was not approved until 25 March 2011.[17] The fifty-year licence for the 14-megawatt dam was approved without the legally required free, prior and informed consent from the Lenca community, as established in ILO 169 which Honduras ratified in 1995.

The following year, DESA submitted an application to expand the dam's energy capacity, but in July 2012 an official environmental risk study found that expansion could leave the river dry and that the company had failed to consider the impact on vegetation, wildlife or the microclimate.[18] Despite this warning, SERNA's legal director, Aixa Zelaya, downgraded the project risk category that October, and in January 2013 Vice-Minister Roberto Cardona granted a 50 per cent expansion to the dam's generation capacity without consulting Congress. This paved the way for a massive increase in potential profits for DESA, with knock-on implications for the ENEE budget which had committed to buying the electricity. The deal also entitled DESA to further tax exemptions, with fiscal consequences unaccounted for by Congress. It was win-win for DESA, less so for state coffers. DESA also needed a construction permit from the municipality or local mayor's office, but at a town hall meeting in October 2011 the Río Blanco community voted 401 to 7 against the dam. Intibucá Mayor Martiniano Domínguez threatened to jail community leaders who had tried to stop construction by snatching a tractor, and then issued the permit in December 2011, alleging popular support for the project.[19]

Agua Zarca was among forty-nine projects approved on Lenca territory that Berta reported as possible crimes to the Special Prosecutor's Office for ethnic groups and cultural heritage. It's one of the smallest, most underfunded teams in the public ministry, but the chief prosecutor, Jany del Cid, is the only prosecutor Berta trusted. Jany and Berta grew up on the same street in La Esperanza. They smoked fake cigarettes after playing football, and choreographed dance routines to 80s classics like 'Footloose' to perform at competitions. 'Kids from rich families always won, it was unfair, but Berta insisted we took part. She had her ideals even then, and never gave in,' so del Cid told me.

Jany del Cid's team charged Mayor Domínguez with abuse of authority in that he had issued the construction permit without properly consulting the Lenca community.[20] The charge was initially dismissed on bogus grounds by a local judge, and then languished in the Appeal Court, until being revived after Berta's murder amid international pressure on the government to do something. Two SERNA vice-ministers, Roberto Cardona and Jonathan Laínez, were also charged with abuse of authority for approving licences without consultation.[21] The evidence gathered by Del Cid's team became part of the internationally backed state investigation into possible criminal wrongdoing in the licensing of the Agua Zarca dam. This resulted in the Gualcarque fraud indictments against the sixteen. All denied wrongdoing, but the judge ruled that prosecutors had enough evidence to proceed with the investigation.

Follow the Money

Berta wrote to the Dutch development bank FMO in October 2013, amid rumours that an international consortium was considering investing in Agua Zarca.[22] Berta detailed multiple ILO 169 violations with regard to the land sales, licences, permits and contracts, and explained how the project was being imposed on indigenous territory amid a campaign of violence and criminalization. She asked the bank, which prides itself on social responsibility, to withdraw from the project. At the time the FMO refused, but changed their mind after Berta's murder.[23] Berta believed other tax dollars were also being invested in the dam. She couldn't prove it before she was killed, but she was right. Agua Zarca was partially funded by the World Bank Group, which has a mandate to give socially responsible development loans to alleviate poverty. In fact, the poor, it claims, are its ultimate clients. By channelling development money through local intermediaries, the World Bank almost got away with keeping its role in Agua Zarca quiet. In Honduras, this brings us back to the elites.

Camilo Atala Faraj appeared on the Bloomberg billionaire list in 2015, after his Ficohsa Financial Group expanded its banking empire by gobbling up regional Citigroup operations. The acquisitions made him Central America's richest banker, worth an estimated $1.4bn. In 2011, before the lucrative takeovers, Banco Ficohsa Honduras received a $70m cash injection from the World Bank's private lending arm, the IFC (International Finance Corporation). The IFC also held a 10 per cent equity share in Ficohsa Honduras between 2010 and 2018. During that period, every Ficohsa loan was in effect an IFC loan.

In October 2013, Berta asked the IFC ombudsman to

investigate whether World Bank money had been invested in Agua Zarca. The following January, she was told that they could 'find no other link between the DESA project and the IFC'. The CAMIF investment fund, another IFC partner, *had* considered loaning money to DESA, but pulled out amid growing international coverage of the controversies and conflict. A fact sheet published two months after Berta's murder said: 'Some organizations have called for the World Bank to withdraw funding for the construction of the Agua Zarca hydroelectric project in Honduras. But the World Bank Group has never invested in the Agua Zarca project.'[24]

Yet, company documents suggest CAMIF's about-turn left DESA with a financial hole it needed to quickly fill or risk losing around $44m from the international consortium. Phone data uncovered as part of the murder investigation suggest that Ficohsa stepped in.

Ficohsa Honduras loaned $1.996m to Inversiones Las Jacarandas, the majority shareholder of DESA, in 2014. Las Jacarandas belongs to the Atala Zablah family — part of the same clan as Atala Faraj.[25] Ficohsa's Panama operation loaned Las Jacarandas $6m on the same date in 2014.[26] The eight-year repayment plans were signed by Las Jacarandas board member José Eduardo Atala Zablah — who is also on the DESA board.

Inversiones Las Jacarandas is a holding company with multiple business interests. However, messages exchanged in February 2014 between DESA president Castillo and financial manager Daniel Atala, José Eduardo's son, that emerged as part of the murder investigation, suggest the Ficohsa loans went to DESA:

Castillo: How much money is left of the loan ... from Ficohsa ... of the 8 million?

Atala: 1.4.
Castillo: Plus the 5 from Ficensa?[27]
Atala: Correct.

Through its US lawyers, Ficohsa denied providing loans meant to finance Agua Zarca or DESA, but the loan contracts I obtained do not stipulate any restrictions: general unrestricted loans can be used by borrowers for any project or purpose.[28] I know that senior management at Ficohsa gave the ombudsman the same reassurance, but refused to provide any paperwork. The ombudsman chose not to pursue the issue. The IFC explanation echoed Ficohsa's: 'IFC has neither invested in nor allocated any funding *with the purpose* of financing the Agua Zarca dam or its developer DESA. Jacaranda is not an IFC client' (emphasis added). But the problem, according to its own rules, is that when the IFC holds equity in a bank that then lends money to the owner or majority owner of a high-risk project, its strict environmental and social standards must apply.

I shared the evidence with David Pred, whose organization Inclusive Development International monitors development loans. He called the World Bank denial a 'half-truth': 'The World Bank didn't invest in the project directly, but that doesn't make it any less responsible ... A general corporate loan is a loan without conditions which means it could be used for Agua Zarca or any project. IFC standards apply to the entire portfolio of the bank; what the company does is the bank's and IFC's responsibility.'

It's never been easy tracking these loans, and it's getting harder, according to Nadia Darr, another development loan watcher, from Oxfam International. The IFC increasingly loans money through intermediaries – banks and private equity funds – which accounted for over half its lending in

2017. This has enabled the IFC to lend more money, more quickly, but at a cost.

'This is taxpayers' money, but we don't know where it ends up, it just goes into a black hole. There is no accountability or transparency for communities like Berta's,' said Darr. There are dozens of communities in resistance in Honduras, hundreds beyond here, that can vouch for that truth.

Agua Zarca wasn't the first project in Honduras in which the IFC arguably violated its own standards. It invested in Ficohsa despite widespread reports by local activists and international human rights groups such as Human Rights Watch and Earth Rights that a major client, Miguel Facussé's Dinant Corporation, was orchestrating private security guards, paramilitaries and soldiers alleged to have killed scores of campesino leaders in the Bajo Aguán.[29] Dinant claimed campesinos had initiated violence against its security guards, and denied any use of excessive force. State authorities have repeatedly failed to investigate the violence which by 2019 had claimed the lives of more than 150 campesinos, including many leaders. In another case, a consortium of regional banks, led by Ficohsa, contributed $20m to the five-star Indura Beach and Golf Resort on the Caribbean coast, which became part of the Hilton's luxury Curio Collection in 2016.[30] The flagship resort was built without community consultation, even though it encroaches on ancestral Garifuna land and ancient burial sites. The small community which lives in beach shacks in the resort's shadow suffered a wave of oppression including attempted illegal land grabs, trumped-up criminal charges, and false claims by the attorney general that Garifunas are not natives and therefore not entitled to be consulted.[31]

After Berta's murder, her daughter Bertita Zúñiga, elected as coordinator of COPINH in 2017, sent a new complaint to the IFC ombudsman in May 2018 calling for an investigation to establish whether taxpayers' money ended up in Agua Zarca. The complaint was rejected, having arrived a few days after the IFC relinquished its equity share in Ficohsa. Bertita said she considered the World Bank an accomplice in her mother's death.

After the Rivers Were Sold ...

DESA has two corporate shareholders: Inversiones Las Jacarandas and junior partner Pemsa Panama,[32] to which David Castillo was named president and given power of attorney in 2012. Pemsa was a majority shareholder of the internationally financed solar energy company Proderssa when it signed a twenty-year contract with ENEE on 16 January 2014. An alleged frontman for the drug trafficking cartel Los Cachiros, who was indicted in 2018 in Honduras also founded Proderssa. These complex dealings are laid out in a detailed dossier about Castillo's business ventures called *Violence, Corruption and Impunity in the Honduran Energy Industry* published in 2019 by a coalition of US rights and legal groups.

That January day in 2014, when Lobo had twelve days left in office, was a good one for solar and wind entrepreneurs as Congress approved thirty energy contracts (averaging 100 pages each) for twenty-one companies in one quick sitting. There was no bidding process, and the twenty-year purchase price agreed was 50 per cent higher than the market price at the time; this will end up costing the taxpayer at least $2bn by 2034.[33] In 2018, a leader of Los Cachiros testified in a New York courtroom that he gave bribes to Lobo in exchange for contracts favourable to companies he owned.

'After the rivers were all sold, they started on wind and solar contracts,' said investigative reporter Germán Reyes.[34] On the day of the coup, ENEE reported a surplus of $7m, its first time in the black in many years.[35] By mid-2018 the debt stood at $1.8bn, equivalent to almost 10 per cent of the country's GDP.

Tax Breaks

A common argument for capitalism is that wealth creation trickles down to the bottom of the pyramid. In the post-coup landscape, new political faces and entrepreneurs got into the energy business while others profited by greasing the right wheels. Some families in affected communities have benefited from land sales and low-paid jobs as builders, cooks and guards, while security personnel – including *sicarios* and paramilitaries – have also prospered. But wealth generation is mightily skewed, partly thanks to a tax system ranked the region's most regressive.

Honduras boasts more than 200 tax exemption laws, which cost state coffers around $1.5bn (36bn Lempiras) each year. Renewable energy entrepreneurs have benefited enormously, saving a whopping $1.4bn between 2012 and 2016, according to investigative reports by Reyes, at a time when spending on health, education and rural development was slashed, and forced migration spiralled.[36] DESA benefited from $450,000 in tax breaks in 2013, and almost $400,000 in 2015. Another dam on Lenca territory, linked to National Party high-flier Gladis Aurora López, qualified for $3m in tax breaks in 2013. In the post-coup landscape, the meteoric political and economic ascent of Gladis Aurora López and her husband Arnold Castro looms large. Berta clashed with both.

López comes from an important military-political family[37] in picturesque Marcala, where almost every resident is connected to the award-winning coffee industry, and also has a story to tell about the power couple. They met at the state-owned El Cajón mega dam: she was a secretary, he worked in security. The newly-weds fell on hard times in the 1990s and ran a very modest eatery, Cafetería El Hogar, where Castro waited at tables and López cooked traditional fare like *baleadas* – similar to burritos and the closest thing Honduras has to a national dish. Castro then got into long-distance trucking, and was accused of being linked to a coffee contraband scam exposed by local radio journalists in 2004.[38] In August 2008, their middle daughter Gracia Maria was abducted as she left a shopping mall in Tegucigalpa, tortured and murdered. Amid the outpouring of public sympathy, López's old friend and distant cousin, Captain Oswald Pompeyo Bonilla, a former security minister,[39] saw a political opportunity and proposed her as a National Party candidate for Congress in the post-coup elections. She won. The novice congresswoman was immediately appointed secretary of Congress. In this capacity she helped to authorize scores of renewable energy concessions and contracts, some going to her husband's companies, for dams on Lenca territory. In 2017, Castro told me they had done nothing wrong and, what's more, out of respect for the Constitution, his wife 'did not participate in the session when [one] contract was approved'. In 2018, the American Bar Association brought a case against Gladis Aurora López under the Global Magnitsky Act – which allows the US government to impose sanctions on foreign officials implicated in human rights abuses or corruption – arguing that she misused her public office to enrich her family. By late 2019, the State Department had not yet made a decision.

Accompanied by Martín Gómez, founding member of MILPAH (Independent Lenca Indigenous Movement of La Paz), a splinter group which broke away from COPINH in 2012, I visited two communities in La Paz affected by dams linked to the López family. Martín is short and quietly spoken, with a dry sense of humour, and always wears a hat. We drove to San José on a hot, dry day just before Easter 2018, skirting lush, hilly terrain dotted with coffee crops, to reach La Aurora dam. The dam has left four miles of the El Zapotal River bone-dry and the surrounding forest bare.

It wasn't meant to be like this. López and Castro promised three trees for each one culled, as well as electricity in every home, a health clinic, paved roads, an ambulance and jobs, in exchange for land sales and support for the dam. Back then the community was not informed about indigenous land rights, and La Aurora started generating electricity in 2012 with few of the promised benefits.

It was a different story in Santa Elena, where another company controlled by Castro obtained licences and permits to construct the Los Encinos dam in the vast, arid, mountainous area bordering El Salvador. This time, communities organized a roadblock after heavy machinery appeared without warning one night in 2012, stopping construction on the Río Chinacla. Berta came with COPINH to support them, and the communities demanded an ILO-compliant consultation. Instead, hundreds of Salvadoran nationals were bussed in for a town hall meeting to sign a decree in favour of the dam.

The community refused to give in, and as a result suffered terrible consequences: three defenders were tortured and murdered amid a wave of state-sponsored violence and bogus criminal charges; as a result, the struggle was taken up by Amnesty International. In addition, on 22 October 2015, two pregnant women were severely beaten by a heavily armed group of civilians, police and soldiers from the nearby 10th Battalion, causing one, Victoria González, to suffer a late miscarriage. I met her cousin María López, who told me how life unravelled after this: Victoria's husband was detained arbitrarily as part of the same wave of repression, and the children were taken into care after she became severely depressed. 'The repression destroyed the family,' said María, another MILPAH leader. Victoria died in July 2017 – a month before her husband was freed and the charges dropped. The crimes against the communities have never been properly investigated.

López was promoted to vice-president of Congress, and also replaced Juan Orlando Hernández as party president. It wasn't long before Marcala's power couple were travelling by helicopter amid mounting rumours of corruption, plastic surgery and properties in Miami. She was re-elected for a third term in 2017. But her US visa was revoked after she was indicted by Honduran prosecutors, along with five other serving and ex-members of Congress, for embezzling $879,000 from a presidential fund via a fake foundation called Planeta Verde.[40] Meanwhile, husband Castro is among thirty-eight entrepreneurs and high-ranking politicians charged by Honduran prosecutors in the Pandora's Box case, in which $12m was embezzled from the ministry of agriculture via two foundations, and some of the money used to finance the 2013 National Party election campaign. Multiple allegations have since emerged about how numerous National Party election campaigns were financed by millions of ill-gotten dollars.

López's American visa was revoked in early 2019, after a US State Department report to Congress listed López among dozens of senior officials from Honduras, El Salvador and Guatemala as being 'known or credibly alleged to have committed or facilitated corruption'. The report also states that the Honduran Congress had taken steps to pass legislation undermining corruption investigations and prosecutions.[41] Hugo Noé Pino, the former finance minister, said: 'Locally powerful figures like Hernández and López came to power thanks to elites, and then got rich through corruption, state contracts and tax breaks like the elites. These are symbiotic relationships.' The pair have protested their innocence.

Anti-Development Rhetoric

Opponents of 'clean energy' projects such as the bloodstained dams in Chixoy in Guatemala,[42] and Los Encinos and Agua Zarca in Honduras, are frequently branded as anti-development by politicians and investors. But in my experience of reporting across Mexico and Central America, this is not the case: what communities want is control over their own destiny, which requires access to accurate information about the consequences and benefits of each proposal. Berta was not opposed to cleaner, cheaper energy. She opposed the imposition of energy projects – of any project – on protected indigenous territories without proper consultation and compensation for affected communities. This is because clean mines do not exist, and dams are never environmentally harmless. Redirecting river flows can leave communities without fresh water for livestock and crops, fish and medicinal fauna; dams can also flood fertile plains most commonly inhabited and farmed by indigenous, Afro-descendant and peasant populations. Globally, dams have forced countless communities to abandon traditional, sustainable lifestyles. Berta demanded free, prior and informed consultations, which meant the right to say no and veto projects. Leonardo

Alvarado, who worked with the UN's Special Rapporteur on indigenous peoples, said: 'Solar, wind and hydroelectric power plants can be the greenest projects, but if imposed using the same dynamic as always, it will be the end of indigenous peoples. Communities have a legal right to reverse decisions made without prior consultation and prevent others being imposed in the future.'

The problem is that, though ILO 169 was ratified in Honduras in 1995, successive governments promised but failed to follow up with guidelines on what a consultation should look like. That doesn't matter, say people like Jany del Cid: the convention became law as soon as it was ratified, and compliance isn't optional.[43] Not so, say insiders like energy entrepreneur and industry spokeswoman Elsia Paz: in the absence of national guidelines, energy companies should not be penalized for following industry norms, and communities cannot veto development projects – a position the ILO appears to support,[44] and the IACHR rejects.

Amid the legal uncertainty, the industry buzzword is socialization, not consultation.[45] For Paz, socialization means educating communities about the benefits of an energy project, such as jobs and company-funded roads, classrooms and water tanks, as well as disproving the 'myths' circulated by opposition groups. But critics argue that at its heart, socialization is little more than a propaganda tool that talks up the benefits of a project and minimizes or ignores the potential negatives. It requires profiling influential community members and winning them over with jobs, money, or small gifts like school supplies or clothes, and then using them to convince their neighbours and to defend the project against naysayers. It's a modern take on the divide and conquer strategy.

Company documents confiscated after Berta's murder

reveal that DESA spent thousands of dollars on socialization consultants in Río Blanco, weakening the social fabric there and in surrounding communities. After the roadblock was set up on 1 April 2013, community leaders Chico Sánchez and Tomás García reported being offered large sums of money by DESA in order to support the dam, but both men turned them down.[46] On 5 September 2013, Daniel Atala, the company's financial manager, messaged a friend: 'Look where I was yesterday … Lenca communities supporting PHAZ [Agua Zarca] … with about 80 Indians that I brought from the project … So they would go to tell the president that just because of a couple of extortionists they were losing the opportunity for development.' Atala also sent pictures from the Casa Presidencial showing DESA executives signing a deal with a new local group,[47] which the company said proved that Río Blanco communities now supported the dam. The agreement got plentiful media coverage. Meanwhile, in Río Blanco itself, the resistance continued.

6

The Criminal State

Agua Caliente, October 2013

Berta was on the run. She'd holed up at an old friend's house in a hamlet called Agua Caliente in the department of Santa Bárbara, an hour's drive from Río Blanco. The gated property on the sleepy main drag belonged to Edna Bovadilla, a schoolteacher who'd trained with her at the *normal* in La Esperanza in the late 1980s.

A month earlier on 20 September, a judge had given bail to fellow COPINH leaders Tomás Gómez Membreño and Aureliano 'Lito' Molina, but made a point of sentencing Berta to jail. After heavy machinery owned by DESA was set on fire, the three were charged with trespass, incitement and causing over $3m of criminal damage. To avoid the arrest warrant issued on 10 October, Berta went underground.

The case generated worldwide attention for the Agua Zarca struggle, as criminalization and defamation increase the risks of physical violence against human rights defenders. Human rights groups dismissed the criminal charges as spurious, and Amnesty International announced it would consider the COPINH leaders as prisoners of conscience if they were jailed.

DESA's security chief, Douglas Geovanny Bustillo, had started the ball rolling.[1] 'I saw Señora Berta bringing people to the tractor in her car, she's the one behind the fire,' Bustillo testified at the initial hearing. He accused Berta of inciting the 'ignorant people' of La Tejera, the Río Blanco community that would be most affected by the dam, to violently oppose the project. 'My job was to coordinate the police, military and private security forces in order to protect the lives of 200 Chinese and local workers *from* COPINH,' he later told me, claiming the protesting campesinos posed a threat. The job was Lieutenant Bustillo's first civilian post after eighteen years in the army. His service included six months in military intelligence, a stint guarding the Estado Mayor (senior command), where he first met DESA's future president David Castillo, and his career high point of fifteen months in charge of security for Pepe Sosa Lobo, president of Congress at the time.

Bustillo had been forced to retire after failing three physicals. Having been unemployed for months, the DESA security job was a lifeline. Bustillo immediately put his military intelligence skills to work, identifying and cultivating several informants in the communities. He saw Berta as a personal threat to his livelihood, not just to DESA. 'She's no innocent lamb. She masterminded many crimes against DESA,' Bustillo told me.[2]

The criminal investigation against Berta and other COPINH leaders kicked off soon after press reports that Lisa Kubiske, the US ambassador to Honduras, backed judicial action against roadblocks and land occupations affecting big business. Kubiske stated that 'the government should guarantee a functional justice system to proceed against those who encourage campesinos to invade lands.' A few months later Kubiske used her speech on International Human Rights Day to give tacit support to the crackdown, singling out Agua Zarca and the Bajo Aguán, according to an op-ed by US law professor Lauren Carasik. '[In December 2013] Kubiske decried pervasive impunity in Honduras as the single biggest threat to human rights... however, despite her own admission that the Honduran legal system is dysfunctional, Kubiske blamed those being oppressed by that impunity for taking the law into their own hands to defend their rights.'

After the 2009 coup civil disobedience was pretty much the only tool campesinos and indigenous communities had left to defend their territories from expropriation and environmental destruction. It's a risky business, as those with money and influence in government and security circles often manipulate the criminal justice system. Years later, at Berta's murder trial, a text message sent on 19 July 2013 by DESA's financial manager Daniel Atala was presented as evidence in court: 'I spent a lot of money and political capital for those three arrest warrants.'[3] Not only did DESA want Berta in prison until her trial, the company, it would be revealed in evidence, also pulled strings with local police chiefs and high-ranking officials to ensure peaceful protesters were criminalized and dispersed. US interference in the matter – Ambassador Kubiske had effectively green-lighted the criminalization of peaceful protests – infuriated Berta.

The house in Agua Caliente where Berta lay low was a spacious colonial-style ranch with grand pillars and decorative Moorish floor tiles. Occupying the modest guest room off the cool back patio, she worked on her laptop at an old school desk next to tall sacks of maize kernels. There was a lot to do: preparing for court hearings, organizing resistance to dozens of other megaprojects licensed on Lenca lands without consultation, dealing with threats against COPINH, investigating banks.

Berta often stayed up all night, fuelled by cups of sweet black coffee from the Thermos flask which Edna refilled every couple of hours. Nearby stood the medication she needed to alleviate the pain of spinal hernias, exacerbated by long hours perched on the white plastic garden chair.

One night, a DESA employee came to Edna's security gate and introduced himself as an engineer. Berta could hear the conversation from her room.

'Don't get involved in problems,' the engineer told Edna. 'Berta Cáceres is a *vieja pícara* [common criminal]. She's going to jail for damaging our machinery. If you hide her here, you'll be in trouble too.'

Edna wasn't so easily intimidated. 'This is my house, Berta is my friend, and you have no right telling me what to do or who I can or cannot invite onto my property,' she said firmly, before asking the engineer to leave.

'*Gracias compa*, you handled that well,' Berta said, emerging from her room with a smile. 'But don't worry, I'll be gone in a couple of days.' They sat for a while chatting about the future. Edna recalled her guest's philosophical approach to having been discovered: 'If they kill me, the struggle for justice will go on. The world is more powerful than these criminals.'

The Criminalization of Protests

Río Blanco was militarized in May 2013, soon after COPINH agreed to help oppose construction of the Agua Zarca dam. Private security guards, police and soldiers from the 1st Battalion of Engineers arrived to patrol, intimidate, and sometimes terrorize the campesino communities. The soldiers were commanded by Colonel Milton Amaya, a graduate of the US School of the Americas (SOA), where scores of military high-fliers from across Latin America have been trained in repressive counterinsurgency tactics.[4] The use of military force against civilians resisting big business was nothing new, but in Río Blanco it was particularly flagrant. The soldiers slept, ate and operated out of the company encampment, creating the impression they worked *for* DESA.

Berta spent long spells in Río Blanco giving rousing speeches at the roadblock, denouncing capitalism, corruption, imperialism and globalization. Berta's sharp analysis and confrontational style of resistance made the world take notice. At home, it made her an instant target, and she was branded a criminal and an enemy of development. The events that led to Berta going underground began mid-afternoon on 24 May 2013, not far from Edna's house. Berta and her right-hand man, Tomás Gómez, were stopped at two military checkpoints en route to Río Blanco for a community meeting. At the second checkpoint, fifteen soldiers forced them out with their hands on their heads and searched the COPINH vehicle, while calling for police back-up. Berta was arrested for illegal possession of a .38 revolver, which soldiers claimed to have found in the boot. The pair were taken in separate patrol cars to the police station in Santa Bárbara. Tomás was freed around 1 a.m., Berta was held overnight and charged with illegal possession of a weapon.[5] In Santa Bárbara, Berta was forbidden to leave the country as part of her bail conditions. She was shaken a few weeks later when David Castillo, the president of DESA, called her with an offer to stall the case so she could attend her daughter's graduation in Cuba. 'How does he know about Bertita? Who does he know that high up?' Berta asked friends. A local lawyer told me that he'd spotted Castillo dining in the El Chalet restaurant in Santa Bárbara with two judges, one of whom was hearing her case.[6]

DESA had a network of paid employees and informants

within the Río Blanco communities. Some were employed as promoters or community links, like Héctor García Mejia, an ex-infantry sergeant who was appointed director of a DESA-sponsored group, CONGEDISBA, purporting to represent the real views of the community. The pro-dam, anti-COPINH press releases by that so-called grassroots group were signed off by Héctor but sometimes written by a PR and reputation management guru based in Miami. Héctor was paid 7,000 Lempiras ($270) by DESA each month. However, the best eyes and ears belonged to spies within families opposed to the dam, as they could freely attend COPINH meetings and pick up intelligence useful to the company.

DESA managers Bustillo and Rodríguez had a key informant in Salvador Sánchez, the thirty-something nephew of moustached community leader Chico Sánchez. He was paid at least 500 Lempiras ($20) a week to report back on COPINH, and specifically on Berta's next moves, as was revealed by the phone data. The inside information allowed DESA to ensure that state and private security forces were deployed to confront peaceful mobilizations and protests, Sánchez would admit at the murder trial.

Meanwhile, on 17 April 2013, DESA lawyer Carolina Castillo wrote to Daniel Atala, the company's finance manager: 'We were just informed that members of COPINH are going to the presidential palace ... I just submitted a criminal complaint to the prosecutor's office ... do you know if your uncle was able to speak with the minister of security?' Two of Daniel's uncles, Pedro and Jacobo Atala Zablah, as well as his father José Eduardo, are on the DESA board.

On 11 October, in a company group chat, the security chief Jorge Ávila wrote: 'I contacted Deputy Commissioner Casco from Santa Bárbara, he did not answer me ... I contacted General Commissioner Ivan Mejía,[7] he will talk to Casco and give the order.' 'Let me know if they don't respond,' replied Pedro Atala. But it was fine – Casco agreed to send reinforcements. This access to the powerbrokers behind the criminal justice system was called upon time and time again, before and in the aftermath of Berta's murder.

First Blood in Agua Zarca

The makeshift roadblock at El Roble, set up on 1 April 2013, was manned in twelve-hour shifts by men, women and children gathered round the wood fire over which they slow-cooked black beans and toasted tortillas on a *comal*, a smooth flat griddle. The roadblock was little more than a glorified human barricade intended to halt building work by physically obstructing the company's machinery. Like campesinos the world over, most of the men carried a machete over their shoulder or in a hip sling. The camp was decorated with Honduran and COPINH flags and surrounded by a stick-and-wire fence and hand-dug trench. On several occasions troops ransacked the site, chasing people out and kicking over the pots of food. But they kept coming back, joined by solidarity supporters from all over the world, singing protest songs to keep their spirits up.

On 15 July, day 106 of the protest, 200 or so community members broke through a gated entry to march on the DESA compound to demand talks. Several shots were fired in the air, and then a soldier opened fire with his assault rifle. Kevin Yasser Saravia shot dead Tomás García,[8] an outspoken opponent of the dam, who days earlier, as we've seen, had turned down 20,000 Lempiras ($900) to switch sides. The forty-nine-year-old father of seven was a kind man, said mourners, who never left home without his white sombrero and machete.

He bled to death on the porch of a green wooden cabin where Chinese construction workers were accommodated.⁹ In the immediate aftermath, Daniel Atala messaged David Castillo: 'The military have killed an *indio*.' He then instructed him to pay an HCH TV journalist 1,000 Lempiras owed from the previous week, plus another 1,000, and to round up other friendly reporters to ensure the company's reaction got ample coverage. 'Shall I get my old man to talk to Arturo Corrales [the security minister from May 2013 to December 2014]?' wrote Atala. Castillo replied in the affirmative, adding: 'and Pompeyo Bonilla [security minister from October 2011 to April 2013] ... It's done ... they're mobilizing people.'

Bustillo, DESA's security chief, assured me that the soldier had acted in self-defence, as Tomás was armed with a machete. By his own admission, Bustillo wasn't there – but multiple eyewitnesses said they saw the soldier fire without provocation. In December 2015, Saravia was found guilty of murdering Tomás, but absolved of the attempted murder of Tomás son Allan. DESA paid 100,000 Lempiras ($4,000) towards the officer's defence.

Tomás was buried in the forest in a spot marked by a simple white cross where his spirit, Lencas believe, will return to Mother Earth as part of the cycle of life. 'I'm so sorry you've lost your husband and the father of your children,' Berta told Tomás's wife, Briselda Domínguez. 'The struggle has lost a brave fighter, but we cannot give up, this isn't over.'

Allan García, one of their sons, was shot in the chest, but survived after emergency surgery. The bullet just missed his heart and left the quiet sixteen-year-old's lean torso horribly scarred. 'We were protesting peacefully, so why did they kill my father? I want the soldier to face the full weight of the law because he didn't kill an animal; he killed a human being,'

Allan told me several months later, on my first visit to Río Blanco in 2013.

Allan arrived for the interview in muddy rubber boots after a long day working in the fields. He just wanted the dam to go away, so he could grow crops and tend his family's few chickens, ducks and pigs in peace. We sat outside on a hand-carved wooden bench surrounded by glorious pines and lush green fields, watching two workhorses munching the grass. 'If they take the river, where will we go, what will we eat?' he wondered aloud.

The July 2013 attack generated tremendous fear about the lengths DESA and the security forces would go to in their attempt to crush opposition to the dam, and numerous people pulled out of the resistance or changed sides as the violence increased. But Allan and his siblings refused to submit.[10]

On that first visit to Río Blanco, dozens of people came to tell me what life was like before the dam. 'We women used to go to the river with our children, to wash clothes, bathe and enjoy ourselves. Now, that is impossible, the dam has turned neighbours against neighbours, families against families,' said Rosalinda Domínguez. Another woman described how armed police came to her home, claiming to be looking for her husband, and forced everyone, even the children, out at gunpoint. It was the middle of the day, so the officers knew he would be working in the fields. But encouraged and trained by Berta, the women didn't cower, they maintained a dignified attitude and participated in every mobilization.

I left Río Blanco clinging on to the back of a pickup truck as it raced along unpaved winding roads through the pretty, fertile valleys. Police officers stopped the taxi-truck at the El Barreal checkpoint, a community where there is some support for the dam. The police post was installed at the behest of DESA and officers patrolled together with the company's private security guards. DESA paid for their food. The police searched the truck and after I told them I was a journalist, demanded my ID. Irritated, I photographed them as one officer filmed me on his phone. 'What business is it of yours getting involved in a community dispute?' the commander, in his mid to late twenties, wanted to know. 'Why are the police and army here if it's just a community dispute?' I snapped back, still thinking about Allan. The commander didn't respond, just waved us on impatiently, and returned to his half-empty bottle of cheap rum in the police hut.

Berta was in La Esperanza when Tomás was killed. A few hours later, sixteen-year-old Cristian Madrid from El Barreal was shot dead. Without offering the slightest evidence, Bustillo, the security chief, accused Berta of masterminding the shooting. Nevertheless, the circumstances surrounding the teenager's death were unclear. He was shot far from the DESA protest, but the Madrid family publicly blamed COPINH, which helped reinforce the notion that it was a violent organization, and any conflict arose from personal vendettas rather than from the project.[11]

The Madrid family are a big deal in Río Blanco: big fish in a small pond. The arrival of this mestizo clan in the 1970s triggered the first land conflict, driving the Lenca communities to organize to defend their sacred earth. Later on, the Madrids supported the dam, and made plenty of money selling prime land to DESA.[12] In numerous cases, cattle belonging to the Madrid family mysteriously got onto land farmed by poor neighbours and munched through precious maize and bean crops. The police were informed but took no action, several affected families told me. Facing bankruptcy or starvation, they sold the land at below market price to the Madrid clan, who then sold it to DESA.[13]

The land is crucial to the conflict, since without it DESA could not build the dam. Lenca leaders say communal ejido land cannot legally be sold, while the mayor's office claims that due process was followed. But, according to indigenous peoples' prosecutor Jany del Cid, who has investigated land disputes across the country, it's not hard to obtain land titles in Honduras, as checks on existing titles are lax, government decisions are hard to appeal, and the system is open to corruption.

Honduras Goddamned

Honduras is the second largest of the seven countries in Central America, and, with around 9 million inhabitants, also the second most populous. It is blessed with fertile soil, and is rich in water and minerals; tropical fruit and sugar cane flourish in the steamy plains and coffee thrives in the temperate mountains. This abundance has always attracted adventurers, entrepreneurs and bandits. In recent times, its porous northern shoreline and corruptible law enforcers have made Honduras an ideal midway destination for drug producers in South America and drug consumers in the north.

Honduras's role in the international drug trade dates back to the 1970s, when criminal groups known as *transportistas* were contracted to move mostly cocaine through or round Honduras. That is, until the meteoric ascent of Juan Ramón Matta Ballesteros, identified by Insight Crime as the original Honduran drug capo, whose rise and fall were linked to US foreign policy.[14]

If you've seen *Narcos* on Netflix, you'll know that Matta played a crucial role in connecting Miguel Ángel Félix

Gallardo's fledgling Guadalajara cartel in northern Mexico with Pablo Escobar's start-up in Medellín, Colombia. The US considered Matta a 'Class 1 DEA violator', but that didn't stop the CIA doing business with him. Matta's airline company SETCO freely moved cocaine bound for US streets from Honduras to Mexico. In return, the State Department contracted SETCO to move weapons, ammunition and Contra fighters into Nicaragua between 1983 and 1985.[15] The CIA gave Matta a free pass, because after all, the end justifies the means. For a while Matta navigated both criminal and counterinsurgency realities, until he was no longer useful.[16]

Matta's rags-to-riches story depended on his deep pockets and a steady supply of corruptible military and government officials. It also illustrates important power shifts happening at that time in Honduras: the armed forces were no longer mere brawn protecting the interests of landowners and merchants, they had now earned a seat at the top table to forge their own economic and political projects, thanks to expedient alliances with landowners, politicians, smugglers and criminal networks.

And, hot on the heels of the counterinsurgency state, the repressive apparatus designed to target subversive opponents was redirected to support the evolving criminal state. Ideological pretexts were abandoned. Instead, crime lords and businessmen employed bribes, threats and violence to take control of judges, prosecutors, politicians and security forces in furtherance of their own interests, whether drug trafficking, stealing land, quelling uprisings by killing community leaders, or all of the above.

Impunity, Crime and Power

Berta met the lawyer who would defend her against DESA at a demonstration against institutionalized corruption in Honduras, eight years before her murder.

On 7 April 2008, public prosecutors Víctor Fernández, Jari Dixon, Soraya Morales and Luis Javier Santos went on hunger strike to protest political meddling in corruption cases. The most high-profile case being obstructed involved National Party veteran Rafael Callejas, and dated back to his presidency between 1990 and 1994. The charges against Callejas – the politician widely credited with unleashing neo-liberalism on Honduras – included theft of $20m from the petrol fund, to pay off party debts and for personal gain.[17] 'Corruption cases against powerful people were effectively frozen,' said Dixon, as we talked one Sunday evening at a roadside diner. 'We had to run them past so many senior people that most never ended up anywhere near court. But those filters only applied to cases against the powerful, never the poor. That was the unwritten rule,' added Dixon, who was president of the National Association of Prosecutors in 2008.[18] (In March 2016, Callejas pleaded guilty to his role in the international football corruption scandal inside the governing body FIFA, and at the time of writing he has still not been sentenced.)

The hunger strike morphed into the country's first anti-corruption movement, as thousands of people from across the social, economic and religious spectrum flocked to Congress in support of the prosecutors' campaign. Satellite hunger strikes erupted across the country. In the capital, COPINH set up camp in solidarity. Karla Lara, a singer and activist who'd been in El Salvador and Nicaragua during the 1980s, bonded with Berta on those long nights outside

Congress. 'She was completely in agreement with the anti-corruption struggle, she was all for it, but she also loved eating and thought the hunger strike was madness,' Karla told me. The singer stayed on hunger strike for twenty days. Meanwhile, Berta, on a full stomach, led protesters to the house of the attorney general, demanding his resignation, then went across the city, from house to house, demanding the resignation of other allegedly corrupt politicians.

It was during these demonstrations, which lasted thirty-eight days, that Berta met Víctor Fernández,[19] who became her close friend and lawyer. He would go on to defend COPINH against DESA. Later, after her murder, Fernández prosecuted mayors and ministers over the Agua Zarca dam and represented Berta's family at the murder trials.

Almost a decade after the hunger strike, a report by the Carnegie Endowment for International Peace upset the country's elites because it found that major crimes, such as Berta's murder, are committed with impunity in Honduras thanks to institutionalized corruption. Sarah Chayes, the author of the academic investigation, says institutionalized corruption is the operating system set up to serve the interests of the elite. She describes Honduras as a prima facie example of intertwined transnational kleptocratic networks linking the public sector, private sector and criminal elements. In other words, powerful international entrepreneurs and criminal organizations with international ties have corrupted state institutions at various levels, with little resistance from public officials, who often benefit from the graft through kickbacks or hush money. It's this circle of corruption that underpins a mafia state that maintains the power and privilege of the ruling elites and powerbrokers. The extent of the mafia state was later exposed via criminal prosecutions brought by US authorities, which implicated serving and former presidents, lawmakers, ministers, mayors, soldiers and cops in drug and arms trafficking, bribery and murder.

Berta was fighting not just Agua Zarca but battles on multiple fronts in the war against neo-liberalism. In 2015 she got involved with a new anti-corruption movement – Los Indignados, the indignant, in reaction to a scandal emerging inside the health and social security system (IHSS). Massive sums,[21] it transpired, had been embezzled by public officials and their cronies. The orchestrated demise of the IHSS helped usher in full-blown privatization promoted by the IMF, while bankrupting a healthcare system relied upon by 1.6 million Hondurans. Some of the stolen cash was allegedly laundered through the five-star Indura resort; another payout helped Hernández to steal the 2013 election.

The scandal had everything you expect from a racy telenovela: drive-by shootings, insipid middle-aged officials turned criminal masterminds with model girlfriends, flashy cars, sham companies, electoral fraud and international fugitives. Scams included overpaying almost $400,000 for ten ambulances, bribes to ministers for bloated contracts, and buying overpriced medicines which were then repeatedly stolen and resold to the IHSS. This was a glaring example of 'institutional corruption', said investigators, which left patients without medicines, equipment or nursing care. One doctor I interviewed in Tegucigalpa, on the day of the November 2013 elections, claimed candidates had funded their campaigns with money intended for hospital supplies. He knew it, but he couldn't prove it. The scale and audacity of the scam only came to light in 2015.[22] 'A functioning hospital system was dismantled and sick people died unnecessarily in order to win an election and justify privatization,' said veteran union leader Carlos H. Reyes.[23] 'This is criminal and the IMF knows it.'

As the drama unfolded, President Hernández accused opposition parties of whipping up the revelations merely to destabilize the government, until a cache of documents leaked to Globo TV made these official denials sound like lies. It turned out that in the run-up to the 2013 elections, the National Party received cheques worth millions of Lempiras from sham companies which had been given medicine and equipment contracts by Congress – led at the time by Hernández – during more of those late-night parliamentary sessions. His sister Hilda Hernández co-managed party funding at the time.[24] Hernández was forced to admit that his presidential campaign received money from companies linked to the scandal, but denied any personal knowledge of the affair, even after cheques emerged bearing his name. But although families, doctors and activists counted almost 3,000 avoidable deaths by mid-2015 as a result of the scam, there was no official investigation.[25] It was around this time, it would later emerge, that the DEA launched a major drug trafficking and money laundering investigation into the president, his sister Hilda, younger brother Tony and other presidential advisers. *No pasa nada*, nothing happens, as they say in Honduras.

The Indignados movement united veterans like Berta and Reyes with disaffected youngsters, conservative Church groups and middle-class families, demanding an anti-impunity organization like the UN-backed CICIG (International Commission against Impunity in Guatemala). For a few months there was hope, but Honduras ended up with a much weaker anti-corruption body, which, shortly after Berta's death, would open an investigation into DESA's finances and government contracts.[26] But for now, the heat on Berta and COPINH was about to get hotter.

Follow the Money

In the last few months of her life, Berta was investigating possible sources of corruption and dirty money behind several unwanted development projects similar to Agua Zarca. She was trying to find clues to the kleptocratic structures behind the proliferation of profitable megaprojects like mines, dams and tourist resorts threatening the existence of her Lenca people and other indigenous communities.

If she could connect the dots, Berta told several confidants, she was going to pass the information to US prosecutors in the hope they would probe further. But the overlap between criminal gangs and the state can be so deep and so extensive that it's hard to tell the good guys from the bad guys. Berta had trouble unpicking who owns what, thanks in large part to opaque land registry, banking and accounting procedures. At the time of her death, friends believe the relevant documents of this research were saved on her laptop, which was never returned to the family by investigators. It fell to others to try and uncover the criminal structure behind Agua Zarca. It would become clear that, as with classic organized crime, the success of such projects depends on violence, influence and money.

The rise and fall of two criminal gangs – Los Cachiros and the Atlantic cartel – and their links to the Rosenthal banking family provide a glimpse of how they, and therefore Honduras, operate. This was possible when key members of the drug clans flipped.

In autumn 2013, around the time Berta was forced into hiding, Devis Leonel Rivera Maradiaga, one of the brothers behind the Los Cachiros gang, started recording his conversations with stalwarts of the Honduran establishment.

US prosecutors in the Southern District of New York describe Los Cachiros as a 'prolific and violent criminal syndicate that relied on connections to politicians, military personnel, and law enforcement to transport cocaine to, within, and from Honduras'. The group worked closely with Mexico's Sinaloa cartel, led by Joaquín 'El Chapo' Guzmán. Cases were brought against numerous cops, soldiers and politicians (and their relatives), whose criminal dealings with the Cachiros helped put huge amounts of cocaine on American streets.

Each time one of the Rivera Maradiaga brothers took the stand in New York, they named names. For instance, in 2017 one jury heard that the Cachiros paid bribes amounting to at least $500,000 to Porfirio 'Pepe' Sosa Lobo as he campaigned for the presidency in 2009 in the aftermath of the coup.[27] And during Lobo's presidency Los Cachiros moved tons of cocaine through northern Honduras and killed at will without fear of arrest or extradition.

Lobo's son, Fabio, was given the job of acting as middleman between Los Cachiros and state officials. Lobo junior personally escorted at least 1.4 tons of cocaine after it landed on his home turf of Olancho, the wild west of Honduras, with protection from soldiers armed with AR-15 machine guns and pistols. Fabio was in so deep that he was nicknamed 'El Comando'.

It was later alleged that Lobo had encouraged Leonel Rivera and his brother Javier to set up front companies to benefit from government contracts. After Lobo's term ended in January 2014, Leonel claimed to have met with Antonio 'Tony' Hernández, the new president's younger brother, to discuss how his family company Inmobiliaria Rivera Maradiaga SA (Inrimar) could recoup money owed for construction and maintenance projects carried out for Lobo's government.[28] Bribery was the answer, according to Leonel Rivera on the witness stand. Tony Hernández denied it, his family denied it, but Tony was in deep, and we would hear much more about him, the Hernández family and the National Party at the end of 2018, as Berta's murder trial was wrapping up.

On another occasion, Fabio, Leonel alleged, charged an extra $50,000 as a sweetener for Julián Pacheco Tinoco, known as 'The Chief', when he was Pepe Lobo's director of state intelligence. Pacheco had previously served as battalion chief in the department of Colón, the Cachiros stronghold, when it was governed by Juan Gómez.[29] It was the assassination of Gómez, the gang's main political mediator, in January 2015 that convinced the brothers that game was over: the political tide had turned against them, most likely in favour of a rival group. That's when they fled Honduras into the arms of the DEA, and Pacheco was appointed security minister. Pacheco and Pepe Lobo vehemently deny all wrongdoing, and by the end of 2019, had not been charged with any crime.[30]

The Rivera Maradiaga brothers delivered a treasure trove of photos, recordings and phone messages implicating scores of police, military, businessmen and politicians, in exchange for the safe passage of relatives to the US and shorter sentences: a highly controversial move by US prosecutors, given that the brothers had confessed to trafficking 130 tons of cocaine, to the murder of seventy-eight people including policemen, judges, lawyers and journalists, and to the attempted murder of twenty-eight others. The brothers will never face justice for the blood they shed in Honduras.

Luis Javier Santos, one of the prosecutors who went on hunger strike in 2008 and would later lead an anti-corruption unit, outlined the Cachiros' modus operandi for me.

The criminal clan, who started out as cattle smugglers, controlled the northern departments of Olancho, Colón,

Atlántida and Yoro for over a decade. Like every gang, they bought political influence in order to operate their drugs business in peace, he explained. They secretly contributed money to election campaigns of mayors, deputies and at least one president on the understanding that if elected, the favour would be returned.

It's the same old mafia story. A politician's success rests in the hands of those who fund the campaign. Undeclared money from criminal bosses and legit companies helps win elections, and thus guarantees the donors protection, political favours and public contracts, which in turn guarantee bribes for the elected politicians. Round and round and round the corruption cycle goes. That's why the CICIG call illicit campaign financing the 'original sin'.

During Lobo's government, the Cachiros won a bunch of lucrative contracts from the Office of Public Works, Transport and Housing (SOPTRAVI) – a ministry with a large budget and long track record in corruption.[31] The bidding process was rigged. The clan created dozens of fake companies to submit overvalued bids they were guaranteed to win. This let them make clean (taxpayer) money, and launder dirty money, said Santos.

The Renewable Energy Projects Unit (UEPER), created by Lobo, was another cash cow and money-laundering vehicle for the criminal group. UEPER supervises and awards contracts for dams and solar and wind stations, as well as auxiliary projects. Companies linked to the Cachiros won thirty-five overvalued contracts from UEPER worth at least $9m via companies including Inversiones Aropolis, COMSSA and Lutopas, according to the National Anti-Corruption Council.[32] Contracts were amplified without due process, which got them big money maintenance, rubbish collection and domestic services projects. These three Cachiros companies were allegedly fronted by lawyer Francisco Mejía, who was given legal powers and free rein by Leonel Rivera Maradiaga. Mejía's wife, Waldina Salgado, and their son, Roberto Arturo Mejía, were also involved in running the companies.

This family trio are also involved in the solar energy company Proderssa. This is noteworthy because several DESA executives, including David Castillo, Roberto Pacheco Reyes (former security minister and DESA board secretary), Daniel Atala (finance manager) and his father José Eduardo Atala Zablah (board member) have at different times had links to Proderssa, company files show.

Another Honduran drug trafficker making big money thanks to dirty contracts came from the La Mosquitia coastal region. Wilter Neptalí Blanco Ruíz, alleged leader of the Atlantic cartel, was based in the isolated north, where he operated seafood export firms and threw extravagant parties for politically important friends. Blanco and the Cachiros appear to have united for several high-profile killings, including the infamous 2009 slaying of drug czar Julián Arístides González. Blanco allegedly ordered cops on his payroll to kill González as payback for having thwarted his plan to steal 143 kilos of cocaine belonging to a rival local trafficker, using corrupt police officers. Blanco escaped Honduran justice, despite recordings from a police station known as the Slaughterhouse (Casamata), which captured moonlighting officers planning the assassination. The cop who obtained the recordings was murdered. Once, in 2015, Blanco was picked up in Honduras on money laundering charges, but soon released. He was finally arrested in October 2017 in Costa Rica – a month after the US embassy in Tegucigalpa took the unusual step of publishing a list of suspects under investigation for drug trafficking and corruption.[33] He was extradited to Florida to face charges dating back almost two decades, settling on twenty years in jail in exchange for naming more names.

The relentless stream of high-profile suspects, including judges, deputies, mayors, military officials, businessmen and cops, under investigation by US prosecutors after Blanco and the Maradiaga brothers developed loose lips, provides further evidence of institutionalized criminality – rather than a state tarnished by a few rotten apples. It's what prosecutors in New York would in 2019 call 'state-sponsored drug trafficking'.

Criminal gangs need reputable financiers to move dirty money into the banking system. Banco Continental, controlled by the Rosenthal family, was one of many that provided this service, no questions asked. The bank helped Los Cachiros launder money and access international financing through a myriad of front companies, according to the US justice indictments. To some, the downfall of the Rosenthal family was a victory scored against white-collar criminals profiting from organized crime; to others, they were victims of political persecution.

Born in San Pedro Sula in 1936 to a Romanian Jewish father and a Salvadoran mother, the family patriarch Jaime Rosenthal was one of the region's most influential and wealthiest men, with a family fortune estimated at $1.2bn by Forbes in 2013. I contacted Jaime – a former Liberal vice-president and congressman – through his official biographer, the historian Rodolfo Pastor. He initially agreed to an interview, but then cancelled on the advice of his lawyers, and never fulfilled his offer to answer questions in writing instead.

In an indictment, US prosecutors claimed Jaime, his son Yani Rosenthal and his nephew Yankel Rosenthal helped the Cachiros launder drug money and access international loans through various business ventures for over a decade.

In one alleged scheme, the Cachiros would buy cattle at

auction and sell it to a meat processing firm affiliated to the Rosenthals.[34] The meat was then exported to the US among other countries. The meat deal also involved Fabio Lobo.

Banco Continental lent the drug traffickers money to fund other businesses used as money laundering fronts, including the Joya Grande Zoo, a mining company, a palm oil production plant and the construction company Inrimar, the indictment detailed.

Yani, a congressman and a Liberal minister during Zelaya's presidency, pleaded guilty to money laundering for the Cachiros during his political career. He was sentenced to three years. Yankel, a former Nationalist minister of investment under Hernández, admitted trying to buy a $1m Florida property on behalf of a lawyer linked to the Cachiros. Yankel also funnelled hefty bribes from licit and illicit entrepreneurs into campaign contributions for cousin Yani and laundered money through the family's Marathón football club, the department of justice said after Yankel's guilty plea. He was sentenced to twenty-nine months.

When this all went down, the Rosenthal conglomerate, Grupo Continental, had multiple business interests including real estate, cattle ranches, a crocodile-skin nursery, tourist resorts, palm and sugar cane plantations, and a cable television and internet company, all of which had accounts in Banco Continental. The bank was shut down and the companies seized.[35]

Jaime denied any wrongdoing. He maintained that the family didn't know the Cachiros were drug traffickers: sure, they'd heard rumours, but all their paperwork was in order and besides, they were depositing cheques from state coffers which showed the government was happy to do business with them. And when the bank opened the accounts and made the loans, neither the Cachiros nor its businesses had yet been named as targets by the US.

Jaime died in January 2019, still a wanted man in the US where he was a designated drug kingpin. He was never extradited, due to outstanding corruption charges in Honduras and thanks to friends in high places, his biographer Rodolfo told me. No one of his position in Honduran society, nor any figure of the political and military establishment, had been prosecuted at home, until Pepe Lobo's wife, Rosa Elena Bonilla de Lobo, was convicted on corruption charges in 2019.

Banco Continental was not the only bank to launder drug money, the anti-corruption prosecutor Luis Santos told me, but it's the only one to have been punished so far. (In early 2019, a US arbitration court admitted a billion-dollar lawsuit filed by the Rosenthals against the state of Honduras, in an attempt to recuperate the financial losses suffered as a result of the asset seizures.)

The light sentences faced by the Rosenthal clan contrast starkly with those of a group of female inmates I met at La Ceiba prison in 2018. A glamorous woman wearing a cerise skirt and jacket made friendly small talk at the entrance while a police officer registered my details for a prison visit. On my way out, she was sitting on a concrete ledge outside with three other women, and I stopped to ask what job she had at the prison. 'I don't work here, I'm a prisoner.'

The four women, in their thirties and early forties, were sentenced to fifteen years for being money mules. They were caught at the airport, where they'd met for the first time, about to fly to Panama with banknotes strapped to their bodies. All four were first-time offenders, poor young mothers recruited to smuggle cash for a few hundred dollars. For that, they missed seeing their children grow up.

Another prima facie case of selective justice involves Miguel Facussé. Allegations of drug trafficking links dogged the palm oil baron – before and after his death in 2015[36] – with little consequence. In the same New York courtroom, Leonel Rivera claimed that in 2013 his criminal group helped Fabio Lobo smuggle more than a ton of cocaine from Venezuela, using a private airstrip on Facussé's Farallones ranch, a stone's throw from the Garifuna enclave Vallecito, where the community reported hearing planes landing at night.

Almost a decade earlier, in March 2004, a classified cable headed 'Drug plane burned on prominent Honduran's property' was sent by the US embassy in Tegucigalpa to the State Department after a ton of Colombian cocaine landed on a secret airstrip in Farallones. The cargo was offloaded onto a convoy of vehicles guarded by some thirty heavily armed men, after which the plane was incinerated in broad daylight at the side of the runway. Facussé was at home while the deal took place, wrote Ambassador Larry Palmer. The wreckage was then apparently buried using a bulldozer. A few days later Facussé told local police that an unauthorized plane *had* landed on his property and burst into flames when his guards shot at it. His version was contradicted by several other officers. 'Facussé's property is heavily guarded and the prospect that individuals were able to access the property and, without authorization, use the airstrip is questionable,' wrote the ambassador.

This was the third time that major drug traffickers had used Farallones as a landing strip in just over a year. Knowing Facussé's links to drug trafficking didn't stop the US from doing business with him.[37]

Our Man on the Ground

I first heard about Olvin Gustavo García Mejía shortly after Berta's murder. He was a man widely feared by COPINH members in Río Blanco. Born in 1986, he lived with his family in Valle de Ángeles, a Río Blanco canton which became a virtual no-go area for those opposing the dam after Olvin sold a plot of his family's riverside land to the company.[38] Several other families also sold their land to DESA, after being convinced by promises that the dam wouldn't affect the river, but many more were 'convinced' by Olvin. 'People are terrified of him, he's capable of extreme violence and he's protected,' said Brigitte Gynther, who documented the threats and attacks against community members.

The fear was palpable. Everyone I asked about him later instinctively dropped their voice before describing chilling encounters. Olvin boasted of keeping a hit list of community leaders regarded as ringleaders by DESA. Berta was on it. Olvin spoke of Berta with venom, calling her an old witch and worse, and often muttered about one day killing her along with the other 'heads' he would claim. She was scared of him. He was the reason she didn't want her children in Río Blanco.

For years Olvin's neighbours and victims claimed he was working for DESA. His older brother Héctor was paid as a community link and as president of the DESA-backed community group (CONGEDISBA), his younger brother Armando worked as a security guard – but Olvin's role was different. He was spotted in company cars with DESA's security detail, and targeted dam opponents, seemingly without fear of repercussions. He felt secure enough to walk around with a .9mm gun in one hand and a machete in the other. In March 2015, Olvin used his machete to chop off the fingers of an anti-dam community member. The victim didn't dare report the attack to police, but immediately withdrew from COPINH and the dam protests. I tried interviewing him on several occasions, but he was too scared.

Others, who felt they had little left to lose, told me their stories about Olvin.

Don Justino is a campesino in his sixties from Valle de Ángeles, with a weathered face and mournful eyes, who was living in COPINH's training centre Utopía when I met him in 2016 – a year after his house was burned down by Olvin and his goons. The following account is a mix of what Don Justino told me and his written statement to the public prosecutor. Don Justino thinks he was singled out as a troublemaker back in 2013, when security chief Douglas Bustillo took his photograph at the La Esperanza courtroom where he'd come to support Berta. After that, he was frequently harassed and threatened for refusing to support the dam.

One afternoon in May 2015, Don Justino was walking home when seven men, including Olvin, cornered him in the doorway of a *pulpería*, a small general store. He'd known most of them since they were babies. 'What's she saying, that *hija de puta,* what plan does she have for the dam?' demanded Olvin, pulling out a handgun and firing two shots into the air. He pointed the gun at Don Justino and threatened to shoot him dead if he didn't answer. Don Justino, thin but farmer-strong, managed to break free and run home. Some of the group, including Olvin and Héctor, followed him, and again threatened to kill him. Don Justino was terrified and fled to La Tejera for safety. When he returned a few hours later, the house was a smoking shell. All his possessions, clothes, furniture, supplies, were destroyed. If no one was hurt, it was only because his wife and children had left months earlier, unable to take the constant harassment.

Drug capos like the Cachiro brothers and small-town thug Olvin García represent two ends of the criminal state continuum. The Cachiros had cops, judges and politicians on their payroll, and so paid for protection directly. In Olvin's case,

DESA paid a hefty price to protect their man on the ground who got results: he scared off dam opponents and silenced others, until DESA could claim Valle de Ángeles supported the project.

On 27 December 2015, Olvin was arrested for illegal possession of two unlicensed guns. It transpired that he was already wanted for the October 2014 murder of Río Blanco resident Bernardo Pérez. Pérez was slashed twenty-three times with a machete, including eighteen blows to the skull, in front of his teenage son, who identified Olvin as the attacker. The arrest warrant related to the murder was issued by a judge on 14 January 2015, but never executed by police and prosecutors. (As there are about seventy houses in Valle de Ángeles, the suspect would not have been hard to find.)

The day García was arrested on the weapons charge, Sergio Rodríguez reported via WhatsApp to Castillo that a lawyer who 'knows the people at the public prosecutor's office well will handle the case' and that Jorge Ávila, the DESA security chief, would coordinate with her upon his arrival in La Esperanza (where García was detained and where the hearings would be held). The next morning, Ávila wrote to Rodríguez that the murdered man's young son was an eyewitness in the case and sent the name of the adolescent and his mother, indicating it was necessary 'to work on the witness', and that he needed a money transfer. Rodríguez requested the money from Castillo, who instructed him to contact Daniel Atala to arrange the deposit. Castillo also instructed Rodríguez: 'Talk to the lawyer so that they do not try that boy [Olvin García] . . . he is our best security at the dam site.'

Castillo was unhappy with the lawyer's fee, as she wanted 400,000 Lempiras ($17,000) to represent Olvin in both cases, the weapons and the murder charge. He reminded Rodríguez that the lawyer who defended the soldier killer of Tomás

García had only charged 100,000 Lempiras. Still, the expensive lawyer did her job.

On 31 December 2015, the murder charge against Olvin was conditionally dropped by the judge after the eyewitness – the victim's son – and his mother completely changed their testimony. Rodríguez wrote to Castillo that 'it all turned out fine' and informed Ávila when the child and his mother left the court. Ávila responded that 'they'll need some lunch' and that it was necessary to 'work on' the witnesses carefully to avoid them reporting coercion, threats, extortion or a bribe, lest their testimony become invalid.

Olvin walked free that same day, despite the detention order for the weapons charge, thanks to an improper request by the prison director for the case to be dismissed – a move described by independent investigators as fraudulent. Security chief Jorge Ávila personally collected Olvin from the courthouse in La Esperanza.

The murder charge was eventually dismissed as a result of the eyewitness withdrawing his testimony

Olvin's evasion of justice makes DESA look bad. It highlights the company's unusual influence over the criminal justice system and willingness to use thugs to impose the Agua Zarca project. When I asked DESA about Olvin in 2016, shortly after Berta's murder, Castillo denied any connection to him or knowledge about why or how he was let off the weapons charge. That was before the phone messages which told a different story.

7

The Threats

Tegucigalpa, November 2013

The day before the general elections, Berta Cáceres was downtown in the capital, Tegucigalpa, informing international observers about the wave of violence and criminal persecution that had been unleashed against her, COPINH and the Río Blanco community for opposing the Agua Zarca dam. 'These elections are taking place in a climate of fear,' she warned. 'There is a hit list circulating.'

At the end of the conference, I approached Berta. Though the forty-two-year-old looked exhausted, she smiled and agreed to be interviewed in La Esperanza in a couple of days' time. She was still in hiding from the bogus criminal charges against her linked to the dam. I learned that she rarely stayed in one place for more than a night, and never travelled alone. She was reluctant to give her address or phone number, but promised that if I found my way to the COPINH office, someone would bring me to her.

It was my first visit to Honduras, and with no smartphone or GPS, I got lost leaving Tegucigalpa, so it wasn't until mid-afternoon that I arrived at the COPINH HQ. Berta's deputy,

Tomás Gómez, escorted me to the gated family house where she was waiting, anxious to get on the road before dusk to her safe house for the night. She was solemn but warm, and we chatted for an hour or so in a shady angle of the pretty floral courtyard while drinking sweet black coffee served by Doña Austra, her mother.

The house is located on the corner of an L-shaped residential street several blocks from the small, bustling town centre. It felt tranquil, especially after the draining traffic fumes of the capital, but twice Berta stopped in mid-sentence: 'They're always watching me,' she said. 'Who are?' I asked. 'The army, the police, the government.' Patrol vehicles and cars with tinted windows and no number plates cruise past the house, day and night, she said.

Berta spoke passionately about Río Blanco and the River Gualcarque as she explained how the community had become militarized and terrorized. The murder of Tomás García, shot dead inside the dam encampment a few months earlier, was still raw. 'Who ordered his killing? Which important people and banks are behind the project, where is the money coming from?' she wanted to know.

These same questions would become the crux of her own family's quest to unmask the intellectual authors of Berta's murder: who ordered, planned and paid for her death? Burning questions that public prosecutors would show little interest in exploring.

Berta gave compelling details about some of the threats, racist abuse and harassment directed at those campaigning against the dam. Sometimes the abuse was dished out openly in front of police during protests, but most commonly came via text messages and anonymous callers. 'I'm not free to walk alone, or to swim in the sacred Gualcarque. I'm separated from my children. I cannot live in peace. I am always thinking about being killed or kidnapped,' she said. 'I am a human rights defender. I will not give up the struggle. I love my country, it doesn't have to be like this.'

Truth takes courage, I thought, and real courage means fighting in spite of one's fears.

At that point, Doña Austra came out and put a protective arm around Berta's shoulders: 'My daughter needs to travel before dark, don't take too long,' she said firmly. Berta smiled, and took her hand. 'I am basically repeating what my mother and grandmother did to fight oppression; they also lived with accusations and threats, just like I'm doing now.'

As we said goodbye, Berta made sure I understood how things worked in Honduras. 'The army has an assassination list of sixteen wanted human rights defenders, with my name at the top. I want to live, there are many things I still want to do in this world. I take precautions, but in the end, in this country where there is total impunity, I am vulnerable. When they want to kill me, they will do it.'

Threats Were the Norm

COPINH was founded in 1993, and from the very beginning upset powerful people. 'Military officers into contraband logging, landowners farming indigenous ancestral land, all these local elites hated us because we made a difference,' said Salvador Zúñiga. In the early days, COPINH business was mostly conducted at Berta's family home, and the children remember hushed discussions between their parents after yet another menacing note was delivered by an unknown hand. 'In my earliest memories, I remember threats and insults against my parents,' said Olivia Zúñiga Cáceres, the eldest daughter. 'At school, there were children and teachers who said our parents were thieves, millionaires with houses in Miami.'

Bertita remembers her siblings were playing in the garden once when she was nine or ten, and she and Olivia saw an unknown man outside the house with a gun. On another occasion, their dog Chocolate saved the nanny who was being attacked by someone with a knife. 'After that, Chocolate was our hero,' said Bertita. 'The fact is, there were so many incidents that threats seemed normal to us, maybe that's why we never really believed she'd be killed.' Threats were nothing new; but everything changed in 2013.

Berta perceived the dangers connected to Agua Zarca as something more serious. DESA's first security chief, Douglas Geovanny Bustillo, an ex-army lieutenant, didn't bother to contain his disdain for Berta and COPINH. He was rude and aggressive to people in Río Blanco, harassing community leaders like Chico Sánchez who got so tired of the constant calls and offers of bribes that he changed his telephone number. Bustillo also sexually harassed Berta. 'My life doesn't make sense without you,' he wrote in a text message on 20 September 2013 – a week after testifying against her in court.

The company president was different. David Castillo was a privately educated, bilingual, charismatic, retired military intelligence officer, who never directly threatened Berta. He was much too clever for that, and that's why she was afraid of him. In July 2013, a couple of days before Tomás García was killed in Río Blanco, Castillo and Sergio Rodríguez, DESA's community and environment manager, went to the COPINH training centre in La Esperanza, expecting a private sit-down with Berta. But she wasn't alone: representatives from Río Blanco and COPINH leadership were also there. 'I don't make the decisions,' said Berta. 'I do what the community wants.'

Castillo offered numerous social projects in exchange for ending the roadblock, but the community said no. Rodríguez complained that while the company was trying to find a solution to the conflict, COPINH didn't really care about the communities, it 'just wanted the project gone'.[1] Berta and the local leaders viewed the offer of community projects in exchange for supporting the dam as nothing more than a bribe.

Not long after Tomás García was killed, Berta asked Suyapa Martínez, director of the feminist Centre for Women's Studies (CEM-H), for permission to meet with Castillo in its office. 'That *maldito* is proposing stuff we don't agree with, but things are heavy, I have to talk to him,' she said. The meeting didn't last long. After he left, Berta confided in Suyapa: 'That one scares me, he's a military man.' A few weeks later, the court issued the arrest warrant against Berta. 'You see, this is different,' she told her daughters.

'She did warn us,' said Bertita. 'She often mentioned Geovanny Bustillo, Jorge Ávila, David Castillo and an unscrupulous family of *sicarios* who operated around Río Blanco. I documented the threats, I put out press releases. But honestly, I never thought anything would happen to her.' Laura, the youngest daughter, agreed: 'We knew she was being monitored and of course we worried, but this was normal, or maybe we just didn't want to believe it.' Hindsight can be agonizing.

A Terrible Year: 2013

I met Berta at the end of a gruelling year. She was dating Aureliano Molina, known as Lito, in her first public relationship since splitting up with Salvador Zúñiga more than a decade earlier. Lito was twenty years younger; his parents joined COPINH in the early days, so he grew up in the organization, and Berta and Salvador had been like family. He played an active role in COPINH until Berta threw him out, for reasons I'm not clear about. Then they got together, and were inseparable for two and a half tumultuous years. The relationship caused a tsunami in her professional and personal life at the worst possible time.

Salvador was furious. He left COPINH shortly before the Río Blanco roadblock, taking key leaders and half the membership with him to a new Lenca organization.[2] Olivia left too. Salvador publicly criticized Berta both professionally and personally, and things turned pretty ugly for a while. Salvador's decision to divide *their* organization hurt Berta more than anything else. Together they had launched the modern-day social movement in Honduras, and when COPINH split, people took sides – including Doña Austra, who picked Salvador. This was deeply hurtful. Berta felt betrayed and adrift from two of her closest, most trusted confidants. And then Río Blanco exploded.

'Río Blanco was the struggle that changed her more than any other,' said close friend Alba Marconi, whose return to Italy after a decade with COPINH left another gap in Berta's support network. 'She knew this dam was emblematic. Stopping Agua Zarca meant not only winning a battle, it meant winning a much bigger war.' Berta was totally committed, but she was distracted by the rifts which made her vulnerable as she geared up for the battle of her life.

Salvador's fury in 2013 wasn't all about Lito. Berta had begun as the junior partner in COPINH, but over time her confidence and standing increased as her vision and analysis evolved. She came to understand capitalism as not only an economic model, but also a patriarchal one, which dominated women in different ways.

That's why she understood that combating patriarchal

capitalism had to start with acknowledging and tackling taboo topics like gender violence, sexual harassment, homophobia and inequality within her own organization. '*Compa*,' she would say to Sotero Chavarría as they drove to meetings, 'you know you're a fucking *machista*.' 'I am, you're right, *hermana*, but I'm trying to change.' They were the best of friends, and every serious talk ended in laughter.

In every space, at every opportunity, she tackled gender violence and discrimination head on. 'It's us women that wash clothes and cook, we need to protect our rivers, we are the heart of our families and the struggle. *Cabrones*, you need to change, all this *machista* shit is old,' she'd urge her listeners at workshops in far-flung rural communities. It was uncomfortable. At times, men stormed out, others insulted her, but this motivated her to do more.

In March 2011, Berta convoked a women-only weekend assembly at Utopía during which she tackled big issues like patriarchy, machismo, feminism, racism, sexual diversity and sexual pleasure, encouraging participants to share personal experiences of violence, discrimination and resistance. 'We have to respect differences, we women can't stay quiet any longer. It doesn't matter if you can't read and write, you're smarter than many who can, your experiences matter, this is how we change things,' she said.

That weekend the women did not cook, or clean, or even make coffee. Instead they were served by male COPINH members, including Salvador. This made both men and women uneasy at first, but generated debate and helped change norms within COPINH. 'It illustrated Berta's political clarity and conviction, and a radical vision no other organization has, even today,' said Gustavo Castro.

A year later, in May 2012, ten women were elected by COPINH's general assembly to serve in the sixteen-member coordinating committee, which historically had been dominated by men. Berta was appointed general coordinator.

In Tegucigalpa during the post-coup demos, she bonded with a crew of feminists and LGBT activists,[3] who would become regular visitors to Río Blanco and La Esperanza. Yet Berta remained sceptical of women-only movements. She believed in change through organizations that reflected people's realities.

'My mum didn't identify as a feminist any more than she identified as an environmentalist or an activist, to her those labels were reductive. More than anything, she identified as an indigenous woman and a *luchadora social*, social warrior,' said Bertita. Perhaps it was her anti-patriarchal evolution which made the turbulent two-year relationship with Lito even harder to understand for those close to her.

Salvador says he left COPINH as a result of the growing influence of Berta's new feminist friends. It seems clear he struggled not only with Berta's critique of patriarchy, but also with her overtaking him as the go-to leader in COPINH. And yet they had grown up together, and remained bonded in many ways. They'd forged a fragile truce in the months before she was killed. 'Call Salvador!' were her last words.

Latin America is the most dangerous region in the world to be a woman.[4] Violence, including sexual violence, is pervasive and perpetrated with almost total impunity. Women and girls who dare report sexual abuse, rape or beatings are routinely failed by the deep-seated machismo that is just as pervasive in public institutions as in the home.[5]

Machismo refers to attitudes, customs, laws, beliefs and behaviours which identify and sustain men as dominant, stronger and more important in every sphere of life, public and private. In a macho world, women are considered physically and intellectually inferior and of lesser worth; such myths are used to justify lower pay, political and cultural exclusion, and violence. Machismo and racism are at the heart of capitalism, a system that thrives on inequalities, with rich white men at the top of the hierarchy and poor women of colour at the bottom.[6]

In Honduras, a woman is murdered every fifteen hours, which is nine each week. Between deadly violence and casual machismo, it's a hard place to be a woman. I love walking in big cities, but in Tegucigalpa that means enduring wolf whistles, hissing and offers of sex shouted from car windows while trying to dodge some of the worst drivers in Central America. I'm not trying to make light of it, it's a hostile environment where I struggle to keep my temper and nerve.

One evening I returned to my friend's tiny terraced house to find several neighbours standing silently, backs against the wall, listening to chilling screams coming from the house next door. 'Help, help, I'm pregnant, he's beating me!' For a few seconds I stood listening too, until the reality of what was happening – and could happen – jolted me into action. We called the cops, not expecting them to show up, but an hour later three female officers arrived. The boyfriend had kicked down two doors before falling into a drunken stupor, and the cops couldn't wake him. They drove the pregnant nineteen-year-old to her grandmother's house. When I returned six months later, she was back living with the boyfriend and their baby.

How significant was machismo in Berta's murder?

Berta's actions caused the Agua Zarca project to be suspended. She refused to go away or be quiet despite the sexual harassment, death threats and criminal charges. She didn't cower and couldn't be controlled. 'They killed her because they could not allow a woman to get away with endangering their business and threatening their investments,' Padre Melo told me. 'She crossed a line, which hurt their egos, and they could not let the "*pinche puta*" get away with it. Berta's murder was fundamentally a *machista* murder.'

Berta's friend, the Garifuna leader Miriam Miranda, agrees. 'They didn't just kill a defender, or an indigenous leader, or an environmentalist – they killed a woman who dared speak out against a patriarchal system, that's why I call it a political femicide.'

Miriam's deputy at OFRANEH, Aurelia Arzú (the all-male football team coach), said the killers wanted to send a message to both women and indigenous communities. 'They had to kill one or the other, Miriam or Berta, because dictators have to dictate.'

Twenty-First-Century Hit Lists: Social Cleansing

Hit lists were part and parcel of military repression in twentieth-century Latin America, used to identify, abduct and kill civilians.[7] The dirty war was barely over when compelling evidence of police-led death squads came to light during the mandate of Ricardo Maduro,[8] elected in 2002 on a promise to crush the US-imported street gangs known as *maras*.[9] He introduced the region's first *mano dura* or iron fist crackdown on the maras, which made being young, poor and male enough to get you jailed, killed or disappeared without trace. Inspired by anti-Nazi legislation in Europe, he outlawed gang membership, sending thousands of alleged young gangsters to rot in inhumane, inadequate prisons. For Maduro, the gangs were a personal issue, and with this new enemy, as with the communists, the end justified the means.

From day one, human rights advocates complained that

Maduro's war on gangs failed to make gang-controlled barrios safer, while providing cover for summary justice: a hit list doesn't need to be written down on paper.

Whistle-blowers brave enough to expose an ugly truth have regularly been fired, smeared or killed in targeted attacks.

María Luisa Borjas was sacked as head of internal affairs for the national police after exposing extreme violence perpetrated and covered up by senior cops in 2002. Borjas was suspended three days after holding a press conference in which she accused the then security minister, Óscar Álvarez,[10] of obstructing an investigation into multiple extrajudicial killings and disappearances of young gang suspects, by police operating as a 'social cleansing' squad.[11] The pattern pointed to state policy rather than lone wolves, Borjas told me. Álvarez denied any wrongdoing, and was never prosecuted or sanctioned.

The cop's cop was ousted with a squeaky clean, twenty-five-year police record, no pension, and a mountain of dirt on high-ranking officers and politicians.

Talk of a hit list targeting social leaders first emerged in the chaotic months after the coup, with Berta, Carlos H. Reyes, Padre Melo and Miriam Miranda among those rumoured to be on it. When I met Berta in 2013, she'd received more detailed information about the list, that's why she and others denounced it publicly. But again, *no pasó nada* . . . it wasn't taken seriously.

Hit lists are designed to generate maximum terror. The goal isn't to kill everyone on the list. Some will abandon the cause, flee or flip; others are included to divert attention or cause chaos. 'Hit lists remind us that the state killing machine remains active and ready, and they maintain an atmosphere of constant anxiety within social movements,' said Padre Melo.

At the same time, living under constant threat can start to feel normal, in part because it's impossible to function otherwise. This can also lead to poor choices in chronically high-risk situations, as the threshold triggering the body's usual stress warning system is so high. This is one reason why a person facing serious threats may sometimes take incomprehensible risks.

Ethnic prosecutor Jany del Cid tried to persuade Berta to accept police protection. 'She told me more than once that she was afraid, but she wouldn't accept police guards, because she didn't trust them.' She argued to Jany: 'What's the use of a police escort when they're the ones persecuting me? They'll know where I am, what I'm doing, who I'm with, no, I feel safer with COPINH, and in the communities.'

Brigitte Gynther from SOAW sent Jany a chronological list of threats and incidents which she'd compiled. Berta denounced threats in press releases, on social media and in interviews, and filed complaints about racism and ILO 169 violations; but she never formally testified about the threats she received, which meant no criminal investigation was ever opened.

Wasted Opportunity

Berta was a strong voice among the *refundacionistas* (reconstructionists) – those who backed the ambitious project to reconstruct the state by reforming the Constitution, to open up political power structures hitherto dominated by the economic, political, military and religious elites. That dream was shattered by the coup. The *refundacionistas* vehemently opposed conversion of the post-coup united resistance, the Frente, into a political party. As Berta put it, 'We can't be a political party, we're the social movement.' But that's what happened. Zelaya, backed by disaffected Liberal Party supporters and a hotchpotch of civil society groups, wanted to regain power through the existing party-political structure. Libre (Liberty and Refoundation) was created in 2011 and promptly absorbed the national grassroots movement, generating a collective sigh of relief among the coup plotters and sympathizers.[12] Berta refused to join, but the change hit her hard. 'She knew they were jumping into a dark hole,' said Gustavo Castro.

And she was right. The move destroyed or at least mortally wounded the social movement. After the bubble burst, everyone retreated to their own corner. A decade later the movement still hadn't recovered: travelling across Honduras to research this book, the hurt, anger and divisions still felt raw. For veteran Carlos H. Reyes, it was an opportunity wasted. 'What hurts me most in life is that we failed to take advantage of the post-coup movement to change the country. As soon as Libre agreed to participate in the elections, the coup resistance was over, and hope died.'

The Bajo Aguán

After interviewing Berta in 2013, I went to the Aguán, where campesinos were fighting to recuperate land fraudulently obtained by the Big Three palm magnates. The drive from the relative rural calm of La Esperanza to the tropical 'city' of Tocoa was unforgettable: miles and miles of uniform rows of towering, robust African palms, crater-sized potholes, a puncture close to dusk, a flat spare tyre, and the start of a three-day monster storm. I was travelling with another reporter, and we were met at the petrol station on the edge of Tocoa by Vitalino

Álvarez, alias Chino because of his silky thick hair, reputed at the time to be one of the most committed and beleaguered campesino leaders in the Aguán. Vitalino introduced us to some victims of the violence perpetrated by paramilitary groups allegedly working for the palm conglomerates.

We met Dominga Ramos at her tiny house set within a plot of African palms, maize and lanky beanstalks, and sat outside on plastic chairs as the rain lashed down on the patio roof. Dominga quietly told us about her husband Matías Vallé, fifty-one, a founder member of MUCA (Unified Campesino Movement of the Aguán), who had been shot dead by two masked men on a motorcycle as he waited for a bus not far from the house. 'He was an honest, simple man who believed in collective action,' Dominga said. He had refused money from Dinant employees to leave the campesino movement. A few weeks later he was dead. 'I saw a police officer trying to hide a bullet shell in the ground with his foot. We buried him in a secret place so they couldn't remove his head [for a bounty]. I am tired and scared,' she said, looking close to tears. 'My two sons left because of threats. We just want to work our land in peace.'

In those days the Aguán was militarized to the hilt: after hopes of a political settlement collapsed with the coup and desperate campesinos coordinated large-scale land occupations, thousands of troops were deployed. The push back against the campesinos was fast and furious: private security guards, police, army and paramilitaries had during that first visit already killed more than a hundred farmers, while many more were forcibly displaced or silenced. Behind this campaign of terror lay the West's bottomless need for energy: African palms were the most profitable of crops because the oil was sold to North America and Europe for biofuel, and could be traded in the carbon credit market.

Berta in a beauty pageant during the late 1970s

Berta, Doña Austra and Olivia in
La Esperanza in the early 1990s

Berta, Salvador Zúñiga, and Doña Austra
in La Esperanza the late 1980s

Berta with her brother Carlos in La Esperanza

Berta and Salvador with Cuban medics helping in the aftermath of Hurricane Mitch in 1998

Courtesy of the Cáceres family

Berta during my only interview with her in November 2013 in her office at Doña Austra's house in La Esperanza

Berta and her mother Doña Austra at the family home in La Esperanza, November 2013

Berta addressing members of the Rio Blanco communities at the old oak tree, El Roble, in 2015

Berta taping a segment at the COPINH community radio station, Radio Guarajambala, in La Esperanza in 2015

Courtesy of the Goldman Prize

Berta on the banks of the Gualcarque River in 2015

In 2013, Tocoa was chock-a-block with security forces, yet business was booming for Los Cachiros; the Maradiaga brothers were often spotted in heavily armoured SUVs. Vitalino recommended switching hotels every night to avoid *orejas* or snitches, which we did, but after three days the rain was still bucketing down and we'd run out of safe places. It's true that grey skies and relentless rain make everything feel more menacing, but trying to find a way out after the main highway was left impassable by flooded bridges was nerve-racking.

As commander of the Xatruch multi-agency taskforce, SOA alumnus Colonel Germán Alfaro oversaw the post-coup militarization and bloodbath in the Aguán. Shortly after that visit, Alfaro publicly attacked researcher Annie Bird, after she documented dozens of murders and other serious abuses linked to military forces based at the 15th Battalion,[13] where US special forces conducted counter-drug training ops. Alfaro accused Annie of lying and trying to destabilize the Aguán. His comments were widely published alongside her photo, triggering a mini-diplomatic incident as human rights groups condemned the thinly veiled threats. As soon as Berta heard about it, she mobilized COPINH to protest. Berta and Annie went way back, having worked together since the late 1990s. Annie is married to Berta's cousin, so they are also family. But every fight was Berta's fight – she never turned away from injustice. A Xatruch unit would eventually be ordered to neutralize community leaders including Berta, Vitalino and Yoni Rivas, but we did not know that until much later.

Yoni Rivas is a razor-sharp campesino leader whose name was on the hit list Berta denounced in 2013. He's one of the smartest, kindest people I know in Honduras, and his arresting story has to be part of this book. Yoni's problems started when the campesinos turned to direct action to recuperate land.[14] The first roadblock was set up on the Tocoa highway days after Zelaya's inauguration. It brought the new government to the table; promises were made, broken and made again, but nothing changed. In June 2009, 2,500 campesino families blocked access to Facussé's palm oil processing plant, paralysing production. This was days before the coup, and the palm magnates accused Zelaya of siding with communist campesinos after he sent in negotiators rather than security forces. Zelaya flew to Tocoa by helicopter and made a promise to a packed stadium that lands unjustly taken from the campesinos would be returned. Perhaps this was the last straw for the coup plotters, as ten days later Zelaya was on a military plane in his pyjamas. Yoni sat down with Zelaya a few weeks later in Managua. The deposed president told him: 'That land belongs to you campesinos, fight for it.' And they did.

By the end of February 2010, the campesinos had control of 20,000 hectares across nineteen farms, including one in the community La Confianza. This was an unarmed insurgency to take back what was legally theirs, the leaders emphasized, though the media claimed they'd been armed by Nicaragua and Venezuela. The backlash was instant: armed police, special forces and private security guards raided the farms. Those on their troublemaker lists who were captured were charged with trespass and robbery. Farms were evicted but quickly reoccupied by the campesinos. It was like a high-stakes game of Whac-A-Mole. Things got really serious on 7 April 2010, when 8,000 troops were deployed to the area, forcing the campesinos at gunpoint to Pepe Lobo's negotiating table a week later. The offer on the table was faraway virgin land in La Mosquitia, plus compensation from Facussé and Nicaraguan palm magnate René Morales. 'We didn't want money, we wanted *our* land,' said Yoni. 'We were born here, and we're prepared to die here.' The final deal was a sweet one for the palm magnates, as the desperate campesinos agreed to buy back their own land. But when Facussé demanded more than double the market price, the campesinos refused, and the fertile lands turned into killing fields.

But first, military intelligence infiltrated the campesino movement to destroy it from inside. Celio Bautista Rodríguez Ponce, a charismatic former special forces sergeant, returned to La Confianza after several years in the US, was elected president of the farm cooperative, and used the position to generate internal conflicts.[15] It was chaotic and confusing, said Yoni. Celio sometimes wore the uniform of a security guard, but other times was kitted out in military gear and seen with Xatruch commander Colonel Alfaro. 'People knew he had formed a security group but at first thought it was to protect them, not kill them,' said Annie Bird. But when Celio's efforts to destroy the farm completely were foiled by other members of the cooperative, including Yoni, who persuaded others to vote against Celio's plans, he went from provocateur to paramilitary leader, and the killings escalated.[16]

Yoni started receiving text messages warning him to 'think of his family', as soon as the farm occupations began in 2010. The threats escalated into assassination attempts. On 11 March 2011, Yoni, Vitalino and two others narrowly escaped a group of *sicarios* by abandoning their car and persuading a terrified bus driver to ignore fake police checkpoints set up as traps. In September 2012, Pepe Lobo sent a message to Yoni and his colleagues that intelligence services had credible information of a plot to kill them. Shortly after, a MUCA lawyer and evangelical preacher, Antonio Trejo, was shot dead leaving church.[17] The very next day, soldiers surrounded Yoni's house.

Throughout most of these incidents, as friends and colleagues were being picked off, Yoni survived for weeks, sometimes months, in neighbouring countries and far-flung rural outposts with barely enough money to eat. But the hit that changed everything was the slaying of his friend José Ángel Flores, president of MUCA, who was cut down in broad daylight on 18 October 2016. Yoni heard the gunfire from his house. The killers celebrated by ripping off their hoods in front of the many eyewitnesses, enabling them to identify Celio's right-hand man Osvin Caballero Santamaría, alias La Ardilla (Squirrel), as one of the gunmen. Jesús Perdomo, the lead investigator in Berta's murder, was assigned to the case.[18]

'That day the paramilitaries showed us they no longer felt any need to hide what they were doing,' said Yoni. 'It's not the same having an enemy outside the community as having one inside, operating with impunity.' He's barely spent a night at home since the murder of Flores.

This paramilitary structure directed by Celio, with Ardilla as his alleged top killer, was meticulously laid out in a criminal case file leaked to Yoni by an ex-public prosecutor, which he shared with me. The file includes the transcript of a meeting convened in August 2016 to discuss killing Yoni, Vitalino and José Ángel Flores. 'It's inevitable that we're going to kill those *hijos de puta*,' said Ardilla's brother Melkin, in a conversation recorded on a mobile phone. Ardilla's and Celio's families live a couple of hundred metres from Yoni's wife and three sons.

After José Ángel was killed, Ardilla's mother Digna was seen out on the street offering 50,000 Lempiras to anyone who would kill those *hijos de puta* Vitalino and Yoni. When I met Digna in 2013, she played the role of grieving mother, claiming Ardilla had disappeared after being detained by

Colonel Alfaro in La Mosquitia, where he'd moved to farm land. Ardilla was certainly detained in a Xatruch military op, but he fled, not moved, to La Mosquitia after killing his cousin, or so I was later told by a local prosecutor. He was out of sight for several months, but eventually reappeared in a fancy SUV armed with military-grade weapons, having most likely been recruited by the army to kill *sans* uniform. Paying customers, the evidence gathered by police investigators, prosecutors, and local activists suggests, included palm magnates, military chiefs and drug traffickers.

In addition to farm cooperatives like the one in La Confianza, Celio's paramilitary group eventually took over MUCA itself. Vitalino went with them. After twenty-plus years fighting the good fight, Vitalino turned against his colleagues after having been given some land to farm. A couple of years later, as the trial of the first eight defendants accused of killing Berta prepared to get under way, Vitalino would turn the screws on me and Yoni.

Yoni's refusal to give in has come at huge personal cost. His eldest boy dropped out of high school because of panic attacks, and his wife suffered a sudden facial paralysis, a condition linked to extreme stress, weeks after receiving messages from Ardilla threatening to 'pull out her tongue' and burn down the family house. In August 2017, Yoni returned to Tocoa for a meeting and was spotted visiting his ageing mother by a neighbour turned informant. Half an hour or so after he'd left, a white jeep with no number plates was parked outside his mother's house, and Celio's *sicarios* were hovering nearby. On that occasion we left the Aguán together in the back of a pickup truck. Yoni sucked on sour lemons to calm his nerves: he could barely breathe.

There's a good side-story involving Yoni, the Cachiros and the alleged assassin Celio.[19] Yoni was nominated by the campesino base to stand as a Libre congressional candidate in 2013. One early morning in September, Celio came to see him with what he called a once-in-a-lifetime offer. 'Powerful people see potential in you and want to help,' he began. 'You know who I'm talking about, the guys who control things around here. Javier [Rivera Maradiaga, leader of Los Cachiros] wants to give you whatever you need for the campaign, money, vehicles, security.'

Yoni was gobsmacked, and tried to buy some time by promising Celio he'd get back to him after consulting colleagues. 'Not everyone gets an opportunity like this, you're an arsehole if you don't take it,' said Celio on his way out. Yoni never returned Celio's calls, and the Nationalist incumbent Óscar Nájera won the election. Several years later, Nájera was named during the US trial against Fabio Lobo in 2017, after which he admitted knowing the Rivera Maradiaga clan, but denied any wrongdoing. In late 2018, La Ardilla was detained in Mexico and returned to Honduras to face multiple homicide charges; Celio is also wanted in connection with several homicides in the Aguán, but at the end of 2019 he remained a fugitive from justice.

At stake is the plan to convert the Aguán into a lucrative special economic zone, dedicated to mining, agro-industry, tourism and energy. The main obstacle is the social movement, specifically the campesinos and Garifunas. Beyond territorial conflicts, the Aguán is where deals are done to kill people. It's a hornet's nest of *sicarios*. The Aguán has become an intolerable inferno, and many have been forced to flee. I am reminded of this quote from scholar Samir Amin: 'We have reached a point at which, in order to open up a new area for capital expansion, it is necessary to destroy entire societies.'

I worry all the time about Yoni and Miriam Miranda.

The Struggle Never Ends

In 2011, the Central American Institute of Fiscal Studies (ICEFI) published the fascinating book *Fiscal Policy: An Expression of the Power of Central American Elites*. The chapter on Honduras, by the economist Hugo Noé Pino, analyses how economic elites control and manipulate tax policies to their advantage. Briefly, lavish tax breaks and opaque accounting rules are designed by the elites to favour their many and diverse business interests, and implemented with the help of the politicians and political parties they put into power by dint of campaign donations and media coverage. But manipulating public policies isn't enough for them. Laws intended to guarantee the most basic rights of the poor majority are simultaneously violated, and people like Berta, Miriam and Yoni who dare to challenge the status quo are dealt with using a gamut of tactics rooted in counterinsurgency doctrine: bribes, threats, arrests, surveillance, more threats, smear campaigns and ultimately death. The 2017 tourism law demonstrates how this plays out.

Honduras is no tourism Mecca. It has a spectacular coral reef, tranquil Caribbean inlets and some interesting Mayan ruins, but endemic levels of violence, militarized streets and poor transport infrastructure put off the spring breakers and retirement tours. Rather than focusing on these rudimentary deterrents, the government decided a new era of tax breaks was the answer.

Incentives were already generous; for instance, 1998 legislation granted a ten-year exemption on sales taxes for any self-declared new tourism business. Among the businesses to benefit are burger and chicken joints tourists would be unlikely ever to set foot in. The new law extends this sweetener to fifteen years, and offers tax breaks on construction materials, air conditioning and furniture to any self-declared tourism enterprise that is expanding or renovating, without it having to demonstrate it is in fact in the tourism game and not laundering money. This sounds bad, but it gets worse.

The star feature is the Fondo de Inversiones Turísticas (FITUR), a new private–public partnership steered by the big business association, COHEP.[20] FITUR will propose new tourism projects and find investors. It also has the power to take forcible possession of land or water by declaring it an area of common interest. If a rancher, for example, doesn't want to sell, too bad – FITUR will decide on a fair price and that's that. In addition, the new law doesn't apply only to private land; ecological reserves and unexplored archaeological sites are also fair game.

The new law would create 250,000 jobs within five years, promised Juan Orlando Hernández and COHEP, and so it was expedited through Congress without public consultation.[21] How the law would take account of the ILO 169 obligations protecting ancestral lands didn't appear in the press releases, but for the coastal Garifuna people, who've already lost huge swathes of ancestral land to tourism projects, it could be catastrophic.

'This law could lead to our extinction,' said Miriam Miranda in Vallecito – just the sort of coastal oasis that could catch the eye of developers. 'It indiscriminately puts our lands and beaches into the marketplace for expropriation in the name of development, which as a community we have to fight against. Which means more repression, more leaders in jail, more leaders dead . . . It's at times like this I miss Berta by my side. We should be fighting this together.'

8

Resistance and Repression

Buenos Aires: 21 November 2014

Several months into researching this book, I came across a short television interview that Berta gave in November 2014 to Resumen Latinoamericano in Buenos Aires.[1] In twelve compelling minutes, she effectively summed up the repression, power grabs and impunity in post-coup Honduras covered in this chapter. I was struck by her unflinching clarity. 'We're still living the coup. All the power and machinery of the coup remains intact, not only that, it's been consolidated by the oligarchy and transnational powers through the expansion of grand capital in megaprojects. There's been a total surrender of sovereignty, and a level of political cynicism [from Hernández] that we've never seen before, not even with Lobo and Micheletti,' she explained energetically over the noise of traffic.

But a weariness came over Berta when she spoke about the *compañeros* most recently lost. 'There's constant violation of human rights by the government and elites, the criminalization and social cleansing of grassroots leaders: take the murder of Margarita Murillo, who was an important figure in

Honduras and Central America, or the recent cases of *compañero* Juan Galindo and a young COPINH boy in Río Blanco.² These killings are part of a well-planned repressive policy, supplemented by legal mechanisms such as the new intelligence law which brands the defence of territory as a crime, impacting on those of us involved in struggles against mines, energy projects and the privatization of natural resources.' Berta went on to denounce the re-militarization of the country amid increased US intervention. '[The Americans] are now participating in anti-gang operations, attacks against campesinos in the Aguán, and the DEA committed a massacre in La Mosquitia. All this is part of the counterinsurgency plan. We don't call it that anymore, but in Central America the counterinsurgency strategy against social movements was never suspended and that's exactly what's being used now, to decapitate those of us fighting and resisting capitalism in our own territories.' It reminded me of how, for the sponsors of counterinsurgency doctrine, the end always justifies the means.

Berta continued: 'The coup plotters just kept going. And then came the issue of the elections. Hillary Clinton, in her book *Hard Choices*, practically spelled out what was going to happen in Honduras. This demonstrates the meddling of North Americans in our country ... She, Clinton, acknowledged that they didn't permit Mel Zelaya's return to the presidency. There were going to be elections. And the international community – officials, governments, the great majority – accepted this, even though we warned it was going to be very dangerous and would be a licence for atrocity ... and that's what we saw happen.'

During the 2016 US presidential race, as reporters started digging into Clinton's memoir, she was asked about her role in the coup. 'Now, I didn't like the way it looked or the way they did it,' she replied, 'but they [the legislature and judiciary] had a very strong argument that they had followed the Constitution and the legal precedents ... our assessment was, we will just make the situation worse by punishing the Honduran people if we declare a coup and we immediately have to stop all aid for the people, but we should slow-walk and try to stop anything that the government could take advantage of, without calling it a coup.

'Zelaya had friends and allies, not just in Honduras, but in some of the neighbouring countries, like Nicaragua, and we could have had a terrible civil war that would have been just terrifying in its loss of life.'[3]

By then Berta was dead.

Killing environment and land defenders isn't new in Honduras. Environmentalist Jeanette Kawas was murdered in a suspected military operation in 1995 in the tropical department of Atlántida, after saving a coastal strip that was home to more than 400 flora and fauna species from tourism developers. Berta admired Kawas, whose case changed international law.[4] In the early 2000s, ten activists from the Environmental Movement of Olancho (MAO) were killed or forced to flee as they battled to stop deforestation and water depletion by networks of powerful landowners, logging companies and criminal gangs in rebellious Olancho. Father José Andrés Tamayo won the Goldman Prize in 2005 for leading MAO's campaign to stop a highway into the forest to benefit the sawmills. The Salvadoran-born Catholic priest led the 'March for Life' which helped put environmental issues, especially illegal logging and corruption in the national forestry institute, on the political map.

Padre Tamayo was in the thick of the post-coup resistance. It was he who persuaded First Lady Xiomara Castro to lead nationwide protests. Soon after, the de facto government revoked his Honduran nationality and deported him. As the sociologist Eugenio Sosa puts it: 'The state and economic elites have been complicit in the systematic killing of land and environmental defenders who threaten business interests since at least the 1980s ... Back then defenders were called subversives, now they are criminalized. Either way, they're considered enemies of the state.'

After the coup, such violence spiralled out of control. Berta mentioned campesino organizer Margarita Murillo, fifty-six, brutally killed on 27 August 2014 while tending her crops in El Planón, in the department of Cortés. A lifelong advocate for women farmers in a male-dominated world, she had already been tortured for her activism in the 1980s. She was shot dead just days after reporting death threats linked to a tense local land struggle.[5] In Honduras, the number and frequency of threats against male and female land defenders is more or less the same, but, for women, these threats are 24 per cent more likely to convert into physical attacks.[6]

Between 2010 and 2015, Honduras was the deadliest place on earth for those protesting the theft of land and the destruction of the natural world, according to the death tally kept by London-based group Global Witness. Few homicides were investigated and fewer solved. Berta's murder triggered international outrage, but failed to stop the bloodshed.

The targeted post-coup violence wasn't limited to rural areas. Honduras also became the deadliest place to practise law, with at least 151 lawyers killed between 2010 and mid-2018, one in five of them women. The death count includes lawyers working on tax cases, representing gang members, campesinos and human rights activists, as well as some who lost cases and some who simply asked to be paid.[7] Violence against the LGBT community also exploded after the coup. By October 2019, 331 people had been murdered

– an average of thirty every year, according to the LGBT violence observatory Cattrachas, compared to less than two annually between 1994 and 2008.[8] Inevitably perhaps, freedom of expression also came under attack as the government sought to silence dissent. Of the seventy-five journalists murdered between 2003 and mid-2018, 95 per cent lost their lives after the coup, according to the National Human Rights Commission (CONADEH). Journalists are most often targeted when investigating links between corrupt state officials and organized crime. Reporting on Berta's case made me a target too.

Dina Meza is one of my journalist heroes. A courageous campaigning reporter, she was exiled in 2013 but returned to launch PEN Honduras and the online independent news website Pasos de Animal Grande (Large Animal Steps, implying the imminence of something important) where she continues to expose corruption and human rights violations. We met at a roadside fast food café one Sunday evening in August 2017, on what was day forty-seven of a hunger strike by students at the public university UNAH, demanding the rector be sacked. She was absolutely exhausted, and in pain, having broken her arm while running with students to escape an armed assailant. 'It's tough, but the students are terrified that if they're alone, they'll be killed. Police circle the university, we hear shots at night, so nobody really sleeps.' Still, she seemed better than during our last meeting, when she'd been plagued by stress-induced migraines.

Dina told me about an unnerving incident in March that year, when an unknown man approached her on the bus and murmured: 'I'm armed, there's four of us, and we have orders to kill you.' He wouldn't say orders from whom, and then appeared to make several phone calls. 'I've got the woman but she doesn't have blue eyes, what should I do?' he said.

Dina had no idea if he really made the calls or if the whole thing was a ruse. When he tried to take Dina's photo, she stood up and overcoming her fear looked him straight in the eye. 'Pleased to meet you,' she said, before alighting and calling her son for help. She reported the incident to the government's protection mechanism team, ostensibly designed to save lives by acting fast.[9] Four months later Dina was still waiting for action, and came to our meeting by bus as she couldn't afford a taxi. Honduras was the third country in Latin America to implement a protection mechanism, after Mexico and Colombia. In each country, journalists and defenders continue to be slain. Impunity kills.

Truths

The truth behind the crimes in the lead-up to and immediate aftermath of the coup depends on who you ask. Two truth commissions were created in 2010 – one by Pepe Lobo, the other by human rights groups – which helped validate each side's version of the facts, while failing to make any notable political or social impact. It's still not clear exactly how many people were killed, injured, raped, detained or disappeared between Zelaya's ouster and Lobo thanking Hillary Clinton. In one of his first acts as president, Lobo granted an amnesty for coup crimes. It was a rubber stamp for impunity.

One indisputable truth is that between 2009 and November 2016, the IACHR issued ninety-eight protective measures covering 461 human rights workers, trade unionists, lawyers, LGBT people, environmentalists, journalists, indigenous activists and their close relatives, all facing serious and imminent risks linked to their activism in Honduras, a country of 8 million people.[10] But the IACHR lacks authority to force a state to comply, and, in most cases, no adequate measures to mitigate the risks were implemented. Berta was the fourteenth recipient of protective measures to be murdered since 2009.[11] Two others were disappeared during that period, while dozens more fled. The failures and limits of protection measures are not properly understood, but we know that in Honduras the state is designed to protect the economic interests of the elites, not those opposing them. In reality, the only reliable protective measure is leaving Honduras. Berta was unwilling to leave, which her eldest daughter Olivia told me was tantamount to a suicide wish.

The UNAH rector was Julieta Castellanos.[12] During the 1980s and 90s, sociologist Julieta was a prominent anticorruption and human rights campaigner. She created the National Violence Observatory after her twenty-two-year-old son was abducted and killed by the police in 2001. Fast forward to 2017, and the same Castellanos authorized state and private security forces to enter campus; they then attacked peacefully protesting students with metal chains and batons. Castellanos condemned the students and defenders like Dina and another female journalist, Tommy Morales,[13] as agitators and terrorists. She went so far as to threaten Padre Melo with legal action after he organized a concert on campus by the Venezuelan protest band, Los Guaraguaos, complaining that '[Melo] encourages disrespect, anarchy and sets a bad example by invading a state institution where there are authorities to respect.' The hunger strike in mid-2017 was an effort to force her out. The problem dated back to 2014–15, when six students were expelled after speaking out against rising tuition fees, biased admission exams and the curtailment of student representation. One, Dayanara Castillo, fled to Costa Rica after surviving two assassination attempts. Students mobilized across the country in support, and scores were expelled and arbitrarily arrested. At a court hearing in June 2017, an agent from the elite investigative squad ATIC admitted infiltrating the student movement at the request of UNAH bosses. The admission barely caused a stir.

What happened to Julieta? She claimed to be combating a leftist plot to take over the university. A takeover also happened to our country, said her former human rights buddies. The violent crackdown on campus was a microcosm of the militarized authoritarian state.

The post-coup surge in targeted violence took place amid an explosion in violence overall, as the criminal underworld flexed its muscles. Every nook and cranny of every weak institution was exploited and infiltrated as security forces focused on repressing anti-coup protesters first, then communities in resistance. Death squads reappeared and the murder rate surged: in 2010 Honduras was ranked the world's most violent country outside an official war zone, an inglorious position it held until 2014.

Homicide and drug trafficking were already on the rise before the coup, but the ouster of Zelaya led to the creation of a major cocaine route and, by 2012, 80 per cent of South American drug planes bound for the US passed through Honduras.[14] The drug trade fuelled bloody turf wars and the killings escalated. 'Honduras became the most dangerous country in the world because institutions collapsed and high levels of impunity opened doors to even wider corruption and criminality,' said criminal court judge Guillermo López, who was sacked after the coup. 'Politicians were given carte blanche by the US embassy, but it got out of control.' Take Yoro in the tropical north. Here, lawyer Arnaldo Urbina Soto (aka 'Negro' or 'Smiley') used his stints as mayor to tighten the family's grip on political and criminal power.[15] The Urbina

Soto clan started out rustling cattle,[16] just like the Cachiros, before moving into narcotics, and the two families worked in harmony. The Cachiros, with a stack of Nationalist politicians on the payroll, paid the Urbina Sotos to receive cocaine-loaded planes on their patch, store the drugs and convey them to the next drop point. Not so collegial was the Valle Valle clan, headquartered in Copán on the border with Guatemala, and another key link in the cocaine distribution chain. The Valles didn't want to pay rent in Yoro, they wanted to control the city. In the middle of the feud in 2014, the murder rate in the municipality of Yoro was 104 per 100,000, just behind San Pedro Sula, then the most violent city in the world. The Valles were, however, willing to do business with another mayor, Amílcar Alexander Ardón Soriano in north-west Copán, thanks to a so-called mafia pact brokered by alleged drug capo Tony Hernández.

Despite the violent chaos, the Urbina Sotos' political stock boomed. In 2013, Arnaldo was named local campaign manager for Hernández, who saw no irony in pledging a law and order platform while standing beside the corrupt mayor. Prosecutors later found a chequebook receipt in an Urbina Soto car for a payment of 4 million Lempiras ($160,000) to the National Party. Hernández won the election using ill-gotten campaign funds, and Arnaldo was re-elected, allowing him to maintain a firm grip over the land title and logging regulation agencies, lucrative public works contracts and local police.

But all good things must come to an end. In 2017, Arnaldo was convicted of money laundering, while his brothers Mario and Miguel Ángel were acquitted. A few months later, in July 2018, the three brothers were indicted by New York prosecutors for conspiracy to import cocaine and multiple weapons charges.[17] By mid-2019 Arnaldo was in jail in Honduras, appealing the money laundering verdict, and facing almost 200 corruption charges in a separate case; he cannot be extradited to the US until he has been tried at home. Mario and Miguel were on the lam. As the researcher Annie Bird told me, what went down in Yoro demonstrates that institutions didn't exactly 'fail' after the coup. It was worse, in that control was ceded to criminal networks of politicians, judges, prosecutors, cops, soldiers and the actual so-called bad guys, who split the spoils to obtain wealth and power. 'The coup strengthened the criminal state,' said Bird.

President Hernández himself has vigorously denied allegations of narco links, continuing to claim he has an unparalleled record in cooperating with the US in its war against drugs, which includes reinstating extradition. It's true that over forty traffickers have been extradited or turned themselves in during his time in power, and several testified in court against former friends and foes to ensure leniency. For instance Amilcar Ardón would eventually turn himself in to the DEA, admitting to drug smuggling and involvement in fifty-six murders, before becoming the star witness in the trial against Tony Hernández.[18] Ardón's loose lips – along with those of several other self-confessed gangsters – helped build the case against Tony Hernández and his role in what US prosecutors would deem 'state-sponsored drug trafficking'.

As murders and insecurity escalated after the coup, the government had the perfect villains on hand to blame: the maras, the tattooed territorial transnational street gangs like MS-13 and Barrio 18. The maras have caused untold misery mainly in their own poor, urban neighbourhoods, by killing to control pathetically small plazas for drug dealing and extortion rackets, or just for kicks. But as violence soared, almost every grisly crime was blamed on them, a situation in turn used to justify the re-militarization of streets, schools, playing fields, even hospitals as part of the *Super Mano Dura* security strategy. I'm not trying to downplay the malignity of the maras – I've documented too many lives ruined by these gangs. But blaming every atrocity on the maras is well wide of the mark, and gives the paramilitaries, drug traffickers and security forces an undeserved free pass. Though maybe that's the point, said counterinsurgency expert Michael McClintock: 'The coup was such a throwback to the 1980s, except everything is now clouded by the fog of the drug war and gang war, and it's easy to smokescreen targeted killings by general violence.'

In April 2016, a month after Berta's murder, I visited Casa Alianza, a child rights group working with street children, orphans, drug users and migrants, for a story on the re-militarization of public spaces. The shelter is in the middle of old Tegucigalpa, near the bustling central market in the so-called historic centre (which is neither pretty nor historic, but is at least devoid of the ugly malls that blight the rest of the city).

Poor young people are being murdered in cold blood, according to the director, José Guadalupe Ruelas. 'The vast majority of victims are standing on street corners or playing, not in a conflict situation, when they are executed by *sicarios* with professional weapons. Their tortured, handcuffed bodies are dumped in rivers or left on the streets. These are death squads; this is social cleansing.'[19] Ruelas showed me a chilling video he'd filmed a few days earlier. The footage captured four or five stocky men in jeans and t-shirts, forcing a strapping homeless lad into an SUV with no number plate. You hear Ruelas, who happened to be passing, asking who they are, where they are taking him and why, as he records the scene on his phone. As he follows them around the car, you glimpse, just for a second, a skinny uniformed cop in the back seat. The fifteen-year-old homeless kid, who had a solvent habit, survived to tell his ordeal to Ruelas, who recounted it to me.

The cops in civilian clothes drove him to a nearby police base where they accused him of snatching one of their mobile phones a couple of days earlier – which he had done, unaware he was stealing from a cop. Instead of booking him for theft, they charged him falsely with illegal possession of a weapon. They roughed him up a bit and let him go. 'Filming them probably saved his life that day, but for how long? Now, if he turns up dead, he's got a gun charge, so it's easy to write him off as another dead gang member,' said Ruelas.

He added that the maras are a major problem in the big cities, but not the only problem. 'We should be more worried about the corrupt police, army, politicians and businessmen linked to organized crime – they're the ones with the real power.'

After Casa Alianza, I visited a few military police units installed in ordinary houses in some of Tegucigalpa's poorest barrios. The military police were created as an anti-gang force when Hernández was president of Congress. Squadrons were rolled out in gang hot spots formerly patrolled by civilian police, and reports of human rights abuses (including beatings, torture and extrajudicial killings) rolled in just as fast. Their impact on the maras is highly questionable: in one neighbourhood, I found the squad stationed at a recently privatized football pitch, and one officer told me they were there to 'maintain order'. Yet, two short blocks away, at a taxi rank, drivers complained of weekly extortion payments demanded by both Barrio 18 and MS-13. In other words, nothing had changed. It's now routine to find military police deployed at public protests alongside the US-trained SWAT teams, the Tigres and Cobras, even in rural cantons like Río

Blanco. Officially, the US supports civilian, not militarized, policing, and has been at pains to emphasize that it does not directly fund the military police. But US-trained officers frequently train and lead these forces, so the distinction seems convenient at best, disingenuous at worst.[20] For Hernández, his pet project paid off: in 2017 he stood for re-election despite a constitutional ban, and committed electoral fraud to hold on to power, according to multiple independent international and national observers. An exception to this consensus was the US embassy, which backed his victory (the 2015 DEA investigation into him and his family had not yet been publicized). The fraud triggered widespread national protests, suppressed by security forces; at least thirty-six protesters were killed, mostly by the military police in suspected extrajudicial killings, according to the UN and other human rights groups. By the end of 2019, no-one had been convicted.

Migration Crisis

What happens when you mix entrenched corruption,[21] violence and impunity with starvation wages, cancelled subsidies and bankrupt public services? A massive exodus of desperate people who have been forced to make desperate choices. In September 2016 I met Andrea Hernández at a shelter in Tapachula, Mexico, near the Guatemalan border, with eight members of her family. They had fled Tegucigalpa a few weeks earlier, after the seventeen-year-old was abducted by gang members while out on a morning run.[22] She was rescued from her week-long ordeal after her mother pleaded with a relative employed in the public prosecutor's office. Andrea couldn't talk about it. 'I can't,' she said tearfully. 'I've tried but I can't.' 'She hardly eats, she cries at night, she's not the same. My daughter was a model student, she wanted to be an architect. Everything changed in one day, for all of us,' said her mother Isabel. The entire family – Andrea, her parents, sisters and her older sister's husband and three children – fled the country fearing retaliation. 'We left our dogs and cat, all my clothes, I couldn't even say goodbye to my friends. I want to go home,' Andrea said. Her mother added: 'She doesn't understand: we're never going back.' The family were granted asylum in Mexico.[23] In February 2017, at a tiny shelter in the central Mexican state of Hidalgo, I spoke with an emaciated youth from the Bajo Aguán with no money, no phone and a story too crazy to be untrue. He'd moved to La Mosquitia for a farming job that turned out to be a scam, and was trained to kill by ex-Kaibiles (Guatemalan special forces) and forced to work as a *sicario* for drug traffickers who enjoyed military protection. The youngster escaped one night after being ordered to kill an ordinary family over a paltry plot of land. 'I can never go back,' he said.

It's impossible to know exactly how many people left Honduras in the past decade, as no one counts those exiting a country. Migration flow is often measured by the numbers detained or deported by US and Mexican immigration, but caution is advisable in interpreting these figures. A rise may reflect a genuine surge, linked to political unrest or a natural disaster, or it may indicate a crackdown. For instance, in 2010 US border control detained 13,580 Honduran nationals. The numbers jumped to over 91,000 in 2014 under Deporter-in-Chief Barack Obama. Then, in 2015, they fell by almost two-thirds (33,848), thanks to the Plan Frontera Sur through which the US incentivized Mexico to stop migrants and refugees from the ultra-violent Northern Triangle – Honduras, El Salvador and Guatemala – en route to the US border.[24] The 'stop them in Mexico' policy was prompted by a rise in minors fleeing gang violence and forced recruitment, which Obama called a humanitarian crisis. In many cases the 50,000 or so children detained in Mexico between 2014 and 2018 were trying to reunite with parents who'd left years earlier to find work. I've met so many Central American youngsters who grew up without their parents; they seem like another generation of orphaned war victims.

The US endorsed the re-election of Hernández in 2017 despite damning evidence of fraud. The post-election repression and aching impotence triggered another wave of forced migration: the number of Honduran children and families apprehended at the US border jumped 87 per cent between December 2017 and April 2018, while those from El Salvador and Guatemala fell. And four out of five people traversing Mexico in the migrant caravan – the first one in 2018, which maddened Donald Trump and intensified the inhumane policy of children and parent separation at the border[25] – were Hondurans.

As people fled, the government reported the most spectacular crime reduction success story in modern times: a 50 per cent drop in the murder rate, from 86 per 100,000 in 2012 to 43 per 100,000 in 2017. Hernández credited the success to increased security spending for his 'tough on gangs' approach,[26] and the selective break-up of certain drug trafficking groups by US authorities, thanks to his reinstatement of extradition. Then there was the police purge: over 5,000 cops, almost one in three, were removed from duty between 2016 and 2018 for being too old, ailing or inept or for failing lie detector tests, in an effort to oust corrupt elements linked to organized crime and extrajudicial killings.[27] A better educated, better-trained cohort replaced them. Although the purge was popular and necessary, focusing on the police rot also helped Hernández's push to deploy military police on the streets, and kept attention away from the armed forces. If something sounds too good to be true, it usually is, and this record-breaking murder drop doesn't sound right to me. If violence, drug trafficking and police corruption all fell, why are thousands of Hondurans still fleeing for their lives? I wonder how much the exodus impacted on murder statistics: if all or some of those who received threats had stayed, would they have been killed?

Víctor Meza, the ex-interior minister, said the good-news numbers were based on raw data which was woefully incomplete and subject to political massaging.[28] 'We have a set of repressive measures and sweeping promises disguised as a security policy, with billions of Lempiras handed over to police and army officers to do what they think is best, with little transparency, and very little being spent on prevention, rehabilitation or reintegration.'

I've met countless men, women and children with wretched stories of forced displacement, poverty, the lure of the American dream, gang violence, deportation and family separation, but these are also stories of resilience. One thing is clear: political leaders have abjectly and repeatedly failed to tackle the complex root causes of the exodus, which is why it continues apace. Central American leaders pay lip service to the US antimigration agenda to ensure aid keeps flowing, but it's not a domestic political issue. The migrants and refugees who reach a place of safety and employment keep the economy afloat through remittances.[29] As for those who get deported or killed, who cares? Not the Honduran authorities.

US Footprints

In the decade following the coup, the US gave Honduras at least $230m in security aid, according to Security Assistance Monitor, a Washington DC-based group. Honduras became the country in the western hemisphere most visited by US special forces,[30] with twenty-one US missions between 2008 and 2014 – a period when Honduran security forces faced allegations of murder, torture, rape and extortion which went uninvestigated and unpunished. The role of American agents on foreign soil is perhaps the most divisive aspect of its calamitous war on drugs. No doubt that's why the DEA repeatedly lied about its role in a bungled anti-narcotics operation in Honduras that left four innocent villagers dead; it then misled Congress, the Justice Department and the public as it tried to cover its tracks. This was the massacre in La Mosquitia Berta mentioned in Buenos Aires. It took place before my time in the region, but I knew about it from Annie Bird, who documented the eyewitness testimonies that helped expose the DEA's lies in an extraordinary bipartisan investigation.[31]

What happened was this: at 2 a.m. on 11 May 2012, Honduran police officers under DEA command fired at sixteen poor unarmed Miskito passengers on a taxi boat on the Patuca River in the municipality of Ahuás, near the Nicaraguan border. The shooting took place after the passenger boat accidentally collided with a disabled vessel carrying law enforcement officers and large quantities of seized cocaine.[32] The DEA claimed that two Honduran officers on the disabled boat fired at the river taxi in self-defence after coming under gun attack. Not true. The officers shot first, and even aimed at passengers who had jumped or fallen into the water. At least one DEA agent in a circling State

Department helicopter ordered a Honduran door gunner to fire at the travellers. There is no evidence to suggest any shots were fired from the taxi boat, or that the victims were involved in drug trafficking. The self-defence motive claimed by the DEA was based, at least in part, on fabricated testimony from a confidential informant and suspected human smuggler who later admitted lying. After the incident, the US-led mission rescued the cocaine and its agents and returned to base. It took community members two days to recover the victims: Candelaria Trapp Nelson, a forty-eight-year-old pregnant mother of six; Juana Jackson Ambrosia, twenty-eight, a pregnant mother of two; fourteen-year-old Hasked Brooks Wood; and a twenty-one-year-old former soldier, Emerson Martínez.

The DEA lied about almost every detail, brazenly claiming that its agents acted purely as mentors and advisers. Honduran agents did not have direct access to intelligence information or the necessary equipment to command such an operation. They received orders from the DEA, they did not give the orders. The man giving them was Richard Dobrich, who went on to mislead Congress about the events – before being promoted to DEA chief in Colombia, arguably the highest-profile post in Latin America.[33] Dobrich's lies were exposed by the damning report, published in May 2017, which lambasted almost every aspect of the DEA's actions before, during and after the incident. The State Department didn't come out looking good, either. And yet there was no mention of compensation or justice for these prima facie drug war victims. I spoke to a survivor, a twenty-one-year-old campesino called Lucio Nelson, who had been returning home after visiting his mother. 'They called us *narcos*, but it's a lie. It was a massacre of innocent people.' Lucio was shot in the right arm and lower back, and despite four bouts of surgery suffers from severe limb weakness and chronic pain.

The boat's owners, Hilda Lezama and her husband, Melaño Eulopio Nixon, were also injured and are still impaired. Juana Jackson's two sons are being raised by her older sister, Marlene. 'We wanted the truth, but we also want justice and compensation – or don't they care what happens to the children?' Marlene messages me every so often, mostly with uplifting Christian proverbs, sometimes asking for help.

If a DEA agent or supervisor faced any consequences for the bungled operation, lies and cover-up, the public wasn't told about it. My specific requests for more details were not answered; I was told only that the DEA had implemented changes in light of the report's findings. What we do know is that the DEA refused to cooperate with the criminal investigation in Honduras, where a local cop went on trial after forensic tests matched one of the bullet casings to his gun. (The other casings recovered didn't match Honduran weapons, but the DEA refused to allow tests on its firearms.) In June 2018, on the day of the verdict, a government vehicle crashed into the car of the victims' lawyer's mother, the celebrated magistrate Tirza del Carmen Flores – one of the four justices who were sacked post-coup. She was badly hurt and in a coma for several weeks. The verdict was postponed for a few days, but came back 'not guilty'.

The Goldman Prize

Berta was awarded the Goldman Prize for environmental defenders at a time when Honduras was ranked the most dangerous place on the planet to defend land and natural resources. The six 2015 winners – one from every continent – were informed in October 2014. The prize is a prestigious one, sometimes described as the Nobel Prize for environmentalists, but Berta took longer to accept than any previous nominee. The money and attention didn't seem right to her, so she asked everyone what they thought, eventually being persuaded that elevating the Río Blanco struggle to a world stage could help protect them.

At the end of January 2015, the Goldman film crew experienced first hand the hostility she customarily faced. Their vehicle was stopped in Agua Caliente by police, soldiers and an angry mob looking for Berta. A few days earlier Berta had received messages from an anonymous good Samaritan: 'Be careful when you have meetings, there's a grass who gives information to the company engineers and they want you arrested ... be very careful when you go through Agua Caliente.'

Later that day in Tegucigalpa, Berta asked Goldman researcher Ryan Mack what would happen if she died before receiving the prize money. 'No one had ever asked me that before,' Ryan told me. 'Berta knew the seriousness of the threats against her life. If anyone understood that time was running out, it was her.'[34] The award gave Berta a platform. She met with top White House advisers and the Democrat leader of Congress, Nancy Pelosi. 'She was eloquent and diplomatic, but unbashful in her bluntness,' said Ryan Mack. 'And she made sure they took away a clear message about the reality she and her people were facing.'

On 19 April 2015, clad in a sparkly, lacy pink dress, Berta gave an electrifying acceptance speech to the jam-packed San Francisco War Memorial Opera House. 'Wake up! Wake up, humanity! We're out of time,' she implored her captivated audience of 3,000 notables in evening dress. The hairs on my arms stand up whenever I watch her speech.

She continued: 'The Gualcarque River has called upon us, as have other gravely threatened rivers. We must answer their call. Mother Earth has been militarized, fenced in and poisoned – it's a place where basic rights are systematically violated. It demands that we take action. Let us build societies that coexist in a just and dignified way that protects life. I dedicate this award to all the rebels out there, to my mother, to the Lenca people, to Río Blanco, and to the martyrs who gave their lives in the struggle to defend our natural resources. Thank you very much.'

The applause was deafening, the audience on its feet. In Honduras, nothing changed.

The Farewell Tour

In November 2015, Berta and Miriam embarked on a three-week speaking tour across the US after receiving the Óscar Romero Award from the Rothko Chapel in Houston, Texas. The organizers said the two indigenous leaders shared the spirit of the murdered Salvadoran archbishop who fought against social injustice and poverty. It was a fitting tribute. The two women were closer than sisters, and the trip gave them time to reminisce about the crazy times they'd shared over twenty years. As Miriam recalled, 'We talked about our families, our organizations; she told me the dam company had spies in COPINH, leaking information. About what we'd do next.'

Miriam and Berta liked to have a good time, and one night in DC they practised asking for a beer in English on the way to some bar. It turned out there was no need – the barman was Honduran. 'We cried, drank beers, and laughed together, we had fun . . . That trip was our farewell tour, we just didn't know it then,' Miriam told me.

The final question Berta was asked in the 2015 Buenos Aires interview was this: did she fear for her life? 'Yes, oh yes, we are scared,' she exclaimed. 'It's not easy living in Honduras, it's a country where you see brutal violence, the threats and attempts are constant. While the risk of being imprisoned is very real, the greatest risk, I feel, is of losing my life, of being physically and emotionally attacked. Besides the huge media campaigns directed against us, it's not the same being a female leader as a male leader, and we see the main media owned by the oligarchs directing smear campaigns against us to discredit us, accusations and infamies against us. So yes, we fear for our lives, we know there's a risk but I want to say categorically that this fear is not going to paralyse us. And even if it happens, I want you to know that the Lenca community and Honduras will continue the struggle and I'm convinced that things will get better.'

9

The Investigation

'Berta, don't die, don't go!' pleaded Gustavo Castro, holding his friend close. But Berta Cáceres was bleeding from three gunshot wounds. She took her last breath in his arms. Gustavo gently laid Berta's bloodstained body on the floor and crept into the bedroom where he had been shot just a few minutes earlier. He was afraid to make a sound in case the killers were close enough to hear. The clock said 11:45 p.m.

Berta's last words were 'Call Salvador! Call Salvador!' Gustavo found Salvador Zúñiga's number on Berta's phone, but her ex-husband didn't answer. He called Tomás Gómez, no answer. He called Berta's lawyer Víctor Fernández, no answer. He tried again and again, but no one picked up the phone. The minutes ticked by.

Just after midnight, Gustavo started sending text messages to Berta's friends and colleagues. 'Help ... this is Gustavo. Berta has just been killed. I'm hurt ... I'm alone in her house, nobody knows, please tell Salvador.' Dozens of calls and messages went unanswered. He was surrounded by silence.

It was 1:21 a.m. when Karen Spring, from the Honduras Solidarity Network, called and promised to send help. The killers had left a hundred minutes earlier. Tomás Gómez woke up, saw the missed calls and messages, and set off for Berta's house on the opposite side of town. On the way he called Juan Carlos Juárez, the police liaison whom Berta had messaged minutes before she was killed.[1] The cop didn't pick up or call back. Tomás stopped at the police station in the centre of La Esperanza. 'Hurry, they've killed Berta Cáceres at her house, come quick,' he urged. Tomás arrived just after 2 a.m. He shouted and honked the horn to wake the security guard who had to lift the wooden barrier so that he could get into Colonia Líbano, the gated community where Berta's house was.

Tomás parked in front of the house and sounded the horn again, until Gustavo came out clutching a small rucksack containing his passport and laptop. His grey t-shirt was covered in blood, his left ear still bleeding. But the metal door in the fence surrounding Berta's house was padlocked shut, and Gustavo couldn't find the key. Shivering, he managed to squeeze his bag under the wire fence and climbed over. 'Are you sure she's dead?' asked Tomás. 'Yes, I'm sure.' They embraced and got into the COPINH pickup.

The security guard snarled at Tomás as he yelled at him to hurry up and open the gate again. On the main road towards town they passed a police truck. Gustavo was in shock, wounded and afraid, but didn't want to go to a clinic or to the police, so Tomás headed towards the training centre Utopía. En route they bumped into members of COPINH walking towards Berta's house, so they turned around and took some of them back to Colonia Líbano. The gate was open, the guard had gone. They went back, ferried another carload, and parked in front of the house. Police were at the scene, but the house wasn't cordoned off when the press started to arrive. Soon after, images of Berta's bloody corpse were circulating on social networks.

Gustavo stayed inside the pick-up, close enough to the house to connect to the Wi-Fi and send emails to worried family and colleagues. He heard journalists send breaking news bulletins, talking about him, the missing Mexican. Berta's COPINH colleague Sotero Chavarría, whom she had asked to rush back from the Tegucigalpa clinic, entered the house and saw two footprints – one on the outside door leading to the kitchen which had been kicked in, the other on Gustavo's bedroom door. 'I'm one hundred per cent certain these were military issue boot prints,' said ex-soldier Chavarría. Several police officers and COPINH members entered the blood-splattered crime scene with the forensic doctor at 3:30 a.m. 'It was a burglary,' one cop told Tomás.

It was 5 a.m. and still dark when Aureliano 'Lito' Molina, Berta's ex-partner from whom she'd split up a few months earlier, arrived with his father and brother-in-law, having driven almost three hours from their home in San Francisco Lempira. By then, military officers were on the scene. Jany del Cid, the ethnic prosecutor, saw images of her slain friend on the TV news and called Gustavo: 'I'm on my way, don't go with anyone, not the police or military, wait for me.' Investigators from ATIC, the high-impact crime force, the Police Crime Investigation Unit (DNIC), and, most oddly, the inspector general's office,[2] were on their way from the capital. The US embassy offered to assist. By daybreak the crime scene was packed. Tomás drove Gustavo to a safe house where ATIC agents arrived with a forensic sketch artist. Gustavo described the gunman who'd shot at him: he was tall, dark-skinned, with short hair, big eyes, wearing a black top and white scarf. Yet when the sketch was finished, it looked nothing like the assailant. Gustavo protested, the illustrator made a few alterations, it still wasn't right – but

Gustavo was worn out and conceded. The agents returned later with photos and videos of COPINH members, to see if Gustavo recognized his killer among them. 'No, it wasn't anyone I know from COPINH,' he insisted.

When the black and white sketch was published in the papers, its resemblance to Aureliano immediately drew attention. Furthermore the security guard claimed it was Aureliano who had left Colonia Líbano with Tomás at 2:15 a.m., not Gustavo. Aureliano was arrested: the authorities had nailed a suspect and a motive. In Honduras, news soon spread that the murder had been a crime of passion.

I was on holiday in Baja California, and woke up to a string of missed calls from my *Guardian* editor. 'Berta Cáceres has been murdered, call me as soon as you get this.' I sat down to write about meeting her in 2013, and looked back at the photos taken that day of her with Doña Austra. 'If they can kill Berta Cáceres, they can kill anyone,' I said to my friends.

Aureliano was not the only suspect; others included Berta's closest colleagues. Their phones were tapped, and Tomás Gómez and Lilian López – COPINH's financial coordinator whom Berta had entrusted with the arrangements if something were to happen to her – were interviewed several times. 'The interrogations were very hostile: they were looking for evidence of internal conflicts within COPINH which didn't exist,' said Lilian. Tomás was pressured to make a statement without a lawyer. 'When they took my shoes, I knew I was a suspect. Berta was dead and now the state wanted me and Lito in jail, to leave COPINH without leadership. If it wasn't for international pressure I would be in jail for the murder,' he told me a few weeks later.

The crime scene experts arrived from Tegucigalpa just before midday on 3 March, led by Sub-Commissioner

Rolando Casco Torres. He had previously commanded the Santa Bárbara police force and would send officers to cover COPINH protests whenever DESA asked, the phone evidence would later reveal. Bullet casings, Gustavo's bedroom door, and several foot and fingerprints were taken away as potential evidence. A few hours later, the autopsy took place in Tegucigalpa. The family's request for a medical observer was rejected. They immediately called for independent international investigators to take charge of the murder inquiry.

Colonia Líbano is a newish gated community situated south of the town centre off an unpaved road, with a view of pine-forested hills. The houses are arranged in small clusters with no street lighting, ringed by a mix of wire and wooden fencing. Berta's three-bedroom bungalow has two flimsy outside doors that respectively open into the kitchen and the lounge, with her en suite bedroom the furthest away at the end of a narrow angular hallway. Just before midnight on 4 March, Gustavo, now a protected witness, was cloaked and taken back to the house, the crime scene, to help investigators reconstruct the murder. Bizarrely, they were accompanied by the prime suspect, Aureliano Molina. Gustavo, who had barely slept or eaten in over forty-eight hours, repeated what he remembered about the shooting. He was told he was free to go home to Mexico the next day.

Berta should have celebrated her forty-fifth birthday on Friday, 4 March. Instead, the following day, thousands gathered in La Esperanza for her burial service, which was led by two Catholic priests, Padre Melo and Fausto Milla. Her spirit was helped on its way by traditional Maya, Lenca and Garifuna smoke ceremonies. Miriam Miranda came flanked by bodyguards, fearful that she'd be next. Ambassadors took flowers to Doña Austra. The Río Blanco people wept. 'She gave her life for our *pueblo*,' said feisty community leader

Rosalinda Domínguez, herself the object of threats and harassment from members of her own family, the Madrids, who supported the dam.

Berta's father, José Cáceres, attended the funeral. The pair had become reconciled after he was diagnosed with cancer, and José had recently lent his daughter money to help cover Doña Austra's medical bills. The other siblings were less forgiving, especially after José, a staunch Nationalist, gave a TV interview emphatically denying that politics or the National Party could have played any role in his daughter's murder.

As mourners packed the streets, ATIC investigators in Colonia Líbano obtained the CCTV footage from a security camera pointing towards the main road. Mobile phones, a laptop,[3] several hard drives and USBs were taken from Berta's house as evidence, as well as money. At Tegucigalpa airport, Gustavo was unexpectedly surrounded by police, and forbidden from leaving the country for thirty hours. The following day, Monday 7 March, he was driven back to La Esperanza where investigators wanted him and Tomás to confront the security guard, Ismael Lemus, in court. The guard's testimony fell apart under questioning. 'I don't know who's pressuring you, you're lying,' said Gustavo, struggling to breathe under the cloak protecting his identity. 'It was dark and the vehicle has polarized windows, so how can you say it was Lito?' The guard conceded that he could be mistaken. Immediately after that court appearance, he disappeared from La Esperanza and was never further questioned about his testimony, which wrongly pointed the finger at Tomás.

At the end of the tense hearing, Gustavo was told he could not leave Honduras for another thirty days, a move his lawyer described as 'illegal and arbitrary'.[4] 'It was a state kidnap,' Gustavo told me. 'The plan to blame Lito didn't stick, blaming COPINH didn't stick, so they took my suitcase and boots and bought themselves thirty days to frame me. I was plan C.'[5] Gustavo was eventually allowed to return to Mexico almost a month after being shot. As international pressure for justice mounted, he and his family went into exile, fearing that those behind the murder could have the means to reach them in Mexico.

As investigators focused on Berta's inner circle, DESA president David Castillo called an emergency meeting to plan the company's security and communication response. 'This is a crisis for us,' he wrote to shareholders and managers. Sergio Rodríguez, the community and environmental manager, urged immediate contact with the banks, while project manager José Manuel Penabad spoke with a local police chief who pledged his support and promised to keep DESA informed of developments. 'He recommends we issue a press release distancing ourselves from the incident,' reported Penabad. The police chief kept his word and the company received regular updates, starting with the initial police report with details of the crime scene, cause of death and suspects: Aureliano, Gustavo and COPINH leaders.

DESA personnel closely monitored press reports, and some started to get nervous as Berta's family and colleagues blamed the company. On 7 March, the financial manager, Daniel Atala, urged Rodríguez to relax. 'You're so negative. Everything will be fine, you'll see. Don't panic and transfer this to others. The minister of security [ex-colonel Julián Pacheco] today told Pedro [Daniel's uncle and a shareholder] that it was a crime of passion . . . we have to wait a few more days and then they'll go down. We just have to keep working as normal.'

The murder made headlines outside Honduras. While at home the mainstream press focused on the crime of passion hypothesis, there was mounting outrage abroad at the killing of the region's most celebrated defender and Goldman Prize winner. 'Award-winning indigenous rights activist Berta Cáceres killed,' said the BBC headline. 'Berta Cáceres, one of hundreds of land protesters murdered in last decade,' wrote the *Guardian*. The killing sealed Honduras's inglorious reputation as the most dangerous country in the world to defend land rights and the environment.

I flew to Honduras a month after the murder, and headed straight to Doña Austra's house. She was distraught. 'My daughter was brave, but she was scared and hardly ever rested even though her back was so painful. "Mama," she would say, "these sons of bitches could kill me at any moment." I'd tell her, *hija*, don't make jokes. She was always working, it's like she knew time was running out,' said Austra, wringing a sodden handkerchief. 'Why ever did she have to move to that isolated house?' As well as buying a reliable pick-up truck, Berta had used the $170,000 Goldman Prize money to pay for back treatment, a tattoo, and the bungalow in Colonia Líbano, her first home of her own. But she was worried about upsetting Austra, who was in poor health, so kept the house purchase secret for several months until the children came home for Christmas.

At Austra's house I met Berta's daughters for the first time. They said their mum had always told her children that she expected them to return home one day and fight for a better Honduras. 'I imagined my life here with her, in the struggle together,' said Laura, then twenty-three and extremely articulate. 'She spoke with such political clarity and certainty, sometimes I couldn't believe that she was my mum. I've lost my mum and we lost a leader.'

By this time, a few weeks after the murder, they were already convinced that it would be up to them to seek justice for their mother. 'DESA hated her,' said Bertita. 'They were the main source of threats, they hated her because she was a woman, and because they couldn't stop her. They tried but couldn't jail her, so they killed her. We know it was DESA but the question is, *who* in DESA? It's going to be down to us to find out.'

I went to Colonia Líbano.

Berta's green and gold bungalow is situated 150 metres slightly uphill from the security barrier along a dirt road, with a gaudy ceramic frog in the garden. The two security guards worked twelve-hour shifts, from six to six. I spoke with the day watchman, Don Ronny, who said that before the murder he'd let in FUSINA (US-trained special forces) patrols on several occasions. Ismael Lemus, who fingered Lito and Tomás, was by this time long gone.[6] The neighbours claimed not to have heard or seen anything suspicious; one woman told me that she and Berta fed stray dogs together every morning, while listening to the birds.

At the nearby cemetery, I found journalist Sarai Alvarado sitting with Julissa Villanueva, the country's chief forensic doctor, on Berta's grave.[7] Julissa assured me that the forensic evidence, including the gunpowder residue, pointed to Aureliano Molina. 'My public ministry sources confirmed it was him,' said Sarai. They seemed so sure that I assumed Aureliano's arrest was imminent. I met the twenty-six-year-old in Tegucigalpa a few days later. He was agitated, and worried about being framed. 'They took my clothes, my shoes, my hat . . . but the last time I saw Berta was two weeks before she was killed,' he said. In the end, Aureliano's alibi proved solid: his phone put him three hours away from the crime scene, and the gunpowder residue mentioned by Julissa wasn't mentioned again. Even so, DESA's legal team would continue to allege his involvement.

Berta loved the river and lush forested hills of Río Blanco and dreamed of retiring here one day. When I visited Río Blanco, people were visibly scared when talking about Olvin García Mejía from Valle de Ángeles, the alleged *sicario* whom DESA had helped avoid prison just a few weeks earlier.

Berta was here a day or two before the tense river protest on 20 February, and had told the community that she was worried about Olvin. 'She told us to keep our eyes open, be alert,' said Rosalinda Domínguez. 'Of course we're scared, Olvin celebrated after the murder; but for Berta and all our martyrs' sakes, we will never allow our river to be sold or negotiated.' The community was broken, but not beaten.

For many, DESA was the obvious suspect; but Víctor Fernández, Berta's old friend and lawyer, was keeping an open mind. In his view, 'COPINH was involved in multiple land struggles which made Berta many enemies, so we don't rule out any individual or any group, legal or illegal. Berta's murder is part of a wave of murders of leaders across Latin America to cause terror and crush organizations which endanger economic interests.'

In mid-April, indigenous and community leaders from across the region gathered at the national sports stadium in Tegucigalpa for the Berta Vive (Berta Lives) gathering. The homage closed on 15 April with several hundred mourners travelling to the banks of the River Gualcarque to take part in spiritual ceremonies. The phone data show that Sergio Rodríguez was warned about the gathering by his informants in Río Blanco, while an intelligence source told DESA's security chief Jorge Ávila to expect twelve to fifteen buses.[8] The Agua Zarca project manager, José Manuel Penabad, told Rodríguez to rally community members at several strategic points,[9] 'especially those from

Valle de Ángeles, at the river!!', and call in elite SWAT cops from the Tigres or Cobras[10] to guard dam infrastructure and equipment. 'The public [security] force has to carry riot gear, and a large quantity of pepper spray,' wrote Penabad, asking Ávila to relay his instructions to police commissioners. Ávila was a busy man: Castillo also wanted him to speak to police contacts to make sure the buses were stopped at various checkpoints. 'The longer they're delayed at the checkpoints, the less time they get at the project site,' wrote Castillo. In addition, the company's PR team briefed a select group of journalists to report positive testimonies about the dam and to focus on filming any vandalism: that way they'd get their expenses covered.[11]

The buses made it to Río Blanco despite the company's best efforts. But the Berta Vive delegation came under attack by locals organized by DESA and armed with rocks, machetes, sticks and guns in plain sight of security forces – who ignored Bertita's and Laura's pleas for help. Berta's right-hand man Sotero and the journalist Tommy Morales were among those injured by the armed group, which included Héctor Mejía, Olvin's brother, from Valle de Ángeles.

That evening, as the buses left for Tegucigalpa, Sergio Rodríguez wrote: 'In the end we achieved our goal: they couldn't get to the dam even though they tried. Around fifty people ... stopped them with the help of police with anti-riot gear. In my opinion, this will have a psychological effect, not being able to reach the dam, and we reaffirmed that the Valle [de Ángeles] and Chorrera communities defend the project and they [in Tejera] are afraid of them.'

Reviewing the phone messages, it's clear that at no point did company executives express any sympathy. Instead they seized on the memorial event as an opportunity to paint COPINH as vandals and to criminalize community members opposed to the dam.¹² Six weeks after the murder, it was business as usual.

Berta's murder put a spotlight on Honduras not seen since the 2009 coup. This didn't stop the bloodshed. COPINH member Nelson García, thirty-eight, was shot in the face by unidentified gunmen on 15 March 2016, following a violent eviction carried out by the military police and the Cobras. Nelson was killed as he returned to his family home in Río Lindo, a Lenca community in Cortés, about 100 miles south of La Esperanza. His family fled and were granted asylum overseas. Three months later Lesbia Yaneth Urquía, forty-nine, who opposed the La Aurora dam in San José La Paz, was beaten to death in the coffee-growing town of Marcala. Her body was found near a rubbish dump the day after she left home on her bike.

As the days and weeks passed, Berta's family travelled across the world demanding an independent investigation that would respect their rights as victims. IACHR proposed a team to probe not just Berta's death, but the deaths of all the defenders murdered in Honduras while they were subject to protective measures. The IACHR had previously sent an expert group to Mexico to investigate the forced disappearance in 2014 of forty-three trainee teachers in Guerrero state.¹³ No thanks, said the Honduran government: our prosecutors, with US embassy help, are doing fine. A few days later the first arrests were made.

On Monday 2 May, just after daybreak, four men were arrested and ten properties raided as part of the official investigation called Operation Jaguar. Two of the detainees were familiar names: Douglas Bustillo, the ex-security chief who supposedly stopped working for DESA in July 2015, and Sergio Rodríguez, the community and environment manager. The other two were unknowns: Edilson Duarte Meza, reported by the local press to be a former army captain, and Mariano Díaz, who the army confirmed was an active special forces major and military police trainer. At Díaz's house in Tegucigalpa, one soldier had a conflict of interest: 'The major is my instructor, I can't arrest him.' 'You've got the wrong man,' Díaz protested. 'It's the manager of DESA you want – he paid Bustillo 500,000 Lempiras for the murder.'

There was a fifth arrest that we didn't hear about for a day or two: Emerson Duarte Meza, Edilson's non-identical twin brother who lived in the house next door in Colonia Pizzaty, a poor neighbourhood in the coastal city of La Ceiba. A gun allegedly linked to the crime was found in Emerson's house. What did the twins have to do with Berta's murder? Two raids in the Bajo Aguán that same day didn't lead to any arrests; who were the investigators looking for?

Also on the same day, 2 May, DESA's offices in Tegucigalpa were searched. The raid was held up until the arrival of the company's lawyers, who signed the paperwork 'under protest', indicating they considered it illegal.[14] By contrast, Berta's family's lawyers were not invited and so had no idea why or what information was seized.[15]

In Honduras, criminal cases are conducted in phases, involving different courts presided by judges rather than juries. At the initial hearing shortly after the arrests, prosecutors played snippets of conversations and showed text messages from Díaz's phone allegedly referring to the murder. It turned out that Major Díaz had been under investigation for drug trafficking and kidnapping since 2015, and his phone was tapped. The five men pleaded not guilty, but the judge ruled that prosecutors had enough evidence to proceed. Bail was denied.

The authorities reckoned, I think, that these arrests would appease the chorus of international critics, including US lawmakers, calling for aid to be suspended. They miscalculated, for if anything the clamour to expose the masterminds behind the crime intensified. Then, a bombshell dropped. 'Berta Cáceres's name was on a Honduran military hit list.' This was the headline on my *Guardian* story published in June 2016. It caused a diplomatic storm.

I'd written for Al Jazeera about the hit list Berta mentioned to me in 2013, but this was different. This time there was an eyewitness, an army deserter who'd not only seen the list but was part of the elite unit ordered to eliminate the social, environmental and land activists named on it. The insider was Rodrigo Cruz,[16] a young military police officer assigned to a sixteen-man squad in the multi-agency taskforce Xatruch based in the Aguán. His commander, a twenty-four-year-old deputy lieutenant, deserted rather than comply with the order, and the unit was dismantled. Berta was murdered, and First Sergeant Cruz fled the country, fearing for his life. I interviewed Cruz via telephone and video calls, and spoke with several people – lawyers, community leaders and activists – who confirmed his identity and military background. 'If I went home, they'd kill me. I'm one hundred per cent certain that Berta Cáceres was killed by the army,' Cruz told me in May 2016.

We met several times after the story was published, and talked for hours. I also interviewed his family, and others who knew him before and after his short military career. I don't know for sure that Berta was killed by the army, but I am convinced her name appeared on a military list not long before she was gunned down.

Berta fought her whole life against militarization. The armed forces are full of impoverished youths with few other options. In corrupt countries like Honduras, soldiers are deployed to repress poor communities, not unlike the ones they come from, to protect corporate interests. With this in mind, Cruz's military experience was eye-opening.

Cruz grew up in a campesino community that had been militarized after the coup. He was impressed by the soldiers' swagger. Asked why he'd enlisted aged eighteen against his parents' wishes, he said simply: 'I liked guns.' After basic training, Cruz was among sixteen high achievers selected from diverse battalions (Tigres, infantry, navy, air force, Jaguars) for the military police.[17] He completed two specialist trainings so gruelling that most soldiers couldn't manage them. He was hospitalized with dehydration and badly blistered feet after the three-week Cascabel jungle survival course, but it turned out to be a breeze compared to Tesón (Specialized Troops in Jungle and Night Operations).[18] For sixty days they slept outside, eating the squirrels, birds and reptiles they hunted with knives. Cruz showed me his back, scarred by beatings with plaited boot laces, a treatment designed, he said, to build physical and mental strength. The final phase in La Mosquitia included lying on an ants' nest and explosives training. Only eight of the 200 graduated; the rest were withdrawn sick, exhausted, starving or mentally broken. The graduation ceremony included killing a dog, eating the raw meat, and getting a hug from the commander. From there, straight to military hospital in Tocoa, where Cruz lay unconscious for four days. During his hospital stay, mysterious daily injections started, which continued after his discharge, and which altered his sense of right and wrong.[19]

In November 2015, Cruz's unit was assigned to the Xatruch taskforce[20] – one of two multi-agency forces in Honduras specialized in counter-narcotics and anti-gang operations. Xatruch is headquartered in Tocoa and covers the Caribbean coast, while FUSINA operates nationwide. As a designated driver, Cruz witnessed several shady ops during his six weeks with Xatruch.[21] The unit was frequently deployed to patrol 'red zones' where campesinos were involved in land struggles against palm magnates. 'One of our main jobs was helping private security guards protect Dinant land,' said Cruz. He recalled seeing ex-special forces officer Celio Rodríguez Ponce (the alleged violent paramilitary leader involved in La Confianza and gunning for campesino leader Yoni Rivas), at the Xatruch base.[22] The squad was also assigned special missions, like the clean-up job at a tiny canton called Plan de Flores, in the department of Colón, where a military outpost was being moved to another farm. Here, Cruz said, they were ordered to shovel decomposing human remains into sacks which they took to an isolated forest reserve, doused them in diesel, petrol and rubbish, and burned. 'We followed the order, no questions asked.'

But what Cruz saw at Corocito, also in Colón, made his 'blood turn cold'. The small base consisted of several derelict houses, one set up as a holding cell, another as a barracks, another as a makeshift torture chamber. 'There were torture instruments, chains, hammers and nails, no people, but fresh clots of blood.' Another mission took them to Agua Amarilla near the port city of Trujillo, where naval colleagues handed over plastic bags containing human remains. Later that night they tossed them into a river heaving with crocodiles. Soon after, Cruz saw the list.

They were en route to deliver supplies to another outpost, this time in Sico, Colón, when the deputy lieutenant ordered them to stop in the hamlet of Icotea to buy sodas. As usual, the crew got out to safeguard the commander, and Cruz was left alone in the driver's seat. Suddenly he spotted some papers that must have fallen out of his commander's vest. It was a list: five pages stapled together, with photos and personal details on each page, front and back. He quickly flicked through and recognized a few names including those of several campesino leaders:

Juan Galindo, Jaime Cabrera, Vitalino Álvarez, Yoni Rivas, and Berta Cáceres, pictured sitting on a rock by a river. 'I knew her name because she was famous, but I didn't really know *who* she was,' said Cruz.

The name that transfixed him was that of an old family friend, Juan Galindo, who'd been shot dead the previous year.[23] The idea of elite forces working off actual paper lists seems a bit passé, but when Cruz saw the black X through Galindo's name, he knew what the list meant, and that he was in deep. Cruz tossed the papers back onto the passenger side before his commander returned. 'Did you read it?' 'No,' said Cruz. They drove off in silence. In mid-December 2015, the unit commander gathered his subordinates in the middle of a football pitch in Tocoa. 'We've been ordered to look for these heads,' the commander announced, holding up several sheets of folded paper. 'I'm a Christian, I can't kill any more decent people, any of you disagree?'

'He [the commander] said the order came from "above", which always meant the joint chiefs of staff, and he was under pressure from the Xatruch commander to comply,' Cruz told me. I still needed convincing. 'How do you know the list came from the joint chiefs?' I asked him, probably a dozen times. 'That's where all orders came from, everyone knew that, it's a hierarchical structure.' For that reason, Cruz believed the same order would have been given to FUSINA. 'If we had the list, so did they, because FUSINA is Squadron 1, Xatruch is number 2, we answered to them.'

Shortly after, Cruz was sent on extended leave. He was trying to wean himself off the pills prescribed by the army doctor, slowly recalling the horrors of what he'd been involved in. He grew increasingly scared and decided to tell his father about the list. A few weeks later Berta was dead, and the image of her by the Gualcarque was plastered across every

TV channel and newspaper. Cruz's father persuaded him to tell trusted campesino activists about the list; they in turn persuaded him to speak to the human rights group COFADEH in Tegucigalpa. After that he fled, crossing borders overland illegally as the army still had his ID card. A hero to some, a villain to others, it's unlikely ever to be safe for him to go back home.

I myself attracted some stick after publicizing Cruz's evidence in the *Guardian*.

In Tegucigalpa, the defence minister, Samuel Reyes,[24] held press conferences and issued communiqués with my photo attached, claiming my allegations were false and constituted an attempt to tarnish the armed forces. The Honduran ambassador in London submitted a written complaint on behalf of Reyes, requesting a retraction.[25] No corrections were necessary, but this didn't stop a flurry of bots, trolls, insulting blogs and an advert for a fake 'media terrorism' conference with me as a guest speaker; the photo was the same one used in the defence ministry communiqués. It was after this that I started travelling to Honduras overland, to avoid more formal airport controls where other unwelcome journalists and activists had been turned away.

My pre-publication questions to both Honduran and US authorities had gone unanswered. Once the piece was out, the US ambassador to Honduras, James Nealon, moved to discredit me and the story through 'background' briefings. He was especially irked by the claim that FUSINA received training from 300 US marines and FBI agents in 2015, even though the 'Rapid Response' training exercises had been announced by his deputy, Julie de Torre, at a joint press conference with Reyes in Tegucigalpa.[26] Nealon, who regards anti-communist zealot John Negroponte as a mentor, told me that there was no evidence of a hit list, but admitted that the embassy had not spoken to anyone cited in my article, not even Xatruch commander Colonel Jovel, as part of its purported investigation launched after the hit list story. It's worth noting that in 2015, the State Department's own human rights report stated that 'unlawful and arbitrary killings and other criminal activities by members of the security forces' remained one of the most serious problems in Honduras. Despite this, US security aid kept flowing. Months later Nealon told me Berta's murder case was the biggest priority for the embassy, and it was my responsibility to hand over the hit list, which he wrongly assumed I had, or else I would be responsible for any further deaths.[27]

More Arrests

On 8 September, Elvin Rápalo Orellana, alias Comanche, was arrested in the rural town of Zacapa, Santa Bárbara. He was twenty-one, and the sixth detainee. Wearing handcuffs, baggy jeans, baseball cap and stripy polo shirt, he looked like a gangly schoolkid. The seventh was ex-special forces sergeant Henrry Javier Hernández, arrested on 12 January 2017 at his brother's barber's shop in Reynosa, a dangerous Mexican border city. Hernández was the first and only defendant to admit being at Berta's house the night she was murdered. A month later, thanks to Hernández's testimony, Óscar Aroldo Torres a.k.a. Coca, was arrested as he walked out of prison in La Ceiba.[28] Tall and tattooed with big, close-set eyes, he looked something like the gunman Gustavo had described.

By the first anniversary of Berta's death, eight men from different regions and walks of life were in jail charged with the murder. Who were they? How did they know each other? If these were the guilty men, who did what and why? Did any of the suspects link the murder to the military hit list? Who gave the order to kill Berta, who paid for it? These were the questions nagging at me when, soon after, I received a cache of leaked court documents presented by public prosecutors in the initial hearings. These documents provided some answers, some clues, but honestly, raised even more questions.

The court papers confirmed that the three suspects with military links, Mariano Díaz, Douglas Bustillo and Henrry Hernández, knew each other and were in regular contact by phone around the time of the murder. I was most curious about Díaz, a decorated active major. After his arrest, he was rapidly given a dishonourable discharge: so much for innocent until proven guilty!

He enlisted in January 1994, the same day as Bustillo, and they served together before Díaz was selected for the special forces in 2002.

Military records show that Díaz attended cadet leadership courses at the notorious School of the Americas in Fort Benning, Georgia, in 1997, fought with coalition forces in Iraq in Operation Freedom, participated in joint exercises with US special forces in 2004 and received counter-terrorism training at the Inter-American Air Force Academy in 2005.[29] His case is emblematic of how US tentacles in Honduras stretch long and deep. In 2012, Captain Díaz was head of personnel at the 15th Battalion in the Aguán,[30] the main site of US special forces training, where he met Henrry Hernández. In 2013, Díaz was head of ops at the 1st Battalion base in Copán, at a time when the Cachiros were trafficking vast amounts of cocaine in that region. His first posting as major was to Western Sahara in 2014 as a UN peacekeeper, after which he returned to the 1st Battalion in Tegucigalpa as intelligence chief in 2015.[31] Díaz was an army high-flier, who when arrested for Berta's murder was on track for promotion to lieutenant colonel (despite being suspected of organized crime), and a military police trainer. The latter function matters because the US insists that it does not support or train President Hernández's pet project, the militarized civilian police. But who trains the trainers like Díaz? The US does.

Bustillo's career was not so illustrious. He retired in 2012 with the rank of infantry lieutenant, after his weight problems scuppered promotion to captain. But he also trained at the School of the Americas, completing logistics and artillery courses, while at home he completed two intelligence training courses and did a spell in counterintelligence in 2003. Between December 2003 and March 2005 he was security chief to the head of Congress, future president Pepe Lobo.

Henrry Hernández was a special forces sergeant whose sniper skills earned him the nickname Zapador. He's from the Bajo Aguán, a community called Los Tarros, and spent his 2010 to 2013 army career stationed at the nearby 15th Battalion, where for a time he served under the direct command of Díaz. After leaving the army, Hernández became a private security guard on palm plantations owned by Miguel Facussé's company, Dinant.

The court documents included selective phone communication obtained thanks to the wiretap, which prosecutors believed were coded discussions about the murder. '*Cuando el pez está cheke me dijo Douglas que eran 50 más 50 de él OK*' (When the fish is okay, Douglas told me that there will be 50 plus his 50), wrote Hernández to Díaz on 5 February 2016.

Remember, Díaz's phone was being monitored by criminal investigators, supposedly familiar with codes used by criminals to cover their tracks. This message was presented as evidence of the murder plot at the trial, but, at the time, investigators did nothing to intervene. Could they have prevented the murder?

In the chats, Hernández mentioned money, but who was paying and why? Did DESA president David Castillo Mejía, a US-trained ex-intelligence officer, have links to the other army guys? And what about Roberto Pacheco Reyes,[32] a former justice minister and DESA secretary? What about the politically connected Atala Zablah shareholders – did they know anything? With so many unanswered questions, I went back to Honduras. It was August 2017.

Prison Visits

Tamara is a mixed prison situated fifty kilometres north-west of Tegucigalpa where most of the defendants were detained on remand. In 2017, the newly appointed governor was Major Osman Rodas, who enlisted in the army on the same day as Díaz and Bustillo, and also served in Iraq.[33] When I asked him about Díaz's alleged involvement in Berta's death, he replied with a stony face: 'Everyone follows their own path.' Before this trip, an independent investigator told me that Berta's murder had 'all the characteristics of a well-planned operation designed by military intelligence, where it is absolutely normal to contract civilians as assassins.' This well-placed anonymous source said it was inconceivable that someone with Berta's profile could be murdered without at least implicit authorization from military high command. Thinking about this, I asked to see Díaz first.[34]

Díaz strutted into the interview room and wrote down my full name in his notebook. He was shorter than I imagined, about five feet, six inches, in good shape, greying at the temples, wearing jeans, a white t-shirt and a fancy digital sports watch. He launched into a monologue: 'Berta Cáceres defended the environment. DESA intended to generate energy which would destroy the river basin. Berta was offered bribes to shut up and close down the protest. She accepted, but the money offered was not enough.'

Díaz told me about an alleged meeting in 2015 in which DESA executives, he claimed, asked top-ranking government officials to have Berta killed by an *equipo de limpieza* – an elite group of police or special forces operating as a social cleansing death squad. The request was turned down, said Díaz, so the company turned to Bustillo. 'I told Negro not to get involved. At first he said no, but he was offered a lot of money, a car and a job in Choluteca.' The only detail I could corroborate was the job offer in Choluteca, at Castillo's solar energy project, where Bustillo travelled with Rodríguez shortly after the murder.

Díaz said his ex-subordinate Henrry Hernández contacted him looking for work, as he needed money to travel to the US. So Díaz introduced him to Bustillo, who was head of security for PCI Inc. 'That's how Henrry got involved in the crime. He didn't have *sicario* experience, but did have a lot of contacts in La Ceiba.' The monologue continued with more details of the murder night, many of them accurate, it would turn out, yet he denied any involvement. How did you know so much about it if you weren't involved? I asked. 'Bustillo told me.'

Díaz said that he and Sergio Rodríguez were accused as conspirators to avoid involving the Atala family. 'I am a victim,' said Díaz. He also mentioned a colonel, but wouldn't give me his name, saying he had visited him in jail: 'He told me about a rumour in military circles that I was fucking Berta, but I never knew her.' There's no evidence that Berta knew Díaz.

'Why are you here, Mariano?' I asked. 'I'm special forces, a military police trainer, they needed someone with my connections to show the press.' He didn't mention the drug trafficking investigation, and neither did the armed forces when they fired him. For the purposes of a murder, Díaz could be written off as a bad apple with a personal vendetta or money problems, whereas drug trafficking would implicate other officers and military structures, which would look bad for the institution.

After leaving Díaz, I was escorted to maximum security where most of the others were being held.

Sergio Rodríguez looked like an accountant on holiday in brown loafers, white socks, checked Bermuda shorts, a blue polo shirt and red-framed designer glasses.[35] He also noted down my name, which he recognized from the *Guardian* stories. Polite and well spoken, Sergio claimed to be dumbfounded by his detention. 'This is to keep the international community happy. I was just an employee, and this has destroyed my prestige. I'm the *chivo expiatorio*,' the scapegoat, he said. 'Why are you here, Sergio?' 'Because of false statements by Lilian López and Sotero Chavarría that I threatened Berta.' In the initial hearing in 2016, Lilian said Sergio had threatened Berta at both the November 2015 and the February 2016 river protests. Berta herself published a Facebook post on 20 February, denouncing Sergio by name for threatening the 'emotional and physical integrity of protesters' – a move he called a 'personal attack by Berta' in the PHAZ security chat. But Sergio was in Tegucigalpa on 30 November, and had phone records and credit card receipts to prove it. Lilian said she'd got her dates mixed up under the pressure of his lawyers' questions. Rodríguez alleged she lied to get him arrested.

'I met Berta three times, and we had a cordial relationship. I don't know who threatened her, but the Agua Zarca line is the easiest target because it was her most visible fight against extractive projects. As far as I know DESA never contracted any third party to threaten anyone from COPINH. If the threats were so frequent, why didn't they report them to the authorities, like we did?' Rodríguez would become the only defendant to testify at the trial, so more from him later.

Douglas Geovanny Bustillo was overweight and cocky verging on combative, and didn't bother to hide his scorn for Berta. He too looked like a holidaymaker in a baseball cap, shorts and t-shirt, with an eye-catching squiggly scar on his right arm. I asked why he didn't testify at the initial hearing. 'They have to prove I'm guilty, I don't have to prove my innocence. I didn't kill her, I didn't send anyone to kill anyone.'

I was curious to know how he got the DESA job in 2013. Bustillo said he'd met Castillo years before at the military high command in Tegucigalpa, but they weren't friends and he simply responded to a job advert.[36] His army training helped him hit the ground running, said Bustillo. He recruited six or eight informants, mostly ex-soldiers, and in his new job he applied the human rights principles, he said, which he'd learned on an army course. Bustillo denied having phone contact with Berta. In fact, he claimed it was she who threatened him. 'She was very intelligent. If I'd sexually harassed or threatened her, she would have reported me.' Bustillo blamed Berta for the murder of Cristian Madrid, the teenager from a dam-supporting community killed in Río Blanco hours after Tomás García. 'She was the intellectual author, why wasn't she arrested?' He blamed special prosecutor Jany del Cid for protecting Berta.

Bustillo said he didn't think about DESA again after being fired, and he was happy in his new job at the US company PCI Inc. 'I had some phone contact with David Castillo, Sergio and Claudia[37] about work-related questions, but never met with any of them.' I didn't know it then, but these were lies. (It transpired that his job was over by 2016, and he met with Castillo the day before the murder.) 'So why are you here, Douglas?' 'It's all political, if they let us go the government will lose votes and could lose US aid. Listen, Berta Cáceres was no innocent lamb, nothing happened to her, but me, they want to fuck me over because I worked for DESA.'

Nothing happened to her ... except she was murdered!

Bustillo seemed convinced that this was a short-term crisis, and he'd be out soon. '*Mira* ... I know that Sergio, Mariano and I had nothing to do with the crime. I don't know about the others.'

I visited Emerson Duarte Meza in the hot, humid and overcrowded jail located a block from the seafront in La Ceiba. It was under Emerson's bed that investigators claimed to have found the murder weapon in May 2016, while searching for his twin brother, Edilson. Emerson left his little boy Kenny, his partner and his mother in order to speak with me in a sweltering little room above the main entrance. He was very polite, quite sweet really. He's short, slim, with cropped frizzy hair and a goatee beard, and he was wearing black flip flops, beige shorts, a red polo shirt and a gaudy gold chain. Emerson was transferred here from Tamara to face the gun charge, and had just been sentenced to three years for illegal possession of the .38 found under his mattress. His story was that he'd bought it a fortnight before the raid for 6,000 Lempiras ($250) from an old schoolfriend called Wilmer, after a football match. 'I admit the gun, I accept the sentence, but they want to jail me for a crime I had nothing to do with,' he said with tears in his eyes.

The night of the murder, Emerson said, was just like any other: he got home from work, watched his favourite narco soap, *El Señor de los Cielos*, took food to his dad who was on night shift, came home, locked up the dogs and went to bed.

He didn't notice whether Edilson's blue car was parked next door or not. This is the vehicle investigators believe was used by the *sicarios*. CCTV footage Emerson believed would prove he was at home that night was wiped before his arrest; I later learned that he refused to provide prosecutors or his defence contact with any information about the supposed gun seller.

So why would he need a gun? 'There are many criminals in the neighbourhood, everyone has a gun to deter thieves, it's not a big deal. I couldn't afford to buy one with a licence.'[38] Emerson is one of six children, born and raised in Colonia Pizzaty, a rough neighbourhood with a drug problem. His younger brother Kenny Alberto was murdered aged eighteen in front of the house in 2012. I went to meet his family in Col. Pizzaty, a few miles south of the jail, an area with unpaved potholed roads and more churches than shops or schools. I found four generations living next door to each in single-storey modest houses, from where investigators seized twelve mobile phones, including the one Emerson shared with his long-term partner, Dayra. I spoke with her and his mother Diana on his grandmother's unlit porch at dusk. Both said they didn't know about the gun until the raid.

'We saw Berta's death on the 6 a.m. news, but we had no idea who she was, it was just another murder ... I don't understand why Emerson was arrested, he was here at home with me. We want an international investigation, we don't trust the Honduran authorities,' said Dayra. The family was understandably suspicious: Dayra and Diana spent several days looking for Emerson after he was arrested, checking army bases, police stations and prisons, until they saw him on the news entering Tamara. The police probably kept the twins apart, hoping one of them would crack and confess.

I later figured out why he was arrested: on the day of the raid, ATIC came looking for Edilson, but Emerson returned home first; at that time he had long hair. A witness from the night of the murder had apparently described a long-haired guy checking a tyre of the supposed getaway car, according to investigators. And then the gun under his mattress. That might explain his arrest, but with no evidence placing him with the other suspects on the night of the murder, why was he charged with murder, and what was he really doing with the weapon? Did he really just happen to buy a gun used in the country's most notorious crime in recent years in a deal at a football pitch, or was he covering for his brother, or for someone else?

Back at Tamara, I met Edilson Duarte Meza, who is shorter than Emerson (his nickname was Chaparrito, or Shorty), with a disproportionately large head, a wispy moustache and a cartoon-like smirk. He has three young children, and like his twin, worked in construction. On 2 March, Edilson said he worked from 6:30 a.m. to 4 p.m., then attended his IT night class from 5:30 to 10:30 p.m. After that, he came home to his pregnant wife's grandmother's flat, up the road from the family plot, as their house was being renovated. That's his story.

The suspect phone linked to Edilson was registered in his name, but he claimed to have lost the number when the phone was stolen, and only got it back a few months later, after the murder. People lose and recoup numbers all the time in Honduras, but ATIC investigators confirmed that no such time lapse and reinsertion of the chip (number) showed up on the phone records.

He denied knowing Henrry Hernández, who by this time had testified that Edilson forced him to get involved.

What about the gun, how did he explain that? 'I've no idea why my brother had it.'

Was he paid to kill Berta Cáceres? 'I had no idea who they

were talking about when I was arrested, I don't understand what it is I'm supposed to have done.'

This was an important point. Two years after the murder, the prosecutors still didn't seem to know who did what, or maybe they were keeping it quiet until the trial.

Óscar Torres, alias Coca, is tall and dark-skinned, with a lopsided face, big eyes set close together, thin lips and an endearing giggle. He is covered in tattoos, everywhere but on his face, with odes to reggaeton and rap music and a massive spiderweb all over his left arm and elbow. He started with the tattoos aged seventeen but said he regretted them.[39] 'I'm not interested in the maras, I'm into the *barras*.' The *barras* are unofficial football fan clubs linked to violence (like UK football hooligans), which in Honduras also serve as recruiting grounds for the maras, street gangs. Torres joined the Montagua *barra* aged about thirteen. He had a tough childhood. His mother left when he was five, and he was raised by an aunt. His father was shot dead in a bar brawl in 2008, a few months after returning from the US.

Torres has a criminal past. In 2009, at the age of fourteen, he was the lookout in a botched school robbery in which the night watchman lost his life; he then spent two years in juvenile. After that, he said, he tried to leave the *barra* and turn his life around; he got a job at the Hotel El Estadio, and enrolled in evening college where he enjoyed Spanish literature and social sciences. Torres was likeable but wily. He admitted carrying a gun, but denied ever shooting anyone; admitted being offered money to sell cocaine and marijuana, but never to kill anyone; knew MS-13 gang members but wasn't one. Several times I felt as if he was about to share something, but then changed his mind. Torres said he met the Duarte Meza brothers in Pizzaty, where he was staying with his sister, but denied ever meeting Rápalo or Hernández. 'Were you involved in the murder?' I asked.

'I wasn't there, I was at home with my girlfriend. I don't know anything about it. I knew *Señora* Berta was an environmentalist, but I didn't realize how famous she was until the murder when she was all over the news and internet.'

Torres said he was considering accepting the charge to get a lower sentence. 'Even if they don't have the evidence, here they can convict you, so maybe it's better that I accept it.'

'Are you worried about the phone evidence?' 'I've never had a phone number registered in my name. Do they have recordings of phone calls?' he asked several times.

He was right, the phone linked to him was not registered in his name; Coca is the nickname for almost every Óscar in Honduras, and tattoos are common. Still, Gustavo recognized him from press reports. His lawyers told prosecutors that he was willing to return to Honduras to identify his assailant and testify before the judges. But that was months ago, and the paperwork was still stuck in the attorney general's office.

Before meeting Elvin 'Comanche' Rápalo in person, I'd heard he was gentle and amiable but started killing people to fund a drug habit. Still, I was taken aback by the goofy metrosexual adolescent who swaggered in. Did this kid really shoot Berta Cáceres?

Rápalo is the eldest of nine children from a dirt-poor family in El Ocote, Zacapa, near Agua Caliente, the canton where Berta was holed up at her friend Edna's back in 2013. As with Torres, the phone number linking him to the crime was not registered in his name. 'The telephone links aren't enough to convict me. Henrry Hernández accuses me of being the gunman but it's his word against mine. He's in deep, got something to hide.'

The problem for Rápalo was that he'd boasted of killing Berta to several people while high, and one of those had turned state's witness. '*Esa vieja yo la piqué*' (I topped the old bird), he allegedly told the witness a week or so after the murder. 'It wasn't easy killing that bitch, she tried to fight back, I had to stamp on her.'

To me, he denied the confession: 'I never admitted anything to anyone. I'm a hard worker, I don't kill for money. I've never been to La Esperanza.'

I went to San Pedro Zacapa, a rural municipality spoilt for rivers, to try and understand if and how Rápalo allegedly got involved in the business of killing people. I interviewed several acquaintances of his on condition of anonymity; they said Rápalo had bragged about getting 100,000 Lempiras (around $4,000) for killing Berta, with which he planned to buy a car.

I tracked down the protected witness, let's call her Ana, and she too only agreed to talk on condition of anonymity.[40] Ana knew Rápalo through a mutual friend, not well, but thought he was nice enough until he confessed to murder, late one evening after a chance meeting. Ana said he smelt of booze, solvents and marijuana, and she noticed scabbed scratches on his neck, just below the left ear. This is what she told me he said. On 2 March 2016, they first looked for Berta at Doña Austra's house, but her pickup wasn't there, so they went to Colonia Líbano. Doña Austra's neighbours, whom I interviewed a month after the murder, recalled seeing strange cars that night, some without number plates.

It was a big job. Several cars and motorbikes were involved, radios were used to communicate, and local cops had been paid to warn them about any operatives. Rápalo wasn't worried about getting caught because the order had come from above. Job done, they drove back north, stopping to toss a gun into the Otoro River. Getting rid of only one gun seemed odd.

Remember, Gustavo heard a radio outside the house during the attack; but as far as I knew, investigators were only interested in one getaway car, and hadn't mentioned a bigger operation or a river search. I was looking forward to hearing this protected witness testify at the trial.

Henrry Hernández was the only defendant I didn't interview. He implicated Edilson Duarte, Elvin Rápalo and Óscar Torres, the alleged *sicario* crew, to prosecutors after being extradited from Mexico. After this he was sent to a maximum-security prison, in case his indiscretion made him a target. With no hope of speaking to him, I went back to the Bajo Aguán, Henrry's home turf, the place where deals are done to kill people.

Los Tarros is an unremarkable rural neighbourhood with a reputation for *sicarios*, car thieves and muggers. It's not a place you'd accidentally stumble across or want to get lost in, said my guide, let's call him Juan, who came from a nearby community. Juan has family in Los Tarros, which provided the pretext to drive through and get a feel for the place. Like everywhere in the Aguán, it's surrounded by row upon row of African palms. Here in Los Tarros many men work in private security, which pays better than field and processing jobs. One such man is Hernández's uncle Rigoberto Rodríguez, who by 2018 was still the only security agent, private or public, ever sentenced for killing campesinos since the coup.[41] We visited Las Tarros one hot and sticky Sunday morning about six months after Hernández's arrest; we drove around the area with the windows down, greeting families who sat outside chatting. Lots of young guys, late teens or early twenties, were roaring around on mopeds through the labyrinth of unpaved roads. In May 2016, Hernández was on the run when investigators raided his father's and uncle's homes. I wanted to talk to them, but Juan thought it too risky as he didn't know anyone in that section of the community.

I wasn't in court for Hernández's selective *mea culpa*, but I did later read his testimony from the initial hearing.[42] Henrry admitted being at the crime scene, but swore it was under duress from Edilson whom he'd met while working security at Walmart (though we know he was also acquainted with Edilson's aunt, who lived in Colonia Pizzaty). Henrry said they went to La Esperanza in Edilson's blue car. Edilson was the driver and in charge of the operation; there was also a tall guy with tattoos on both arms, known as Coca, who shot the Mexican, and Chelito (slang for a white guy), who shot Berta. Henrry claimed that he was forced to go along because he'd previously been to La Esperanza with Bustillo on PCI Inc. business, and admitted locating Berta's house – but couldn't explain how or why he knew its whereabouts. Notably, Hernández exonerated Díaz in his confessions, affirming his major had nothing to do with the affair. He didn't know his major's phone was tapped. He also cleared Emerson Duarte.

Parallel Investigations

As the months passed, the case was transferred to the sentencing court in Tegucigalpa – like the Old Bailey in London, with none of its historic charm – but the state's hypothesis about the motive and modus operandi was still unclear. On that August 2017 trip, I met María Luisa Borjas, the cop's cop sacked in 2004 after uncovering alleged police death squads, to talk about the veracity of an internal report into Berta's murder by the police inspector general.[43] This atypical investigation was ordered by Security Minister General Julián Pacheco, the double SOA graduate and former intelligence chief, on the morning after the killing.[44] As always, María Luisa turned up immaculately dressed in a trouser suit with well-coiffed hair and brilliant lipstick, styled more like a private school headmistress than a straight-talking anti-corruption crusader. The internal IG report was leaked to several journalists, including myself, in the weeks following the murder. It read like a who's who of political movers and shakers,[45] and, as far as I could tell, it consisted of facts mixed in with outlandish falsehoods. In Honduras, it's not uncommon for official reports on sensitive cases to be doctored – add a few names, change a few details – just enough to divert or warp an investigation, or purely for political gain. But the IG had no business investigating the murder, its mandate being internal police affairs. Borjas therefore believed it was likely an intelligence-gathering mission to determine who *could be* vulnerable. Information is power, after all.

Borjas was convinced of the report's veracity. 'It's signed and stamped, I believe it's genuine. Why aren't these people under investigation?' I wasn't so sure. Eventually, María Luisa publicly called for those named in the report as 'intellectual authors' of the murder to be investigated, in order to confirm or eliminate them as suspects, she told me. Among the names she read out was that of banking mogul Camilo Atala Faraj, cousin of the Agua Zarca shareholders. He at once filed a criminal defamation suit against Borjas, claiming she'd caused 'irreparable damage' to his reputation, and vehemently denied any involvement in the assassination.

The defamation law has been widely criticized as a tool to stifle freedom of expression. According to the IACHR, 'such laws lend themselves to abuse as a means to silence unpopular ideas and opinions, thereby suppressing the debate that is critical for the effective functioning of democratic institutions.' Still, in January 2019, Borjas was found guilty and sentenced to two years and eight months behind bars, during which time she should, the judge said, be stripped of her seat in Congress. Borjas challenged the verdict, claiming that it amounted to a 'judicial contract killing'. By the end of 2019 the case had not been heard by the Supreme Court, and Borjas continued in Congress.

In 2017, Berta's family commissioned a group of international lawyers to conduct a fact-finding investigation into the murder, possible related crimes, and the official investigation itself, to examine whether those arrested were indeed the correct and only culprits.[46] The investigation concluded that

> partners, executives, managers, and employees of DESA, private security companies working for DESA, and public officials and state security agencies, implemented different strategies to violate the right to free, prior, and informed consultations of the Lenca indigenous people. The objective of those strategies was to control, neutralize, and eliminate any opposition.

Although the lawyers gained access to only a fraction of the state's evidence, they nevertheless identified multiple irregularities in the investigation, possible masterminds who remained at large, and a pattern of criminal conduct which showed the murder was not an isolated incident.

> Despite the secrecy of the Public Prosecutor's investigation, [we have] been able to establish the participation of executives, managers, and employees of DESA; of private security personnel hired by the company; and of state agents and

parallel structures to state security forces in crimes committed before, during, and after 2 March 2016, the day of the murder. Those crimes remain unpunished.

The investigators pointed to three possible masterminds, identified in their report as Executive 1, Executive 3 and the head of security, who had thus far not been indicted by state investigators. Soon after the report was published, the family's lawyers presented prosecutors with a document detailing the evidence included within the trough of discovery files the state also had against the three men: Daniel Atala, David Castillo and Jorge Ávila. Some of the Atala family, including Daniel and his father José Eduardo, sought meetings with state investigators.[47] But nothing happened.

As the second anniversary of the murder approached, some Honduran papers reported that Leonardo DiCaprio would appear at a protest in Tegucigalpa with Rigoberta Menchú, the Guatemalan Nobel Prize winner and one of Berta's heroes. Fake news, sadly, no Leo or Rigoberta. Instead, on 2 March DESA president David Castillo was arrested at San Pedro Sula airport as he was about to leave for Houston.[48] On Twitter, the public ministry announced that 'Roberto David Castillo Mejía is the intellectual author of the Berta Cáceres crime, according to investigations', and published a photo of him handcuffed next to a hooded ATIC agent. 'We were friends, we went to restaurants together,' Castillo protested as he was handcuffed. Arresting Castillo on the second anniversary of the murder was quite a PR coup for the authorities, given that some US lawmakers were again demanding that security aid to Honduras be suspended.[49] Merely a coincidence, investigators told me; they thought Castillo, who'd recently moved out of two properties in Tegucigalpa, had got away. Then he checked into a 9 a.m. United Airlines flight from Tegucigalpa to Houston, but cancelled an hour later. Investigators were reluctant to activate their usual intelligence sources in case of leaks to ex-intelligence officer Castillo, but an airport informant tipped them off when he checked in for another flight.

I met David Castillo six weeks later, by which time he'd appeared in court and vehemently denied any involvement in the murder.

The trip to the Tamara penitentiary is a two-hour trek by taxi, bus and truck, ending with a short walk, which gave me time to imagine meeting the man accused of masterminding Berta's death. By this point I had watched videos of Castillo at COPINH protests, read countless messages he'd written and received, heard his initial court testimony denying involvement, spoken to friends and colleagues who could not believe that such a smart, educated man could be involved in murder, looked into his army and post-army career, and interviewed Berta's closest confidants. By this time, I'd written so many stories about the case that I knew he'd know who I was. I was a little nervous as I waited with my notebook and pen for the guard to bring him into the stuffy office.

Castillo came in, the dark circles under his eyes making him look older than his age. He glanced at me, turned to the warden and said: 'Who's this, why I am here?'

I introduced myself.

'I know who you are, you are the reason that I am in prison,' he said, not quite shouting but with voice raised and nostrils flared. 'There is no way I am ever sitting down to talk to her,' he snapped, looking at the warden. 'The reason I'm here is because of the lies she has written about me and my company. I had nothing to do with the murder, or the logistics, or the planning of the murder.'

'I'm here to hear your side of the story – please sit down,' I said, nervous hands behind my back.

'No, you only write lies. In fact Berta and I had a very good relationship, we went out to bars and restaurants, I went to her house in La Esperanza. We spoke and met two or three times every month. Everything was sorted between Berta and my company. We had a friendship. Her death was a personal tragedy for me.'

'Berta was scared of you, *Señor* David, you were not friends, she was afraid of you. It's true that you met sometimes. How did you always know where she was going to be?'

'I paid for her mother's medical treatment one or two months before she was murdered, my wife recommended the gynaecologist, that's the kind of relationship we had. I went to her house!'

'You did go to her house, but you weren't invited: that is called harassment. She was scared of you. How did you know where she was going to be all the time? You would turn up at malls, events, even the airport …'

'I never went to the airport.'

'Did you use your military intelligence sources to keep Berta under surveillance?'

He scoffed, but for a moment looked flustered. 'She would call me and tell me what her plans were, where she was going to be, we would talk all the time, that's the sort for relationship we had.'

'She was scared of you, *Señor* David … Please sit down.'

But he wouldn't. 'I'm not going to speak to you. If you were an honest, objective journalist you would have contacted my lawyer so that he could have been present today.' Actually I had tried reaching DESA executives to request an interview with Castillo's lawyer, but no one ever got back to me.

'All the lies you've written about my company. We never tricked or forced anyone into selling land, everyone who sold us their land did so willingly, we're a good company, a good neighbour in the community ... You and other journalists like you have reported one-sided stories, filled with lies. I've replied to your questions personally, and you still printed lies and misrepresented us.'

'You responded personally, great, so why did you tell me in May 2016 that DESA had no relationship to or knowledge of Olvin García, who killed several people in Río Blanco and terrorizes families opposed to the dam, when that isn't true?' In December 2015, Castillo referred to Olvin as 'our best security at the same site' in a message to Sergio Rodríguez.

I asked him about paying for Olvin's lawyer, if the company had nothing to do with him. He squirmed but stuck to his story: 'I don't know Olvin ... maybe Jorge Ávila and Sergio Rodríguez did. I'm the president, I'm very high up. As if I would know people in the communities.'

'The evidence proves you knew Olvin and his brothers Héctor and Armando too, both worked for DESA. Jorge Ávila went to collect him in a DESA vehicle from the La Esperanza police station. Did you bribe someone to get him out of trouble?'

He scoffed again, loudly. 'This is what I mean, you're biased, that's why I am here, how can you say that? And what evidence, a report paid for by COPINH, that's not evidence.'

'It's a question, *Señor* David: did DESA pay authorities to get Olvin out?'

'No!' He moved towards the door.

It was over. I took a big breath. The prison guard came in, I gestured to him: 'Give me five minutes please, I need to write this down.'

If Douglas Bustillo was in deep, what about DESA's second security chief Jorge Ávila, who everyone called *el mayor*, the major? Ávila was an ex-police officer, trained in the US, Colombia and Israel, who was dismissed in 2000 after twenty years' service as part of an anti-corruption purge. Ávila joined DESA in mid-2015. He was more refined than Bustillo, with better police connections, but unpopular with the guards.[50]

Before the murder, Ávila coordinated with local police commanders to have officers deployed at COPINH protests, and played a key role in getting Olvin García out of jail in December 2015. On the day of the murder he went to La Esperanza with pro-dam community members from Valle de Ángeles. Later that night, I was told, in the very early hours of 3 March, Ávila received a call over the radio: '*Listo, ya está hecho el trabajo*' (Right, the job's been done), but I never got the opportunity to ask him about it. After the murder he coordinated with police to get updates about the investigation.

Ávila was interviewed by investigators a couple of weeks after the murder, but never under caution. Investigators requested his work record, but the police claimed they couldn't find it. In November 2017, soon after the GAIPE report was published, Ávila suffered a stroke affecting his speech and mobility. He knew he was under investigation, that's what caused the stroke, his wife Tania Zelaya told me.[51]

On the Offensive

In April 2018, the ex-mayor of Intibucá, Martiniano Domínguez, became the first person ever to face criminal trial for violation of ILO 169. The case centred on a town hall–type meeting about Agua Zarca in Río Blanco in October 2011. The meeting did not constitute an ILO 169–compliant consultation, argued the prosecution. It was not free (the mayor was accompanied by security forces and DESA officials), it was not prior (construction work on the road had already started and licences had been issued), and it was not informed (no details were given on the project's size, duration, environmental consequences,[52] compensation or expected profits). When the people voted overwhelmingly against the dam, Domínguez approved the construction permit anyway, claiming community support on the basis of fake signatures.

A Guatemalan anthropologist, María Jacinta Xon,[53] told the court that indigenous territories had been continuously exploited and expropriated since the arrival of the Spanish over 500 years ago. In the case of Agua Zarca, she said, 'the community's crops were destroyed because the state and its representatives do not see indigenous people as human beings. The project generated crisis and conflict in a once harmonious community which has never been the same again. The social fabric was ruptured.'

The defence claimed that most people supported the dam, and repeatedly questioned whether the Río Blanco community is in fact indigenous, and whether it holds the river sacred. In one extraordinary exchange, the defence asked Xon: 'Do you consider the Río Blanco community civilized?'

With other officials around the country facing the same charge in connection with other megaprojects sanctioned on indigenous territories, this was a precedent-setting case and therefore a deeply political one. Domínguez was found not guilty of abuse of authority. COPINH pledged to appeal.

Around the same time, not long after Castillo's arrest, DESA retained the international law firm Amsterdam & Partners, led by Robert Amsterdam. In July 2018, I and other journalists who'd written on Berta's case were sent a report commissioned by Amsterdam and written by the Canadian criminal defence lawyer Brian Greenspan, which claimed to have uncovered 'serious violations of Honduran and international standards in the murder investigation and prosecution of the alleged perpetrators'.[54] Greenspan criticized the state's case as unsubstantiated and biased. He accused GAIPE, the international group commissioned by the family, of violating international fact-finding standards, and showing 'gross disregard for the legal rights of DESA's employees'.

Amsterdam and the family's lawyers agreed on one thing: that the Attorney's General's office had violated due process by withholding evidence it was obliged to share with all parties. By August 2018, a month before the trial was scheduled to begin, prosecutors had on thirty-five occasions refused to comply with four court orders to provide information to Berta's family's lawyers, resulting in the suspension of eight hearings. The prosecutors were never sanctioned for contempt of court. Meanwhile the permissible pre-trial detention period of thirty months was running out.[55]

The refusal to share evidence fuelled the family's fears that the authorities were protecting the real criminal masterminds, and perhaps even their political patrons. 'The court's actions are grossly negligent,' Bertita told me. It clearly wasn't fair on the defendants, and withholding information could open the door to appeals. Yuri Mora, the prosecutors' spokesman, denied that disclosure rules had been violated. 'The investigation to find the remaining intellectual authors [masterminds] continues, but the case is practically resolved,' said Mora. Quite a statement, given the trial hadn't yet begun.

Finally, seventeen days before the trial opened, the attorney general admitted that key expert evidence, including ballistics, phone and computer analysis and financial reports, could not be shared because they still weren't complete or in some cases had not even been started![57] Of the forty-plus mobile phones found, data were recovered from only 30 per cent, and prosecutors admitted to analysing only two of Berta's mobile phones; they couldn't find any record of the third, that her family insist she had on the night of the murder.

The Mariano Díaz question stood out. Why didn't prosecutors send Díaz's gun to ballistics? Not only that, *no* data were extracted from the mobile phones, tablet, computer or hard drive found in Díaz's house.[57] None. He was an active special forces major under investigation for drug trafficking and kidnap: surely prosecutors would want to know everything about him, as he could lead them to a bigger criminal network. Or maybe the point is that they didn't.

The evidence hearing took place shortly after this bombshell admission from the attorney general. This constitutes the last judicial phase before the main event. It's crucial, as the judges decide what evidence, experts and witnesses proposed by each party will be admitted. A case is only as good as the evidence admitted. I was following developments from Mexico.

The victim's lawyers[58] proposed as witnesses the majority shareholders, the three Atala Zablah brothers;[59] Jacobo Nicolás, vice-president of DESA and president of BAC Honduras Bank; and Pedro Wady, a DESA board member and ex-president of Montagua football club. With his brother José Eduardo, another DESA board member and current president of Montagua, Pedro runs the family firm Camosa, a John Deere distributor. The lawyers also wanted to call both José Eduardo and his son, Daniel Atala Midence, DESA's financial manager and vice-president of Montagua. These four, it was argued, were members of group chats in which key incidents before and after Berta's murder were discussed. Daniel could testify about the payment to informants run by

Sergio and Douglas; the brothers about coordinating with ministers and police departments. The court rejected the application on grounds that it was 'excessive'.[60]

Carolina Castillo, DESA's lawyer and former national energy company (ENEE) legal rep, who played a crucial role in securing the dam's permits, licences and finances, was rejected. Carolina also liaised closely with government lawyers Aixa Zelaya and Edwin Sánchez, whose 2013 trip to Washington DC to defend the dam was funded by DESA; they were also rejected. How about Jorge Soto, the USAID manager who worked with DESA before the aid agency shelved the deal after Berta's murder?[61] Rejected.

The family also wanted senior police officer José Rolando Casco Torres, for two reasons: as commander of the Santa Bárbara police base, he coordinated directly with DESA to deploy agents during COPINH protests. Then, thanks to a promotion, he was designated head of the inspection team at the murder scene on 3 March 2016. Request rejected.

Just two cops were accepted: Felipe Ramos, Casco's subordinate who had been sent to police the protests, and Juan Carlos Juárez Bonilla,[62] the liaison officer who received Berta's last ever text message on 2 March 2016 and who didn't respond to Tomás Gómez's call for help. Also admitted were Jorge Ávila, brothers Olvin and Héctor Garcia Mejía, informant Salvador Sánchez, and Spanish COPINH supporter Luis Díaz de Terán.

The court rejected every single expert witness proposed by the family's lawyers, on the grounds that the proposals were *sobreabundante*, excessive or overkill.[63]

This was a blow.[64] The family's case presented the murder as the grand finale of an intelligence-driven terror campaign against Berta Cáceres and COPINH, which could only be properly understood by identifying the whole criminal structure and defining the role played by each person and agency before, during and after. But the court was restricting its focus to the murder as an isolated attack by unconnected individuals. In other words, it had decided only to hear the state's case.[65] I made my way to Honduras.

The Trial: Monday 17 September 2018

By 8 a.m., riot and military police were lined up outside the courthouse. The courtroom was run down and small – fewer than fifty seats, no standing allowed, with phones, laptops and video transmission all banned by the judges. One side of the public gallery was filled with the defendants' families and supporters, on the other side diplomats occupied the front row, leaving Berta's supporters and international observers to share chairs.

The trial was scheduled to start at 9 a.m. At 9:45 the judges opened an unrelated evidence hearing, and for two surreal hours heard arguments in a drugs case while families and lawyers involved in the most emblematic trial in Honduran history milled about in the blazing sun.

Outside the court complex Miriam Miranda led a passionate protest of Garifuna, indigenous and peasant women demanding the criminal masterminds behind her friend's murder face justice. 'They say we're against development, that we're criminals and vandals. They expel us from our territories, and then they kill us. ¡Ya basta!'

Héctor García Mejía, Olvin's older brother, led a counter-protest. 'Sergio we carry you in our hearts', read one placard held high as the defendants arrived in a prison van at 11 a.m., late for their own trial.

At 11:45, we squeezed back into the courtroom. The

hearing lasted ten minutes. The opening of the trial was suspended until the Appeal Court could rule on a petition filed by the family's lawyers to recuse the judges, which accused them of abuse of authority, concealment, denial and delay of justice, and dereliction of the duties of public servants.[66] 'We want, no, we demand justice, but not at any cost. With these judges, justice is obviously impossible,' said Bertita outside the court.

I rushed off to write a story on the recusal petition. Soon, I was bombarded with messages about a communiqué circulating on social networks.

The press release accused me of inciting armed violence in the Bajo Aguán, by encouraging campesino communities to wrongly blame security forces for the death of loved ones. I also encouraged them, it seemed, to give false testimonies in favour of Yoni Rivas and against the paramilitary *sicario* Osvin Caballero, aka Ardilla,[67] who had been detained in Mexico a couple of weeks earlier. Signed by the 'Independent Association of Campesinos from the Aguán Valley', a group no one had heard of, the text advised other communities in Honduras and neighbouring countries to watch out for me, an over-ambitious Mexican (*sic*) journalist representing shady international groups. It called on the authorities to investigate me, and finished by declaring me *persona non grata* in the Aguán.

This was scary. I was being linked to known killers and armed insurgency in one of the most dangerous regions in Latin America. I started making calls.

The main objective seemed clear: to intimidate me to stop covering the trial and leave the country. Honduras ranks 141st for press freedom out of 180 countries assessed by Reporters Without Borders, and the great bulk of murders, threats, harassment and stalking of journalists goes unpunished.[68] Claiming I was using journalism as a front to incite violent insurgency and assist organized crime could also serve as an excuse to deport me from the country.

My heart said, 'don't give in to bullies'. My head reminded me that I was in one of the world's most dangerous countries for women and journalists, where impunity reigns.

The *London Press Gazette* ran an online story under the headline: 'Guardian stringer covering notorious Honduras murder trial shares safety fears amid online smear campaign'. The story went viral. This wasn't the first smear campaign linked to my coverage of Berta's case: I had been targeted after publishing the military hit list story, but this time I was in Honduras. The *Guardian* editors wanted me to leave, but I was reluctant. This is what we do, expose the truth in the teeth of danger. I agreed to leave if things got worse.

Yessica Trinidad from the Mesoamerican Initiative of Women Human Rights Defenders, an old friend of Berta's, published an alert: 'We repudiate and condemn this attack, which places the physical integrity and right to free expression of Nina Lakhani at serious risk, along with the right to information of the Honduran people and the international community.'

Amnesty International wrote to the security minister Julián Pacheco, and the human rights secretariat. 'Although these messages do not refer to the case of Berta Cáceres, it is highly probable that the objective is to put the journalist at risk, taking into account that she is the only international reporter covering the trial ... In Honduras and other countries across the region, possibilities of an attack against a journalist or a human rights defender increase after defamation campaigns.'

I gave Edy Tábora, director of the Committee for Free Expression (C-Libre), authority to represent me in case of any immigration issue or criminal charge, and the state-run protection mechanism opened a case recognizing me as a bona fide journalist – important in the light of the claims I was an insurgent masquerading as a journalist.

Dina Meza wrote a story, the Committee to Protect Journalists (CPJ) in New York issued an alert, so did Verso Books and COPINH, among many others, which helped generate public interest across the world. A freelancer's life is often solitary, especially when writing a book, and the messages of outrage, support and solidarity kept my spirits up during those difficult days.

So who was behind the communiqué?

The Independent Association of Campesinos didn't exist, and the style and phrasing were remarkably reminiscent of a message circulated a few weeks earlier about Yoni Rivas, soon after he turned down help from national intelligence chief and former Xatruch commander Colonel Germán Alfaro.[69]

This brings me to Vitalino 'Chino' Álvarez, the only person in Honduras who thinks I'm Mexican. The hit list given to the Xatruch unit had Vitalino's name on it, and he helped get the army deserter, First Sergeant Cruz, to safety. But since then he'd sold out the campesino movement and was now working within the paramilitary-controlled La Confianza farm. '*Hola mi amiga Mexicana*,' he'd greeted me a few months earlier, *before* I confronted him over lunch in San Pedro Sula, when he told me he'd decided it was 'better to be on the inside'.

I'd asked Vitalino why he'd recently tried to persuade campesino families to register their names and ID numbers with the current Xatruch commander. 'That sounds like military intelligence work, Vitalino, why would you do that?' 'No, you've got it wrong, we only spoke to a few families, I was trying to help them access social projects. *Amiga*, you've been brainwashed by Yoni, he's too radical,' said Vitalino. I never heard from him again.

As we waited for the Appeals Court to rule on the recusation petition, I met with the UK ambassador.[70] I had worried about being denied entry into Honduras ever since the hit list story, and with even more reason now. The ambassador agreed to tell Honduran officials that the UK considered this as an attack on me personally, and on press freedom.

After ten days with no news from the court, a second communiqué was published, this time accusing me and investigator Annie Bird of terrorism. With so many pending appeals and injunctions, the victims' lawyers didn't expect the trial to open until early 2019, so I went home to Mexico for a breather, to await the restart of the trial.

A few days later, on 11 October 2018, 160 people left San Pedro Sula with the intention of reaching the US as part of a migrant caravan. The caravan turned into an exodus. Over 10,000 men, women, children and infants, unable or unwilling to tolerate the toxic mix of violence, poverty, corruption and impunity, left Honduras on a perilous journey towards a hostile country. Donald Trump threatened to withdraw millions of dollars in aid, prompting jeers from the marchers to the effect that they'd never received any help anyway. But it jolted President Hernández into action. He turned Honduras into a giant, if porous, jail by deploying troops to the border in a futile attempt to stop people fleeing.

As this humanitarian crisis unfolded, the recusal petition was rejected and the trial unexpectedly reconvened. The victims' lawyers submitted written arguments explaining they would appeal the decision before the Constitutional Court. The judges accepted the legitimacy of the constitutional challenge, but then, after protests from the public prosecutors and defence lawyers, ruled the trial would open the following day *without* legal representation for the victims. In an extraordinary move, the judges claimed that by not showing up in court, the victims' lawyers had abandoned the trial.[72] Instead, the victims – Berta's family and Gustavo Castro – would be represented by the public prosecutors.[73]

The legal basis for dismissing the lawyers was highly questionable. It was a knock-out punch for the victims, who had fought so hard for justice in an unjust system. On Twitter, Bertita Zúñiga wrote: 'Alert the court has removed our lawyers and left us without representation for the trial of those accused of murdering my mother. I feel devastated.'

Why did they do it? The victims' demands for full disclosure were delaying the trial, and the court was under pressure to wrap up proceedings by 2 November, when remand ended for five defendants – Díaz, Rodríguez, Bustillo and the Duarte twins. Was a fear of looking bad behind the extraordinary decision, or was it a more sinister move to conceal the whole truth?

I made my way back to Honduras overland, nervous but ready. The trial of the eight men accused of murdering Berta Isabel Cáceres Flores opened on 25 October 2018.

10

The Trial

The Courtroom

Three gowned judges took their seats behind a raised wood-panelled desk facing the public gallery. To the right, between the justices and public gallery, were the eight defendants and their fourteen lawyers squeezed in behind an L-shaped arrangement of desks.[1] The defendants accused of planning the attack against Berta and Gustavo were Sergio Rodríguez Orellana, DESA's community and environmental manager; US-trained ex-lieutenant Douglas Geovanny Bustillo, DESA's security chief between 2013 and 2015; Mariano Díaz Chávez, a US-trained special forces major, and his former subordinate ex-sergeant Henrry Hernández Rodríguez. Óscar Torres Velásquez, Elvin Rápalo Orellana, and twins Edilson and Emerson Duarte Meza were accused of the shootings. The defendants were dressed in jeans and white t-shirts, apart from Sergio Rodríguez who wore smart trousers and a dress shirt. Opposite, to the public's left, were four state prosecutors with the case files piled high behind them and an empty space where the victims' six lawyers should have been seated. The court clerk and fourth judge were also on that side.[2] The public gallery was mostly empty, just a handful of embassy reps, international legal observers and defendants' relatives, but no one from COPINH or from Berta's family, who had boycotted the proceedings. The atmosphere felt flat, more like a provincial traffic case than a notorious murder trial. The courtroom was lined by armed prison guards and soldiers assigned to protect the judges and prosecutors.[3] Finally, at 10:30 a.m. on Friday 25 October 2018, the first witness was wheeled out in a tall wooden box, the shape of an old British red telephone box, with a polarized window on the door. I'd never seen anything quite like it, was it a magic trick? No, it was protected witness 268, 'Ana', to whom Elvin Rápalo had allegedly confessed killing Berta. It was a false start: we heard a sob, the box was wheeled back out, a doctor was called.

I'd met all the defendants apart from Henrry Hernández, and most caught my eye, smiled, and mouthed hello. Emerson Duarte, the twin whose charge I couldn't understand, looked downcast, his eyes dull, but the others joked and chatted. The prosecutors and the defence lawyers exchanged banter across the courtroom, and at one point the justices were laughing so hard that Judge Delia Villatoro bent over holding her stomach as if she had a stitch.

As we waited for the protected witness to regain her composure, the forensic evidence got underway with Dr Dunia Hernández, who arrived at Berta's house at 3:30 a.m. on 3 March 2016 and confirmed the death.[4] The crime scene photos were projected onto the faded wall of the public gallery.[5] We saw Berta's body splayed on her bedroom floor, arms stretched above her head, face and torso splattered with red like a Jackson Pollock painting, her hair clumped together by the blood flowing from three bullet wounds. She was in her pyjamas. Rápalo watched the slide show intently. Berta had fought to change Honduras so that poor children like him would have options other than crime or migration. We would later learn that Rodríguez was sent a similar crime scene picture of Berta's bloodstained corpse, by a contact whom he refused to name.

We were also shown a photo of a man's mutilated ear, obviously Gustavo Castro's, whom the court consistently referred to as 'protected witness ABC2016'.

The wooden box was wheeled out again after a long lunch. In the UK and US criminal justice systems, witnesses answer questions, unsolicited information is not allowed, and it's up to the lawyers to extract the best evidence. Not so in Honduras. Ana, her voice distorted to sound like a husky male alien, was invited to testify however she saw fit.

She told the court that around Easter 2016, Elvin Rápalo asked her if she'd heard about Berta Cáceres. 'I said yes, I'd heard it was a crime of passion, which is when he said "No, I topped that old bird," and gestured like he was pulling the trigger of a gun . . . But it wasn't easy, she fought back, so he stood on her . . . he said he was going to buy a car with the $100,000 Lempiras he got for killing Señora Cáceres.'

After the alleged confession, Ana said she found out that Rápalo was heavily into drugs and alcohol. The prosecutor asked: 'What does Elvin Rápalo do for a living?' 'He is, was, a *sicario*. That's what people in the village told me, that he killed people and liked to show people photos of his dead victims.'

The box was wheeled over to the row of defendants for Ana to point out Rápalo, who broke into a half-smirk. Nerves perhaps, or immaturity, or maybe he just didn't care.

Court was adjourned for the weekend after hearing three hours of evidence. I was thinking that we could be here for weeks at this rate, when the head judge, Esther Flores, announced the trial would be over in a week, by 2 November, the last day of remand for five defendants.[6] 'That's impossible,' retorted lead prosecutor Ingrid Figueroa, because the state was still trying to track down several witnesses. I felt dispirited as I headed back to the flat, wondering how Berta's children must be feeling, expelled from their mother's murder trial. The streets felt eerily quiet for a Friday afternoon, as riot police prepared to confront the Marcha de Dignidad, a peaceful march in solidarity with fellow Hondurans under attack in the migrant caravan as it trundled north.

Forensic Evidence

Berta died from a haemothorax, with 850ml of blood trapped between the chest wall and lungs, said the forensic pathologist Dr Etelinda López Castellanos, who conducted the autopsy in Tegucigalpa on 3 March. Three bullets entered Berta's body: one in the middle of the left arm, exiting just above the armpit and re-entering just below it. This one perforated both lungs. The second hit the left shoulder and lacerated the right jugular vein before exiting through the right armpit. The third entered above the left shoulder, and tore through the left lung, diaphragm and stomach, before lodging near the base of the spine. Each bullet damaged multiple vital organs, causing massive blood loss. She survived no more than five minutes.

The gunpowder residue on her olive-green t-shirt indicated that she was shot at close range. The trajectory of the bullets showed the gunman was above her at an increasing advantage, which meant she was most likely standing when first shot, but fell down as he fired again and again. The protected witness claimed to have seen scratches on Rápalo's neck during the alleged confession, but no fingernail DNA evidence was mentioned. The autopsy was co-signed by Dr Semma Julissa

Villanueva, the head of forensic medicine, who had told me at the graveside that the residue implicated Aureliano Molina.

I counted thirteen armed security officers in court during the autopsy evidence, more guns than people in the public gallery.

The ballistics expert presented the findings from the forensic analysis of the US-manufactured Smith & Wesson K-Frame .38 revolver found under Emerson Duarte's mattress,[7] as well as four bullets and fragments recovered at the crime scene, and two from the autopsy. Bullets are like fingerprints, uniquely marked once fired, and Olman García said tests confirmed that the bullets recovered from Berta's body and bedroom were fired by the gun Emerson claimed to have bought after the murder.[8] A .40-calibre bullet was identified, but the gun used to shoot Gustavo was never found. The forty-one bullets found at Edilson Duarte's house were not tested. The .38 found in Díaz's closet had not been tested. Why didn't prosecutors want to know more about the weapon found in the possession of a special forces major suspected of drug trafficking, kidnap and murder?

Colonia Líbano is an isolated, gated residential neighbourhood with one CCTV camera facing towards the only entrance. It was working on the night of the murder and captured three people running from right to left in front of the entrance at 11:38 p.m. It's dark, the footage is grainy, and the suspects are unidentifiable. As they run past the entrance barrier, where the guard is apparently sound asleep in his hut, headlights illuminate the road. You never see the vehicle but the height of the lights suggest a car, not a pickup. The car did a U-turn and drove towards La Esperanza just after 11:40 p.m. Investigators believe the car belonged to Edilson Duarte. It was seized on 2 May, but no evidence linking it to the murder was presented in court.

After watching the CCTV video, ATIC investigators returned and discovered a circular hole cut into the wire fence in front of a cluster of trees. This was the most likely entrance and escape route used by the gunmen. A single muddy footprint discovered in front of the hole was not lifted for analysis.

The Police Work

Henrry Hernández was on the run in Mexico when his house in Los Tarros was raided on 2 May 2016. Investigators found his army fatigues at his father's place and almost 100,000 Lempiras ($4,000) at his uncle Oscar's. Oscar testified that the cash, and numerous mobile phones seized as evidence, belonged to the evangelical church where he was the treasurer, not to Henrry. Although Hernández's selective confession at the initial hearing was not submitted as evidence by prosecutors, several details were followed up by the lead ATIC detective, Jesús Perdomo.

Perdomo looks like what he is: a SWAT team police investigator who spends a lot of time at the shooting range and gym. In Honduras, prosecutors are in charge of a case, but as lead investigator he oversaw the day-to-day police work. He testified for several hours over several days, and came across as a diligent cop who'd done some good police work. Nevertheless there were gaps – leads that should have been followed but weren't – and he omitted crucial details from his testimony.[9] Perdomo said the initial lines of inquiry were crime of passion, internal jealousies within COPINH, a revenge killing linked to a femicide case Berta had fought to get prosecuted – this was new to me – and her opposition to Agua Zarca. One by one, he said, each line of inquiry was ruled out, until the phone data led them to Bustillo and DESA.

At every stage of the case, Bustillo's defence had claimed that the request for phone records was authorized by the wrong court, thus making the phone data and everything else that followed illegal and inadmissible. But Bustillo was in all sorts of trouble.

The raid on 2 May 2016, the day Bustillo was arrested, yielded a treasure trove of evidence that suggested DESA's ex-security chief had been on a spending spree, despite having been unemployed for several months.[10] Recently purchased goodies included a red Honda Civic with a receipt for 165,000 Lempiras ($6,500), an Acer laptop, sound system, printer, portable air conditioner and hair straighteners. Investigators also seized several tablets, mobile phones and memory devices, part of a military-grade M16 rifle, 30 x 30mm-calibre bullets, plus a quantity of bank cards, bank books, deposit slips, cash and paperwork linked to DESA, and newspaper cuttings about Berta's murder. Bustillo, who came into court looking as if he was dressed for a leisure cruise in his electric-blue cap, matching tracksuit top and man-bag, occasionally jotted down notes as the evidence was passed around. Bustillo got Hernández a job at PCI Inc. (where he was still security chief) in November 2015, according to the HR file, and Henrry was sent to work at Walmart in La Ceiba for a couple of months. Investigators believed Hernández was the point man on the night, and recruited the *sicarios*. In his testimony Hernández blamed all his troubles on Edilson Duarte, who denied knowing him. Investigators thought the pair had met through Hernández's aunt in Colonia Pizzaty (Edilson's uncle's partner).[11] But these key connections in the criminal structure – who contracted who – were never explained at the trial.

Rápalo was also in all sorts of trouble: not only was he

named by two witnesses as Berta's killer, he was using another suspect phone number from the crime scene. It was registered to someone else, but the number was active on WhatsApp, and the profile picture was of Rápalo.

Hernández had also tattled on Torres, a.k.a. Coca, describing him as the tattooed guy who shot Gustavo. ATIC found Óscar Torres living with his older sister in Colonia Pizzaty, a couple of blocks from the Duarte twins. Torres and Edilson went way back, yet bizarrely Perdomo claimed the only connection between them was that they both lived in La Ceiba, a city of 200,000 people.

ATIC agents went to Pizzaty in early 2017, where a neighbour turned informer had Coca's number saved on his phone, the same number picked up by the antenna closest to the crime scene on 2 March 2016 and registered to a deceased woman named Rose Bodden. This informer said Coca left the country (heading for the US, via Mexico) shortly after Berta's murder, but had recently returned.

A weak point in the case against Torres, argued his defence, was the lack of evidence linking him to the suspect number on the day of the murder. SIM cards and phones are endlessly lost, stolen and replaced, as most people use cheap pay-as-you-go devices.

After his arrest when leaving jail in La Ceiba in February 2017, Torres told ATIC agents he'd once owned a .40mm, but had sold it long ago to a friend in the Aguán. ATIC followed up the lead, but the supposed buyer was now dead. The weapon was never found.

Investigators also didn't know about Coca's Mexican adventure. Thousands of young men leave Honduras every year in search of a better life; Torres left more or less around the same time as Hernández, and ended up in the same godforsaken place, Reynosa. The move didn't work out. Torres was deported in November 2016;[12] Hernández was extradited two months later. The two denied any contact while in Mexico.

But the most gaping hole was obviously Gustavo Castro. He was the only eyewitness, but his return to Honduras to identify his assailant had been obstructed by the Attorney General's Office.[13] His witness statement, given the day after the murder on 3 March, was only read out in court on the penultimate day of the hearing. His absence was suspicious, several defence lawyers suggested.

One last truth emerged from Henrry's selective confession. He said that the getaway crew were stopped at a police checkpoint on the highway heading north; this is true. Hernández was crying, feeling guilty perhaps. Edilson told the cops that they were returning from Henrry's grandmother's wake. It worked – the car wasn't searched, and they went on their way.

The circumstances surrounding Díaz's arrest caused a stir, in part because the poorly prepared state witnesses contradicted each other on where he was held while the house was being searched. This was important because the executor judge – a fancy title for the prosecutor in charge of the raid – claimed that Díaz told him they had the wrong man, that it was a DESA manager who'd paid Bustillo 500,000 Lempiras for the murder. Díaz made the alleged declaration without prompting, and without a lawyer present. His defence lawyer claimed the whole thing was made up.

Díaz was charged with planning the murder, as was Sergio Rodríguez. (No evidence was presented to suggest they knew each other.)

Perdomo said he took statements from several COPINH supporters who witnessed Rodríguez making threats to or about Berta at the protest on 20 February 2016; this Rodríguez vehemently denied. The contemporaneous Facebook post by Berta accusing Rodríguez was not mentioned by the prosecution. Rodríguez was also implicated by an eighty-second phone call he made to Bustillo at 6:29 a.m. on 3 March 2016, seven hours after the murder. It was the first call between them that year,[14] a fact investigators considered atypical and suspicious, but which Rodríguez claimed was intentionally taken out of context.

The state also argued that Rodríguez monitored Berta's movements through a network of informants, sharing the data with DESA executives and shareholders. This was *necessary collaboration* for planning the murder, prosecutors alleged. The victims' lawyers had always maintained that Rodríguez's role in the criminal structure went far beyond what the state would present, and in fact there was evidence that the community manager manipulated informants and provocateurs to incite community divisions which sometimes led to violence. To help demonstrate this, they had called four community members as witnesses who testified on Wednesday 31 October.

Olvin García Mejía, of whom Berta had said she was afraid in the weeks before her death, took the stand wearing bright blue jeans and a smart black shirt, his hair slicked back with gel. The family's lawyers had wanted to question him about the unlicensed guns which led to his arrest in December 2015; and why David Castillo had referred to him as 'our best security'; how much he was paid by DESA; the murder charge for killing Bernardo Pérez in October 2014, which was dropped after DESA undertook his defence; and the arson attack on dam opponent Don Justino in Valle de Ángeles. The state prosecutors asked him not a single question.

Instead, what we learned from Olvin's testimony was that he sold DESA a plot of family land on the river bank in Valle de Ángeles after negotiating the price with Rodríguez, describing him as a pleasant fellow who promised all sorts of projects for the communities, the latter being unanimously in favour of the dam. Even this falsehood went unchallenged by state prosecutors. He refused to answer my questions outside court. By then, Olvin had reportedly found Jesus Christ and stopped drinking (though he never stopped terrorizing people from Río Blanco). But six months later, in June 2019, he would turn up drunk at a church function wielding a machete and a handgun, and never make it home. His dismembered body was found dumped in a coffee plantation a few days later.

We know from the phone evidence that the Agua Zarca project manager, José Manuel Penabad,[15] specifically asked Olvin's brother Héctor's group, from Valle de Ángeles, to confront the Berta Vive delegation on 15 April 2016. Héctor was there when the group attacked mourners and threatened to kill Tomás Gómez. Héctor was paid 14,000 Lempiras ($600) every two months by DESA as a community 'link', though we never found out what his role involved. Again, prosecutors asked nothing. When Rodríguez's lawyer gave Héctor an open mic, he decried COPINH as a violent organization that shipped in Lencas to oppose the dam earnestly desired by the Río Blanco communities, and he praised Rodríguez as a peacemaker who actively discouraged confrontation. 'It was Berta Cáceres who created destruction and division in the area by opposing the dam,' he said.

Yet the phone messages suggest otherwise. On 13 February 2016, Rodríguez wrote to the Security PHAZ group:

> With respect to the division in La Tejera, Francisco [Chico[16]] Javier's group is now disjointed. Francisco's son Aníbal says that if he retires, thirteen other families would leave. Francisco wants to retire because Rolando Méndez wants to kill him . . . and also wants to machete the coffee farm. I told the informant to continue working on dividing them and persuade him to destroy the farm . . . me and the Major [Ávila] are seeing if

we can add another informant to Rolando's group, a boy from Olvin Mejía's family who lives in Tejera.

Outside court, Héctor told me that he and Olvin 'never' threatened to kill Berta or anyone else. 'Why did DESA pay for Olvin's lawyer in December 2015?' I asked. 'As a thank you for selling them land.'

Salvador Sánchez had been a friend of Berta, someone she considered a *compa*, a partner in struggle. He was visibly trembling as he walked towards the stand, glancing furtively at Olvin in the public gallery. 'I would call Sergio Rodríguez during meetings with Doña Berta, to let him know where COPINH planned to go,' he said. 'Why?' asked the prosecution. 'Because he'd promised me a security job . . . because he was scared of Berta, they went in with machetes and damaged the tractors constructing Agua Zarca. Sergio would get the police in whenever a mobilization was planned.'

What was his reward for the information? 'I didn't get the job, because COPINH didn't let them work.' And that was it.

I followed him out of court. 'How much were you paid, Salvador, 2,000 Lempiras, 3,000 Lempiras?' 'No, not that much, 500 a month,' he said, looking at the floor. 'I have four children.' 'You sold out Berta for 500 Lempiras a month? You told DESA everything about her, and now she's dead.'

'I didn't know that would happen, I regret it,' he said.[17] The phone messages show that DESA regarded Salvador as their most valuable informant and spy, because of his family connections and Berta's trust.

This was the day when it became crystal clear that expelling the victims' lawyers had left little hope of getting to the truth. Who was behind the criminal structure responsible for the wave of crime in Río Blanco that culminated in the murder of Berta Cáceres? From the way in which the lawyers were expelled, after having been repeatedly denied information and blocked from making their case, it was hard not to conclude that concealing the truth was exactly the point.

On the Day of the Dead, a small group of COPINH members including Laura Zúñiga were tear-gassed by riot police as they tried to erect an altar in memory of Berta outside the courthouse. Meanwhile in court, COPINH was painted as a violent organization by some of the defence lawyers, accusations that went unchallenged in the absence of the victims' lawyers. It was a hostile environment when COPINH leaders Lilian López and Sotero Chavarría were called as witnesses. I wondered if they'd appear. Lilian in particular could expect aggressive interrogation by Rodríguez's defence. But they loved Berta, and wanted to testify.

Sotero Chavarría joined COPINH in 1994, a year after it was founded, and she played a key role in obtaining land titles for over 200 Lenca communities. He told me Berta was his best friend. He told the court that these lands were under threat from companies dishonestly promoting megaprojects as development, when they were in fact driving forced migration to the cities and the US. 'We live in a country which is a disaster, in COPINH we work with people who have the least,' he explained.

What does DESA do? asked the prosecutor. 'They make dams and kill people,' replied Sotero incisively, before continuing: 'The case is very clear. DESA tried to jail Berta, then bribe her. David Castillo tried to induce her to clear the way for Agua Zarca. When they couldn't, they killed her. DESA is guilty and we want justice.'

Lilian went on the offensive. 'You're trying to make out COPINH is a violent organization, but we haven't killed anyone, we are the victims. They killed Berta for defending a *pueblo*, they killed her for being a woman. But she's still here, giving me strength, that's why I'm not afraid to tell the truth.'

In cross-examination, Jair López, Sergio's defence lawyer, highlighted the contradictions in Lilian's earlier testimonies, when she'd wrongly said Rodríguez was at the 30 November 2015 protest. He called her a liar three times in his closing arguments. I have no idea why the prosecutors insisted on including this alleged threat by Rodríguez in the case, given his water-tight alibi. 'They say I'm a false witness, but I know the threats, I was with her,' said Lilian. 'DESA monitored her, bought off leaders, paid informants, divided the community, that's why we know it was DESA who killed her.'

Tasiana Pineda, a middle-aged campesina from San Francisco de Ojuera, was called as an alibi witness for Rodríguez. She said that he was at her house the day before she saw Berta's murder on the news, but couldn't remember which day that was. I'm not sure what the point was of this unreliable alibi testimony – but what she told the court next was very interesting.

Whatever the date, on the day in question Rodríguez was at Tasiana's house negotiating damages for land DESA had destroyed to construct a road without permission from the family.[18] 'The mayor gave the company permission, he said it was municipal land, but we were the owners ... they took almost half,' she said tearfully. Rodríguez and Castillo repeatedly insisted that DESA only bought land from willing sellers·

The bulk of the evidence relied upon by the judges was not heard or seen by the accused or the public. It was mostly documentary – reports, authorization certificates, contemporaneous records, inspections and seizures – which prosecutors and defence by and large did not want read out in court. Investigators were summoned to ratify the documents, confirm their authorship, locate their signature, and only answer questions to clarify the content. In most cases, even basic details such as which defendant the evidence referred to wasn't stated. Open questions, which might have given the public and defendants an idea of the content and strength of the evidence, weren't allowed.

My request to read the admitted documents was denied. 'Yes, it's a public trial, yes, the files are public, no, you can't read them,' said the court archivist. She advised me to get friendly with the defence or prosecutors. The lead prosecutor politely refused to divulge even her name, referring me to the press office.

Though I'd followed this case from the start, I often found the evidence difficult to follow. How would we know what the judges would base their verdict on, if we couldn't see the evidence? It was so frustrating, like catching snippets of a conversation through a wall – especially when we got to the money.

The Money

Forensic accountant Wendy Maldonado took to the stand to answer questions on her 150-page report.[19] The eagerly anticipated report may have been fantastic, but she was a terrible witness: inaudible, confusing, and easily bullied by the defence. The evidence was technical, complicated, incomplete,[20] and too fast to follow. In a jury system, the prosecution would have been obliged to present the evidence in a more digestible way.

This is what I pieced together: Rodríguez was contracted by DESA in July 2012 as environmental manager, but the role was later expanded to include land acquisitions and community projects. His $3,000+ monthly salary was paid by four companies created to execute Agua Zarca: DESA until 2015, then PEMSA Panama, the minority shareholder of DESA, then PEMSA Honduras.[21] Following his arrest, his salary continued to be paid by Concasa.[22] Before she was killed, Berta was trying to trace the money behind the Agua Zarca dam. An investigation into possible bribes and money laundering, announced in mid-2017 by the international anti-corruption mission, MACCIH, was ongoing. The forensic accountant detected money flowing in and out of the Agua Zarca companies for salaries and expenses. Was this for tax purposes, or something more sinister?

Sergio received around $100,000 in payments between 2013 and 2016, including personal deposits by David Castillo, which were unaccounted for by payslips, tax declarations or expense forms, said Maldonado, who categorized this as unjustified income. But Rodríguez commissioned his own financial expert who concluded the income was kosher, despite messy accounting due to expenses, bonuses and wages going in and out of both personal and business accounts. Rodríguez's expert found no evidence of direct financial gain from Berta's murder.

Neither financial expert mentioned the monthly payments to community link Héctor Mejía, informant Salvador Sánchez and others, payments which suggested that community support for the dam was largely bought. For instance, the phone data indicate that on 7 January 2016 Rodríguez requested 100,000 Lempiras (approximately $4,000) to deal with a COPINH protest planned for that weekend. This sum, according to the letter Rodríguez sent that day, was needed to bring a notary from Santa Bárbara to file allegations of trespass and possible property damage; to transport a prosecutor and police investigator to the site; to buy food for the police as a goodwill gesture; and to cover two days' pay and food for 'workers' – community members and municipal workers confronting COPINH.[23] The money was approved by company president Castillo and transferred by Daniel Atala.

The car Elvin Rápalo allegedly boasted about buying with his payment for the murder wasn't mentioned, nor was the 500,000 Lempiras Díaz claimed DESA paid Bustillo, nor the $100,000 Lempiras deposited into Bustillo's account in November 2015. The evidence regarding Díaz's financial affairs was impossible to follow.

Mid-trial, during a break from proceedings, lawyers with the international observer mission met with high-ranking justice officials to highlight concerns about the expulsion of the victims' lawyers and the poorly prepared state witnesses and evidence. 'Don't worry, people will be convicted,' they were told. What did they mean, how did they know, when we were only halfway through the evidence? Was this a done deal, a political deal?

Berta's case was supposed to be the litmus test for a justice system that has received millions in US and EU aid. It was meant to prove that Honduras could and would prosecute complex high-impact crimes, following the evidence no matter where it led. Zahra Piñero, coordinator of the EU Justice project, told me: 'There's no interest in increasing the independence of the judiciary, because controlling the careers of judges and prosecutors suits politicians.'[24]

And as if to prove the point, the trial was reconvened a day early without us being told. Key data extracted from Rodríguez's and Bustillo's phones were presented to an almost empty public gallery.

I needed to know which phone chats were admitted as evidence, and politely asked the prosecutor's spokesman, Yuri Mora, on several occasions.[25] A week passed, no response, so I asked him again at the courthouse. 'What are you going to do with the information?' Mora demurred. 'I'll get it for you so long as you promise to be objective ... You seem to be aligned with special interest groups.' 'Is this a public hearing or not?' I said. 'Why didn't you inform the victims about the secret hearing? I thought the public ministry represented them. What are you trying to hide?' 'You mean those victims who say we don't represent them,' he sneered and walked away.[26] That same day Rodríguez's lawyer, Jair López, beckoned me over. 'I'm very disappointed in you, Nina,' he said with a smile. On his laptop was a folder titled 'Nina Lakhani' which contained all my tweets,[27] translated into Spanish, some sections highlighted with comments. He pointed out two minor errors in a thread summarizing the best bits of the previous week's evidence. I thanked him and promised to correct them. Jair wouldn't tell me who the translated tweets were being shared with, or why.

Elsia Paz, the combative spokeswoman for the renewable energy sector, was mentioned in the phone evidence. On 24 April 2013, DESA's in-house lawyer Carolina Castillo messaged Daniel Atala to say that she'd 'just seen Elsia Paz who said that she could easily control Berta Cáceres, that she had her well investigated and she was a blackmailer, but with two phone calls she'd never bother them again.'

I contacted Elsia for comment on this message.[28] Her first response was typically evasive, but that night she wrote again, this time in clumsy English:

> Nina ... I read all the twitters you write and publish ... you are using this case as a moment of fame. you need attention and a way that your book can sell. Your thing is not the facts ... is the way you can make a fantastic ideological story. I truly you respect. You make a living selling stories. Just remember this. there are inocent lives in jeorpardy. Dont

be obsesive about a story, that you are not even sure about the facts. Karma will hit you. There are innocent lives.

On another occasion, we heard the statement by protected witness AAA, Berta's deputy Tomás Gómez, in which he described trying to get police help before driving to Colonia Líbano to rescue Gustavo. Immediately afterwards, Díaz's combative lawyer Ritza Antúnez told the press pack that Tomás should be investigated as a suspect, given that he'd breached the crime scene (not true) and failed to call police (not true). Her inaccurate remarks were not probed, but were circulated widely, illustrating the uncritical and superficial reporting of the case by much of the mainstream media. The country's small independent press did not attend the trial. When I challenged Ritza on her comments, she rejected my criticism and walked away. After that, one court reporter who was particularly chummy with Ritza placed a notebook or sweater on the chair next to her whenever I walked into court, so I couldn't sit down.

As the trial chugged along, an ex-special forces soldier travelling with the migrant caravan told a Mexican journalist in Guadalajara that Berta was murdered by an agent called Herzog Arriaga, who had successfully infiltrated her inner circle by pretending to be an activist.[29] The unnamed soldier claimed he and eighteen colleagues were jailed by order of President Hernández, to stop the truth behind the state-sponsored murder being exposed.

The story coincided in several aspects with that of army whistleblower Rodrigo Cruz, who claimed the hit list was given to FUSINA and Xatruch on orders from the joint chiefs of staff at the presidential palace. Salvador Zúñiga had told me COPINH was infiltrated from the start, and in 2013 lots of new faces were seen as things in Río Blanco heated up. It made me again wonder about higher levels of responsibility yet to be investigated or purposefully left out, like the incredible meeting Díaz mentioned with DESA executives and top-ranking government officials, and the close ties between DESA executives and senior police officers and ministers.

Phones

A well-presented criminal case captivates through persuasive storytelling, unexpected twists and turns, alternative villains, and a clash of legal minds as the prosecution and defence attempt to outsmart each other. That's why courtroom dramas make great television. But these shows depict jury trials, where each side must try to persuade laypeople of its own version of events, hypothesis and evidence. This forces the prosecution and defence to formulate a cohesive narrative, and their expert witnesses to explain technical, complicated evidence in a way intelligible to ordinary people.

In this trial, the state lacked a cohesive narrative, probing questions and context, despite the vast amounts of information collected by the investigation. Prosecutors failed to articulate the roles of the defendants and how they connected to each other. The who did what, why and how was missing – until we got the phone evidence which was the game changer.

The state's case was built on telephone evidence. Even though no data were extracted from 70 per cent of the mobile phones seized during the raids, more than a thousand pages of data were extracted from Daniel Atala's iPhone 5 found at DESA's offices. The data were admitted into evidence on CDs, but prosecutors wanted to show two WhatsApp chats on the projector, one between Atala and Bustillo from 19 July 2013, the other with his partner from the following month.

Rodríguez's defence furiously objected to the latter,[30] arguing that only conversations between company partners, managers and security personnel linked to the monitoring of Berta and COPINH were authorized. The judges overruled this objection. Daniel Atala was not on trial, but we knew he was under investigation. Were the prosecutors preparing for an arrest? The message from Bustillo was about paying an informant. 'Danny can you deposit a thousand Lempiras for two weeks for an informant because he's given 500 per week,' wrote Bustillo on 20 August 2013. 'OK,' replied Daniel. We didn't find out the identity of the informant.

Atala's exchange with his partner was about the 2013 trumped-up criminal charges against Berta, Tomás and Aureliano which suggested political influence.

> Daniel Atala: *I got you motherfuckers*, just found out that one of those COPINH sons of bitches left the country ... asking for political asylum in Norway LOL, *es un maje q foc* ... His name is Aureliano Domínguez [Lito], he's a murderer, I'd like to have a face to face, *le monto verga* [I'd fuck him up] I swear
> Maria Fernanda: Eeeeyyyyyaaaaaa
> DA: I see him in the street and I fuck him up
> MF: Stay away, don't even think about that
> DA: He's leaving today
> MF: But that's good *bello*... that they're scared
> DA: For the 3 ... Berta, Aureliano and Tomás ... three leaders
> MF: Aureliano wants a *wiwow* ... *Cawifornia wowl*
> MF: But why does he want to leave? Because there's an arrest warrant?
> DA: I've spent a lot of money and political capital to get those three arrest warrants

MF: Good

DA: After seeing them commit 500 crimes. It's really something the problem of impunity in Honduras

Atala was right – impunity is king in Honduras, with fewer than one in ten crimes investigated and only a small proportion prosecuted, especially when the suspects are part of the privileged elite. Jair López and Celeste Cerrato shook their heads in angry disbelief. The chat was irrelevant, they argued. Jair told me Daniel was a lovely guy.

Yet the phone data were peppered with casual racist comments by DESA executives and managers, especially Daniel Atala, who on 12 March 2012 wrote: 'I am sitting at a table and two *indios* came to invade my space . . . and there are 20 empty tables.'

On 4 December 2013 he wrote: 'These Indians think that women will become infertile because of the dam', and on 4 March 2014 he called Río Blanco Lencas half-breeds: 'That's what I call *indios* from Agua Zarca . . . to not identify them as Lenca indigenous people . . . I call them Ladinos because they are not legit Lencas.'

Berta and Salvador founded COPINH as a counterpunch to centuries of institutional racism against the Lenca people which destroyed their land, language and cultural identity. Berta frequently denounced public officials for racism. Berta's children regard her murder as a political femicide, a killing motivated by money, machismo and racism. Neither racism nor misogyny featured in the state's case.

The prosecution's star witness was Brenda Barahona, who submitted a 471-page report on the phone evidence and was on the stand for almost a week. A cool, clear, commanding expert witness, with over twenty years in police intelligence, she'd been trained by the US embassy and Colombian intelligence experts. Her long dark hair tied in a bun and traditional blouses reminded me of Frida Kahlo. Barahona's evidence was often compelling, and for the first time the state had a narrative. The defence lawyers hated her.

Barahona immediately endeared herself to the public gallery by explaining key terms: phone taps record the content of all communication in real time, without the user's permission, while data extraction means retrieving content retrospectively;[31] a phone number on the SIM card and the IMEI, the unique handset ID number, are both traceable; the closest antenna usually captures both calls and texts, but topography like high mountains or circumstances like heavy phone traffic can bounce the signal elsewhere. After the unfathomable financial evidence, her willingness to explain the basics was a huge relief.

Barahona's first task after the murder was analysing the phone traffic from the antennae closest to Colonia Líbano, which captured Berta's final calls and messages and Gustavo Castro's desperate pleas for help. However, most of the messages Gustavo tried to send after Berta died failed, because the phone credit ran out.

After eliminating the numbers belonging to Berta's neighbours, other messages and calls from near the crime scene led them to Hernández (two numbers), Edilson Duarte, and numbers registered to the deceased Rose Bodden (Torres) and Dimas Rivera (Rápalo). In addition to these five, calls and texts were analysed from numbers used by Douglas Bustillo, Mariano Díaz, Emerson Duarte, Sergio Rodríguez, David Castillo[32] and Daniel Atala, as well as from two of Berta's numbers. WhatsApp messages from Atala, Bustillo and Rodríguez were also admitted into evidence. (The victims' legal team pinpointed over forty other numbers as suspicious enough to warrant further investigation, but no action was forthcoming.)

DESA personnel discussed Berta and COPINH in multiple chats and conversations, but Barahona focused on the Committee PHAZ WhatsApp group,[33] created on 7 October 2015 by David Castillo (the name was changed to Security PHAZ by Rodríguez). The formation of the group coincided with a new wave of direct action by Berta and COPINH after they realized that construction of the dam was under way on the far side of the River Gualcarque in San Francisco de Ojuera (not Río Blanco). Castillo was worried about a leak via the contractor and asked everyone to be more careful. 'For now we'll manage strategic information and intelligence between us. This will be the Agua Zarca security crisis committee ... so we can react in the best way ... and immediately.'

Castillo informed the group that Berta was planning to come to the project a few days later, on the Saturday, with people from La Tejera. 'They'll invade us for five days.' 'I hope it rains and the river rises,' said José Eduardo Atala, a DESA shareholder.

Knowing that Berta had an appointment in Tegucigalpa the following Monday,[34] Castillo reassured the group that she at least wouldn't be staying past the weekend. Still, he wanted action, and instructed Rodríguez to buy a new mobile and use it to send anonymous messages to community leaders in La Tejera. 'Remember, Sergio, make sure neither your name nor the company's is involved ... and delete the messages.' Shortly after, Castillo reminded Jorge Ávila about the forthcoming scheduled meeting with the government security minister to discuss police support.

On 10 October, community members from La Tejera constructed a makeshift wooden bridge over the river in preparation for Berta's arrival. Next day, Sergio Rodríguez wrote: 'The bridge must be destroyed tonight. There's no one looking after it apparently.'

Pedro Atala, another shareholder, agreed: 'Get that bridge down . . . let nothing be easy for those sons of bitches.' A few hours later it was dismantled: 'Mission accomplished bridge down on both sides', confirmed Ávila. With that, Berta's plan to lead protesters to the new installation was foiled. 'The señora left, it was a failure, with the bridge destroyed by security she couldn't cross the river,' said Castillo. But Berta did not give up so easily. COPINH built another bridge and the protests continued, despite a heavy police presence.

I tracked down a former military intelligence officer, let's call him Joaquín, who was part of DESA's security detail when ordered to destroy that bridge. He resigned soon after, because 'that's not what I signed up to do. DESA had a network of informants and knew everything about Berta and COPINH. I knew they were plotting something, and it felt personal. So I got out.'

The day after Castillo gloated about destroying the bridge – Monday 12 October, the international Day of Indigenous Resistance – DESA security guards fired guns and lobbed stones at community members gathered at the river. Berta was with her mother at a Tegucigalpa clinic, and messaged Castillo thanks for his help in organizing the appointment.

On 29 October 2015, as COPINH kept up the pressure, Rodríguez wrote: 'It's evident that when Tomás and Berta aren't here, the movement is weak, and few participate. Therefore, we should also take actions against them.'

It was around then, late October or early November, that prosecutors allege the decision to murder Berta was taken.

Bustillo was not on the company chat, but he frequently communicated with Castillo despite having been sacked in July 2015. On 9 November 2015, 100,000 Lempiras were deposited into one of Bustillo's bank accounts. Two weeks later, on 22 November, Bustillo texted Castillo that he'd completed '50 per cent', and they arranged to meet at Chili's, a Tex-Mex chain in the Próceres mall in Tegucigalpa. As the two men made their way there, Castillo sent another message: 'Bustillo, get a move on, no partying, and have everything prepared because it could happen at any moment in the course of this day.'

Díaz communicated with Hernández and Bustillo, not surprisingly given that he'd been in the army with both. But the calls and texts intensified in the weeks before the murder, and the contents were captured thanks to the phone tap.

In January 2016, Díaz was recorded chatting and exchanging messages with Hernández and Bustillo about a 'job' ... Berta's name was never mentioned, nor was La Esperanza, because they used coded language common in police and military circles, said Barahona. Hernández addressed his former commander as *señor*, and Díaz his protégé as Zaper, short for Zapador, which is slang for sniper.

On 4 January Díaz and Hernández met at City Mall in La Ceiba. An hour or so later they spoke again by phone, and Hernández enquired whether they would do the job, which Díaz appeared to advise against. Immediately afterwards Díaz told Bustillo that, having spoken to one of his intelligence guys in the area, he couldn't get directly involved; he'd like to but he couldn't, and so would help find an alternative solution. If Major Díaz consulted an intelligence officer to obtain information for a crime, this implicates state resources and therefore state responsibility.

Over the next few days, Hernández and Díaz talked about good business involving *ganado* or cattle, criminal slang for kidnap target, and *carne asada*, roast meat, slang for murder. On 9 January, Díaz informed Hernández that the indecision had cost them the job: *los de arriba* (those above them) had given it to someone else. Hernández blamed Bustillo for the delay, and reminded Díaz that he had a *gatillero*, a gunman, a youngster known as 'Los Dedos' or Fingers who charged 10,000 Lempiras ($400) a hit, in order to keep the three of them out of trouble.

Hernández was broke and desperate to leave Honduras. He needed 15,000 Lempiras to pay a coyote to smuggle him into the US, and asked Díaz to get them back on the job. 'Everything depends on them above, but I'll try,' said Díaz.[35] A week later, on 16 January, Bustillo asked Díaz if he'd got the *avión*, literally the plane, though Barahona said it's also slang for vehicle. Díaz had not.

On 20 January Bustillo and Díaz discussed a plan for that Friday, 22 January.

Bustillo and Castillo communicated by phone on 21 January. Their signals were captured by the same antenna in Tegucigalpa, leading Barahona to conclude they also met in person to discuss the following day's reconnaissance mission. The next day, 22 January, Bustillo and Hernández were in La Esperanza where they stayed until the next morning. During that time, Díaz made no calls or messages from his usual phone, but Bustillo communicated with a contact saved as Díaz 2. Barahona concluded that Díaz was also in La Esperanza for the reconnaissance mission, using this second phone.

No phone data from Díaz 2 were presented. Barahona most likely relied on intelligence sources, but it was an evidential leap inadequately explained.

On 25 January, Castillo called Bustillo, we don't know what about as their phones weren't tapped. But two days later, Bustillo asked Díaz to loan him a gun, *el chispero*, which Díaz agreed to bring him. Four days later Bustillo and Hernández met in Siguatepeque, a picturesque town famous for its strawberries off the highway connecting Tegucigalpa and San Pedro Sula. From here they took the winding road up to La Esperanza, where the two men stayed until 31 January, according to the phone data.

During that period Bustillo communicated frequently with Díaz, who seemed to be coordinating the mission and claimed he was ready to move in case of emergency. Díaz was under investigation for organized crime, and at times seemed to be discussing various illegal activities in code.

After leaving La Esperanza, Hernández went back to Los Tarros in the Aguán and Bustillo went to Tegucigalpa. Díaz meanwhile was busy with classes for his promotion at the military academy in Tegucigalpa.

On 2 February Hernández and Díaz chatted about a hit for the coming weekend: 'I'm going to work with the other guy because you need to stay clean for your career,' wrote Hernández. 'That's fine, *tópala*' (kill the woman), said Díaz. But Hernández was broke, so broke that Díaz lent him money to travel back to La Esperanza for the 5 February job. That job was to kill Berta Cáceres.

Hernández told Díaz that '*cuando el pez está cheke*, once the job's done, he'd get 100,000'. Díaz joked about the stingy amount, but said that for his mates, he'd work for free. Just before 4:30 p.m. Díaz gave one last piece of advice: 'Silence over the radio.'

Bustillo met Hernández in Comayagua, north-west of Tegucigalpa near the Palmerola airbase, and gave him the gun loaned by Díaz. A third person was present, perhaps Los Dedos, whom investigators never identified in court. Bustillo used his phone to find pictures of Berta, including the iconic one at the river and a beautiful one with Doña Austra at the Goldman Prize ceremony. Bustillo returned to the capital, while Hernández and the gunman, *el gatillero*, went to La Esperanza.

But the plan bombed. At 8:30 p.m., Hernández informed Díaz that Berta was not alone, 'there's a lot of people traffic ... he [Bustillo] wants us do it in the early hours.' Díaz was concerned about such a last-minute change of plan. 'You have to wait a few hours after the game, you can't just leave the area immediately ... I'll be there moving directing everything.' Barahona interpreted this as Díaz being ready to fetch them after the crime.

Separately, and seemingly unaware of the unfolding problem, Castillo messaged Bustillo at 9 p.m., telling him to 'remember the accidents and the scene'.

The plan to kill Berta on 5 February was postponed because Laura and Bertita were with their mum. The job required more manpower, said Hernández, and a car, as they were too exposed on foot. Díaz said he didn't want to burn his own car, so they'd need to find a stolen one and make a new plan.

Hernández wanted to take the gun home with him, but Díaz insisted on having it back as it wasn't his. They met in Siguatepeque and Díaz got back the weapon. Bustillo suggested Díaz and Hernández carry out the job on 6 February instead, but that didn't happen.

Later that day, Bustillo informed Castillo about the failed killing: 'Mission aborted today, yesterday it wasn't possible. I'll wait to hear what you say, the thing is I've no logistics, I'm at zero.' 'Copied, mission aborted,' replied Castillo.

Over the next month, Díaz, Bustillo and Hernández communicated regularly. Díaz told Hernández that they'd lost the job, having taken too long. But Hernández insisted, explaining to Díaz in long rambling conversations captured on the wiretap why he was desperate for cash. He'd lost his job at Walmart, was behind on loan repayments, and lost two guns and 26,000 Lempiras when stopped at a checkpoint in San Pedro Sula. He had to *asar la carne*, kill the target.

Hernández told Díaz that he'd found a *sicario* group who would provide the wheels and weapons, but wanted 25,000

Lempiras ($1,000) up front. 'These guys are something else, they know how to kill, they're excellent killers ... We just need to roast the meat and then share out the meal,' he told Díaz. Hernández tried to persuade Díaz that this group was the real deal, he'd gone with them two nights earlier, on 19 February, when they wasted someone with nine bullets, *tata-tatatata*. They were willing to do the job alone, said it would take only ten or twenty minutes, but Bustillo wanted Hernández to go along. Remember, Hernández claimed that it was 'Shorty' (Edilson) who forced his hand.

Díaz, who chatted to Henrry in between classes and research for his thesis, appeared to distance himself from the murder: 'Them above have given the job to other people, they couldn't wait any longer. I'm not getting involved ... I'm not interested, it's too crazy. But I'll try and help you get the money, a loan, as a favour.'

Díaz was worried that the *sicarios* would pocket the money without doing the job, but Hernández reassured him, saying that he'd known one of the group for eight years because his family lived in the same neighbourhood. He was presumably talking about Edilson.

In February, Díaz was all ready: he provided the gun, used intelligence sources to gather information, and coordinated the botched mission. If you take his change of heart at face value, rather than as a smart ploy to avoid detection, the fact remains that here is a decorated active major, soon to be colonel, who knew about a plan to kill someone but told no one and did nothing to prevent it. State investigators listening to the phone tap also failed to intervene. Díaz said he was not involved, yet he continued to ask Hernández about the job, communicated frequently with Bustillo, and agreed to help get a loan to pay the *sicarios*. We don't know from Barahona's report if he came through with the cash or not, but the plan went ahead.

On 20 February, as the plot to kill her gathered pace, Berta led hundreds of COPINH members to the Gualcarque River. It was that tense, chaotic day when Berta was warned by Sergio not to go to the river, and the deputy mayor screamed in her face, 'You old witch, you'll never come back here.' Rodríguez, Ávila and DESA also took steps, documented in the Security PHAZ chat, to press criminal charges against dam opponents.[36] Bustillo monitored the protest and relayed information to Castillo, which contradicts Díaz's claims that the job had been given to another group. Bustillo then went back to La Esperanza on 21, 24 and 27 February, followed Berta around town and took photos of her and a house (the wrong one) in Colonia Líbano on his phone.[37] On two of those days, Barahona thinks Díaz was with him.[38] What about the hit men? There was regular phone traffic between the alleged *sicarios* and Hernández from 26 February, suggesting the job was on. The frequency of calls and messages intensified from 1 March, suggesting final plans were being coordinated.

What about the alleged conspirators? Castillo arranged to meet Bustillo early on 1 March at DESA's offices, to give him the money referred to in the phone message as 'the requested loan'. That day at 2 p.m., Rodríguez informed the Security PHAZ group that fifteen community members had left Río Blanco for training in La Esperanza, where Chico Javier (Sánchez) was going to resign in front of Berta. This was one example of what the state argued amounted to 'necessary cooperation' by Rodríguez. The defence argued that he was merely confirming that Berta would be busy, and not causing problems for the project.

On 2 March,[39] Hernández left Los Tarros to meet Edilson Duarte, Torres and Rápalo in La Ceiba, and together they drove to La Esperanza.[40] In the hours before the murder,

Bustillo searched for more pictures of Berta on his phone. One hour before the murder, Torres, Rápalo, Hernández, Duarte and Bustillo called each other, suggesting they were in different places, perhaps at different lookout points. By this time, Berta was at her home with Gustavo Castro.

Between 11:30 and 11:38 – when the assailants entered the house and shot Berta and Gustavo – Torres, Duarte and Hernández again communicated by phone. If Duarte was in the getaway car, Hernández may have been outside the house; remember that Gustavo reported hearing a radio frequency.

The alleged hit squad's five phone numbers were captured at Berta's residence around the time of the murder, and then they left the area immediately afterwards to head back north.[41] It was the first and last time those phones and numbers were detected in La Esperanza, apart from Hernández's during the alleged reconnaissance missions. Later the phones were in Santa Rita, Yoro, where the squad members stayed the night together after the near miss at the police checkpoint. Hernández communicated with Bustillo, whose phone put him in Tegucigalpa, before and after the murder.[42] The four alleged *sicarios* and Bustillo swapped their SIM cards between various phones, perhaps thinking it would protect them. The phone evidence did not connect Emerson Duarte to the murder, Barahona concluded. Emerson nodded his head.

After the Murder

Rodríguez claimed that he heard about the murder from colleague Claudia Erazo at 5:32 a.m. on 3 March. He immediately called Castillo, then sent a message reminding him to speak to the banks. That was the first concern, the company's investors. Castillo got to work coordinating the company's security, economic and communications response via the Security PHAZ chat.

Bustillo received the 'atypical' eighty-second call from Rodríguez while driving to San Pedro Sula, where his phone was captured en route to the bus terminal.[43] It was here, Hernández had previously told Díaz, that the *sicarios* received payment for an earlier murder. Was Bustillo delivering the money he got from Castillo? Bustillo met Díaz on 6 March at 9 a.m. in Tegucigalpa at the City Mall food court, we don't know why.

DESA closely monitored news reports and court proceedings to figure out who was being blamed. On 3 March, Francisco Rivas, an ex-DESA engineer, messaged Rodríguez: 'I see they sent you to get rid of Berta, what crap.' Sergio agreed: 'Watch how they're going to blame us.' Rivas sent him a link to a Facebook page where the company was being blamed, commenting: 'You need to find out who's behind it.' Rivas was just kidding, claimed Rodríguez's defence in closing arguments.

You can tell from the messages that Rodríguez was anxious. Remember how Daniel Atala urged him on 7 March to relax and not panic, otherwise he would make other people panic – 'the security minister today told Pedro that it was a crime of passion . . . *que hay que esperar unos días para que caigan los hechores y que a ellos solo les queda seguir trabajando normal.*' But Rodríguez was spooked by press reports blaming him and Ávila in particular. On 17 March the pair met with lawyers, and gave voluntary statements to investigators.[44] Maybe the meeting reassured Rodríguez, as the following day he and Bustillo went to Castillo's internationally packed solar plant in Choluteca. Bustillo had been promised a security job there; could killing Berta have been a prerequisite? That's what Díaz told me: that Bustillo turned the murder down until the company came back with an offer he couldn't refuse.

Despite some nerves and growing international outrage, construction of the dam continued, and company officials felt secure enough to employ its influence and resources to disrupt the Berta Vive river march in April.

DESA was unprepared for the arrests on 2 May 2016. Rodríguez was texting with his lawyer Celeste Cerrato, when he saw twenty or so agents outside his mother's house. 'No, get out of there, there has to be an arrest warrant,' the lawyer advised. 'We'll take care of it.' But it was too late, and Rodríguez turned himself in. Barahona said she included this communication as it showed Rodríguez didn't make a run for it; still, it was later excluded from evidence as a breach of lawyer–client confidentiality.

Castillo called the company vice-president, Jacobo Atala Zablah, with news of Rodríguez's arrest. Don Jacobo couldn't believe it: 'For the love of God, today they've sunk us completely.' Castillo reassured him that Rodríguez had nothing to do with it, and the arrest was just a show for the media. Jacobo asked if ATIC was part of the Public Prosecutor's Office. Yes, replied Castillo.

At this point Barahona stopped to ask the judges whether she should play the rest of the call, which dealt with 'personal matters'. The consensus was negative.

And yet the rest of the call *is* in her report. Jacobo wanted to know which authorities he should call for help; General [Julián] Pacheco, the security minister, was considered the best person to start with. But Jacobo worried that Pacheco was dependent on the Attorney General's Office, and anyway he was overseas, so he asked if Castillo's friend (Rigoberto) Cuéllar was still assistant attorney general.[45] He was but had been sidelined, said Castillo, who suggested asking Don Eddy, Jacobo's brother José Eduardo, for advice. How this snippet could be regarded as personal is a mystery, unless of course it was part of the deal to keep politicians out of the trial.

By this time, Castillo had been charged with masterminding the murder, but he was not on trial. Yet the prosecutors and Barahona repeatedly emphasized evidence against him. In the middle of Barahona's testimony, DESA's international legal team published a report containing a cache of WhatsApp messages its experts had extracted from Berta's smartphone, which they claimed contradicted the state's case.[46] The Amsterdam report claimed Berta and Castillo were friends,[47] the investigation into Berta's murder wrongly targeted DESA thanks to falsehoods circulated by COPINH, and Rodríguez and Castillo were in fact political prisoners. The published messages between Berta and Castillo are dated between October 2014 and December 2015, during which period they met several times, enquired about each other's wellbeing, and Berta even wished him happy birthday. She asked Castillo for help in renting a car, he obliged, and on two occasions he tried to give her money. At the end of June 2015 Berta asked Castillo to find out more about agent Elvin Noé Corea Munguía, and provided his licence plates and ID number.[48] I don't know what she was after, it's not in the message, but she must have suspected that Castillo would use his military intelligence contacts. Castillo expressed an interest in Nahua and Mayan astrology, and in her involvement with the Indignados protests. He asked about her plans, sometimes she told him, and these details Castillo often shared in the DESA security chat. Berta told close confidants that she felt shaken after Castillo turned up at the airport just when she was about to travel. The messages show that on two occasions they arranged to meet at the airport.

In early 2014 Castillo had told Berta that he was giving up, had finished arguing with COPINH, and would focus on his solar energy project in the south. There were no signs of construction until August 2015, so perhaps she believed him?[49] That's when Castillo made her some kind of proposal, saying they must find solutions that worked for them both, but he refused to meet in Río Blanco for further discussions. He wanted a neutral location. On 6 October, Castillo told Berta that he considered her a friend. 'I believe that we share certain criteria and of course I hope that one day we will find a midway point where our ideals will meet and leave us with a solution in which we both win.' Berta agreed to discuss it, but warned there were things she didn't agree with. A day later, the Security PHAZ WhatsApp group was created.

It's unclear whether the pair met, as the published messages end on 16 October 2015 – shortly before the decision to kill her was taken.[50] After this the building work stepped up, and so did the resistance. The situation was very tense in October and November, very like 2013, with frequent protests, which triggered threats and police persecution. Shots were fired towards Berta's car in Río Blanco on 6 November, the special rapporteur visited, and Tomás Gómez received calls from the Madrid family threatening to 'fix things with Berta the nice way or the nasty way, once and for all'.[51]

We don't know what Berta said to Castillo during that tense period because DESA's lawyers did not publish those messages. We do know that Castillo messaged Berta on Christmas Day to wish her well. She responded warmly, said she was spending Christmas with her daughters in La Esperanza. He wished her a Happy New Year with her family, and she reciprocated.

The messages suggest that Castillo fished for information while pretending to be Berta's friend. Did Castillo feign friendship just to find out about her movements, or did he hope to convince her – by gaining her trust and even reliance on him for certain things – that the project was okay, there was no need to oppose it? Maybe. In the company security chats he called her *la vieja*, old girl, a somewhat disparaging term.

Berta told friends and family that she suspected Castillo was trying to seduce her. He's handsome and comes across as charming and helpful in the messages, at a time when she was in an abusive relationship. Did she on some level fall for it? Or did Berta, who her friends say was pretty crafty herself, try to play him at his own false-friend game in the hope of gleaning information about the dam? If so, he outplayed her. He won, she lost. The game was over. Barahona's case was clear: the order to kill Berta came from DESA executives. But had this been proved beyond reasonable doubt?

Frequent delays during the six-week trial made small talk inevitable. I often chatted with Díaz's wife Wendy, who was sure that every scrap of evidence against her husband had been manipulated to save more powerful culprits, though she never said who. Wendy wore old clothes, used a cheap throwaway phone, and showed me letters from the armed forces demanding money owed on their house. If Díaz was involved in organized crime, it didn't make his family rich.

I was intrigued by a WhatsApp group called 'Promotion 34' – the 1997 graduating military class, including Díaz, Bustillo and Rodas, the Tamara prison governor who like Díaz served in Iraq, but also David Castillo, who graduated much later in the US. This is the only state evidence linking Díaz and Castillo. Wendy didn't understand it either: she knew the others, but not Castillo. She was close to Bustillo's wife, Lesley. 'Why doesn't she come to court?' I asked. 'She stays at home praying,' Wendy answered.

Díaz's older sister Tomasa, a gentle, retired schoolteacher, said she cried twice after Berta's death: 'First when I heard the news, and again when I heard my little brother had been arrested. I admired Berta Cáceres very much.'

They grew up poor in rural Comayagua, but their grandmother was a domestic worker for the notorious army commander Manuel de Jesús Trejo, who sponsored their father's military education.[52] Like Wendy, Tomasa refused to believe Díaz was capable of criminality, and dismissed the phone tap evidence as fake. '*Mi negrito* has always been with intelligence, going after narcos, and lots of officers *do* get involved. But my brother was never ambitious or vain, his children go to public school and they live in a modest house. Even when he earned good money with the UN, he didn't change.' Perhaps he was leading a double life, given how he'd boasted about multiple lovers to me – that can get expensive – but Tomasa dismissed any extramarital affairs as flings.

Two others who attended regularly were the wives of detective Juan Carlos Cruz and police officer Miguel Arcángel Rosales, who were in jail facing charges of manipulating a witness statement and audio evidence that he had perverted a criminal investigation.[53] The alleged tampered audio evidence implicated some of those mentioned in the IG report María Luisa Borjas was sued over. Both men denied wrongdoing. (The case was dismissed in 2019, before reaching trial.)

Sergio's elderly, coiffed mother and daughter Ingrid, twenty-two, were in court every day, and pretty icy towards me, which I understood. But as the trial approached its end, Ingrid thawed. She told me she was studying law and hoped to do a master's in international relations in London. She brought in some aftershave on the day Rodríguez testified, he was chuffed, it was a tender father–daughter moment.

Missing from the proceedings was Major Jorge Ávila, who

was called as a witness but died a few days before the trial after suffering another stroke.[54] Sergio Rodríguez was the only defendant to exercise his right to testify, and spoke for over two hours. He said everything had been fine, the communities were on board after being 'socialized', until the roadblock in April 2013.[55] It was only after Berta held the El Roble meeting that the community turned against the dam (not true). He said the company won over two key roadblock organizers (true), but then Chico Sánchez took over and violence against the project spearheaded by COPINH escalated (not true).[56] Rodríguez said the decision to move the project to the other side of the river was taken after Tomás García was killed in the DESA encampment in July 2013. With the new plan under way, DESA decided to drop the criminal charges against Berta and her colleagues after they were dismissed at appeal (not true).[57] Berta reappeared in mid-2015, but work on the dam continued unless there was a protest, of which the company advised security forces in advance.[58] He affirmed, and this was key, that the Security PHAZ chat monitored Berta and COPINH's movements *only* to protect Agua Zarca installations. His words had been taken out of context regarding October 2015, when he recommended taking 'action' against Berta and Tomás; he'd meant legal action. On cross-examination he couldn't explain why this would have been necessary if she was no longer a problem.[59] After Berta was killed, Rodríguez said he called Castillo and Bustillo because her death had implications for the dam, but that was all, there was nothing more sinister. 'Berta and COPINH were no longer a problem for us, we had 450 days working without interruption before her murder, apart from 30 November and 20 February . . . there were no economic losses.' The reconfigured project would generate more energy and therefore compensate any losses, he said.

Rodríguez blamed his incarceration on lies by Lilian López and Barahona.[60] 'The charge changed from intellectual author to collaborator, yet the prosecution has the same evidence it presented at the first hearing ... I'm fifty-one years old, I can't be in prison for something I didn't do.'

The End: Saturday 24 November 2018

Prosecutors argued that the motive behind Berta's murder was financial loss to DESA, that the order to kill and the money both came from David Castillo, and that the seven men on trial played crucial roles: Rodríguez managed the paid informants and monitored Berta's movements; Bustillo was the middleman, liaising with Castillo and Rodríguez from DESA, and with Díaz and Hernández to plan the murder. Díaz provided the weapon, vehicle and logistics; Hernández organized the *sicario* group, and participated in the reconnaissance missions and the murder; Edilson provided and drove the getaway car; Rápalo shot Berta; Óscar participated, but they didn't say what role he played.

The state requested thirty years to life for murder, and twenty years for attempted murder for seven of the defendants. The charge against Emerson Duarte was dropped to cover-up (of the gun), which carries a maximum three-year sentence.

The defence teams each argued that the state had failed to prove beyond reasonable doubt the involvement of their client. They all agreed that Brenda Barahona had exceeded her brief as an expert witness, and her conclusions were unfounded and overreaching. The case was made for reducing the crime against Gustavo Castro to assault, given that his life was never in danger, which was rejected.

The Trial

After closing arguments, Laura and Olivia Zúñiga Cáceres came to court to exercise their rights as victims to have the last word. The sisters stood at the gallery railing. Olivia had given birth a month earlier. Laura took the microphone and faced the judges and the accused.

'Berta Cáceres was a person who struggled, who was rebellious, who confronted the Agua Zarca Hydroelectric Project because it violated human rights, a project that caused bloodshed in Lenca territory.

'Today it's up to me to speak, something I don't want to do because no one wants to talk after their mother has been murdered, it's up to me to speak because this justice system didn't allow us to participate in this process, it expelled us. Our lawyers should be here, explaining the context in which this murder occurred, how they hunted her down. From the moment my mum was murdered, we were excluded from the process . . . we've had to fight for information at every moment, every step of the way. We didn't do it on a whim, we did it because we are prepared to do everything necessary to get to the truth because we understand that it's our right, because we understand that it's the right of the Honduran people. We've been meticulous. We have asked for the court to be recused and we have even filed a complaint against the [state] prosecutors because we want the best trial.

'This is an important moment to make legal precedents for the people [of this country], who are fleeing, who are bleeding. This was the opportunity to do it. The struggle for justice for Berta Cáceres does not end here . . . We are not passive victims. We will act because Berta Cáceres deserves it, because the Lenca people deserve it, because they keep on persecuting us even now, because this criminal structure that killed Berta Cáceres is still active.'

The very last words actually went to the defendants:

'I'm innocent, I was not in La Esperanza,' said Óscar Torres.

'I'm sorry to see the grief for Berta Cáceres ... I didn't provide any weapons, money or vehicle. I hope the court brings us justice,' said Mariano Díaz.

'It's been thirty months of suffering for me and my family ... It's unfair, they've tarnished my name and ruined my twenty-five-year career. I feel for her children, in 1992 my father was murdered. They have the right to demand justice and so do I,' said Sergio Rodríguez.

'I'm innocent,' said Edilson. 'I'm innocent,' said Emerson.

'I don't know anything about the Doña,' said Elvin Rápalo. 'The protected witness lied, the number isn't mine.'

'I proclaim my innocence, I didn't persecute Berta Cáceres, my communication with David Castillo was about work. I am a victim ... The public prosecutor manipulated the evidence,' said Bustillo.

'We're accused of the worst thing, in the name of God we ask for justice for the lady ... People look at us as the worst, as criminals. I was in the army, they accuse me and my major but our conversations weren't about Berta Cáceres. God bless you all,' said Hernández.

Court was adjourned until Thursday 29 November, at 4 p.m., for the verdict. I needed a drink.

Verdict Day

The verdict was scheduled for 4 p.m., but by 2:30 there was a long queue outside the locked courtroom which only seats about fifty. Doña Austra got a seat with two of Berta's brothers, as did COPINH's spiritual leader, Pascualita. Héctor

García's Valle de Ángeles crew waited outside the door, squeezed alongside Berta's friends who chanted: 'Berta vive, la lucha sigue' (Berta lives, the struggle continues).

As we waited inside the courtroom for the judges to arrive, crisis talks were taking place up the road at the presidential palace. It had been a terrible week for President Hernández. His younger brother Tony, a former congressman, was indicted in the Southern District of New York, accused of having been a major drugs and arms trafficker since 2004, and having collaborated with the Cachiros and the Sinaloa cartel. His late sister Hilda was accused of running a corruption ring which had embezzled $11m from the ministry of agriculture in order to fund his 2013 election campaign. The National Party was accused of operating as a criminal structure. The net seemed to be closing in. Riot police and soldiers lined the tense streets. What would happen if the defendants were found not guilty? How would the people react, would it be the catalyst for wider protest?

For once the judges were on time. The cameras rolled for live streaming. Judge Esther Flores looked nervous and her voice quavered.

Berta Cáceres, the judge said, was killed because of her leadership in the opposition to Agua Zarca, which was costing DESA money.

Sergio Rodríguez and other company executives hired informants to gather information about Berta and COPINH. The information was used to repress the Lenca leader and undermine her movement. Rodríguez provided necessary cooperation, and was therefore guilty of murder. As the judge uttered the word '*culpable*', Rodríguez shook his head in disbelief, while his daughter Ingrid sobbed loudly.

Next the judge turned to Douglas Bustillo. He conspired with Rodríguez and other DESA executives to eliminate

Berta. Bustillo and his former army colleague Mariano Díaz helped plan and carry out the murder. The judge found Díaz to be an essential collaborator, an active member of the armed forces who could have intervened to save Berta's life. Both were guilty of murder.

Díaz and Bustillo, the judge ruled, had conspired with Henrry Hernández, who recruited the hit men, named as Edilson Duarte, Óscar Torres and Elvin Rápalo. All four were found guilty of Berta's murder and the attempted murder of Gustavo Castro.[61]

Emerson Duarte was cleared.

Seven men had been found guilty of murdering Berta Cáceres. The verdict was just, but was justice done, with so many questions still unanswered?

Outside the court no celebrations were held by Berta's friends, family and colleagues, instead they issued a call to revoke the Agua Zarca licence so the people of Río Blanco could live in peace.

'We demand that the masterminds behind the murder be brought to justice,' said Olivia Zúñiga. 'We demand justice for Berta Cáceres in a country with so much impunity, not just for our family but for the Lenca people, for Honduras, and all the environmentalists who've lost their lives.'

'Our battle for dignity, truth and justice does not end here,' said Laura Zúñiga. 'We will keep fighting – just like Berta Cáceres did.'

Afterword

Berta Cáceres meant many things to many people. She was an indigenous leader, a political radical, and a grassroots human rights defender who refused to surrender to the patriarchal neo-liberal world order. She was smart, kind, funny, provocative, and a rare leader who could listen, negotiate, and bring people together. She died much too young, at only forty-four, at a time when our world's indigenous peoples and natural resources are under sustained attack from unsustainable greed and consumption. The race to save the planet is on, but radical changes are needed and time is running out. Her death was a crime against her family, her organization COPINH, the Lenca people, Honduran society and humanity.

In a way, life and death in Central America were simpler during the Cold War era. Economic and political enemies of the ruling elites were labelled communist sympathizers and neutralized. If Berta had been killed in the 1980s, it would have been considered a political murder mandated by state policy. Today, security forces are still deployed to protect foreign and national business interests, but belligerent community leaders are tarnished as anti-development criminals and terrorists, rather than as leftist guerrillas. Today, the mystery or uncertainty created by generalized violence *is* the state policy. The nightmare that has unfolded in Honduras since the 2009 coup has shown that repressive state structures endured after the dirty war. The elites behind them regrouped, modernized and reactivated their forces to prop up the emerging criminal state. As hundreds of thousands flee, the country's economy is increasingly propped up by remittances.[1] The language has changed, but for those clinging to power and making the money, the end always justifies the means.

In October 2019, I moved to New York to start work as the *Guardian*'s first ever environmental justice reporter. That same week, Amilcar Ardón, the former mayor of El Paraíso and a confessed drug trafficker and killer, told the Southern District of New York Court that in 2013 Joaquin 'El Chapo' Guzmán came to his house to deliver $1m in cash, a contribution to the election campaign of Juan Orlando Hernández, who subsequently became president. The money was said to be a quid pro quo intended to allow the Mexican drug capo to continue doing business in Honduras. Ardón also admitted to giving $1.6m of his own drug takings to the Hernández campaign. If these allegations are true, Hernández won the election thanks to a campaign funded by drug proceeds *and* money stolen from the healthcare system (IHSS) and numerous other public funds.

In the court files, Hernández and his predecessor Pepe Lobo were designated co-conspirators who allegedly leveraged drug trafficking to 'maintain and enhance their political power'. Prosecutors alleged that the National Party had benefited from drug money during the last three elections. Cachiros leader Devis Leonel Rivera Maradiaga backed this up by claiming to have paid bribes to President Hernández and his security minister Julián Pacheco.

As the trial unfolded, Hernández took to Twitter to denounce the multiple allegations against him as '100% false, absurd and ridiculous'. He also sent a diplomatic note to US officials complaining about the denigrating manner in which prosecutors referred to him and his alleged role in what they deemed to be 'state-sponsored drug trafficking'. Regardless, the trial ended with the president's brother Tony being convicted on 18 October 2019 on weapons charges, for lying to the DEA, and for conspiring to import 220 tons of cocaine, crimes for which he faced a mandatory minimum of thirty years' imprisonment.[2] The very next day in Tegucigalpa, President Hernández appeared at a military parade laughing alongside interim US Ambassador Colleen Hoey. The following week, a delegation from the US State Department and Homeland Security met with the Honduran government to discuss ways to stop migrants and refugees reaching the American border. Then, an alleged drug trafficker whose ledgers had provided the prosecution with key evidence about Tony Hernández's drug shipments was shot and stabbed to death in a high-security prison in Honduras. The notebooks reportedly contained coded references to the president. Shortly after, the victim's lawyer was also murdered. No arrests; *no pasa nada*. It's unclear what it would take for the US government to stop propping up an illegitimate government accused of operating a narco state.

By late 2019, neither Porfirio Lobo nor Hernández had been indicted on any charges, and both continue to protest their innocence. But those close to them continued to fall: Lobo's wife, former first lady Rosa Elena Bonilla de Lobo, was sentenced to a staggering fifty-eight years for embezzling around US$800,000 during her husband's presidency. The ill-gotten windfall, deposited in her personal bank account five days before Lobo's term ended in January 2014, was spent on jewellery and paying off credit card bills. This was the first successful prosecution for a case backed by the Organization of American States anti-corruption mission MACCIH. Other cases had fallen foul of a corrupt pact made among lawmakers trying protect themselves, their colleagues and their associates from prosecution.[3]

Billions of tax dollars and aid dollars have been stolen over the past decade while hundreds of thousands of Hondurans have fled the misery of poverty, unemployment, violence and repression. On top of that, we know almost nothing about what happened to the millions made by drug traffickers such as Tony Hernández, Fabio Lobo and the Cachiros brothers. How much of this money was laundered through perfectly legal anonymous corporate structures involved in energy and extractive projects and backed by international financiers? This is just one example of information that global corporate and financial systems seem designed to obscure.

Berta's murder triggered international condemnation but failed to stop the bloodshed. At least twenty-four land and environmental defenders have been murdered in Honduras since 2 March 2016. Latin America remains the most dangerous region in the world to defend land and rivers from megaprojects like mines, dams, logging and agribusiness. Between March 2016 and November 2019, 340 defenders were killed in the Americas, according to Global Witness. Why? These high-impact crimes largely go unpunished. Impunity breeds crime.

At the heart of most conflicts over land and natural resources is the failure to obtain free, prior and informed consent from communities before megaprojects are sanctioned. Despite everything, the Agua Zarca licence has not been revoked and hangs over the Río Blanco community, which continues to face threats and harassment from a handful of pro-dam neighbours. At the time of writing, the Honduran state continues to circumvent international standards enshrined in the ILO 169 convention and UN Declaration on the Rights of Indigenous Peoples; it is trying to push through a so-called consultation law, promoted by a congressman with alleged ties to drug traffickers, which would in fact undermine meaningful participation by communities. Meanwhile the repression continues, yet the government and its economic backers have faced no significant consequences from the international community or from investors, including taxpayer-funded development banks. On the contrary, it's been business as usual, and this complicity has helped fuel corruption, violence, and impunity, which in turn sustain the killing fields. 'Too often companies and investors benefit from corruption and neglect their responsibility to respect human rights,' concluded a UN delegation to Honduras in August 2019.[4]

The killing of defenders is only the crowning macabre finale. The vast majority of victims had previously been subjected to a campaign of intimidation, defamation, threats, attempted bribes, assault and, increasingly, judicial persecution. The use of laws and policies designed to tarnish, criminalize and intimidate defenders, their families and communities is rising and often takes place under the murky cloak of national security. This shows how state apparatuses – police, prosecutors and judges – are employed to protect business interests over citizens' rights. Just one example is provided by the seven ordinary campesinos from Guapinol in Tacoa, Bajo Aguán, where the community has since 2015 been trying to block construction of an iron ore mine owned by the son-in-law of deceased palm oil mogul Miguel Facussé, which threatens to contaminate local rivers. In September 2019, in a case condemned internationally as unjust and unfounded, the men were charged with arson and the illegal detention of a private security manager. The seven defenders were subsequently held illegally for eight weeks in an extremely violent high-security prison meant for gang members, drug traffickers and murderers, thanks to an improper order from the National Penitentiary Institute. It took eight weeks, three writs of habeas corpus and an international campaign to secure their transfer to an ordinary jail, where they remain locked up. At least four other Guapinol defenders fled Honduras and sought asylum in the US to avoid judicial persecution. And so the merry-go-round of misery keeps turning.

In December 2019, a year after seven men were convicted of killing Berta Cáceres, the court finally reconvened to hand down the sentences. The hitmen – Elvin Rápalo, Edilson Duarte Meza, Óscar Torres and Henrry Javier Hernández – were each given thirty-four years for the murder and sixteen years and four months for the attempted murder of Gustavo Castro. Sergio Rodríguez and Douglas Bustillo got thirty years and six months for murder, while Mariano Díaz was found guilty by omission and given thirty years. Justice was partially served, but focusing only on the material authors in crimes like this is 'insufficient to combat impunity and is problematic, as it does not identify powerful groups which may be behind human rights violations', in the words of Michel Forst, the UN Special Rapporteur on the situation of human rights defenders.[5] Meanwhile the case against David Castillo, so far the only person accused of masterminding the crime, rumbles on. In his case, Berta's family and COPINH have been recognized as victims of the crime and therefore authorized to mount private prosecutions independent of the state's case. As part of this, they filed an application to a US federal court to subpoena bank records linked to a $1.4m five-bedroom house in Houston, Texas, purchased by Castillo eight months after the murder.[6]

In the 2018 trial, we saw how the judges curtailed evidence which threatened to expose a wider conspiracy and criminal network. In the Castillo trial, the victims' lawyers will seek to prove that the murder was the grand finale of a state-sponsored criminal campaign against Berta and COPINH. Castillo's lawyers continue to protest his innocence, claiming he is the victim of political persecution. Berta's children continue to speak truth to power. The struggle for justice will be long.

New York
December 2019

Notes

1. The Counterinsurgency State

1 The first families set up home here in the early 1940s, after the fertile land was given to the indigenous Intibucanos by former president Luis Bográn. It wasn't a gift, but payment in kind for building his castle, which now lies in ruins, on top of a steep hill overlooking the nearby town of Santa Bárbara.
2 Gilberto Cáceres Molina, Berta's paternal grandfather, rose to the rank of regional commander after being forcibly recruited to the army as a teenager. He was elected to Congress for one term and served five terms as mayor of Marcala.
3 Visitación Padilla, the first women's organization in Honduras, was created to defend jailed and tortured female political prisoners across Central America. Its coordinator Gladys Lanza, a prominent labour rights organizer and Communist Party coordinator, was detained and tortured in 1984 by state security forces. Lanza, another real-life hero for Berta, died aged seventy-four, six months after Berta herself, still appealing a sentence for libel designed to discourage the group's defence of women's rights. She was posthumously pardoned by the Supreme Court.
4 The imposition of the counterinsurgency doctrine unfolded domino-fashion: first in Guatemala, to prop up military dictatorships allied with US business interests, then in El Salvador against the left-wing guerrillas, and then in Honduras, from where attacks were launched to undermine the Sandinista revolution in Nicaragua.

5 In El Salvador, fourteen families controlled 90 per cent of the land, and largely dedicated to the lucrative coffee cash crop. These families sent their children to exclusive schools in Europe, while paying their mainly indigenous labourers in meagre rations of tortillas and beans. An uprising led by Communist Party leader Agustín Farabundo Martí in 1932 was brutally repressed, the brunt of casualties borne by the indigenous Pipil.
6 In September 1974, Fifi killed as many as 10,000 people in Honduras and destroyed large swathes of the countryside, sparing neither subsistence crops nor banana plantations.
7 Zelaya Senior was convicted for the massacre, along with another landowner and two local army commanders, but amnestied in 1980 after serving just one year.
8 See allworldwars.com/CIA-Psychological-Operations-In-Guerrilla-Warfare.html.
9 Until the Great Depression, Honduras was the world's most important banana-exporting country. The year 1929 was the zenith of Honduras's banana trade, with 29m bunches exported. After that it declined due to the impact of the Wall Street crash on American consumers, disease in the plantations and hurricane damage. See cadmus.eui.eu.
10 The Dulles family was key. John Foster Dulles negotiated the land giveaways in Honduras and Guatemala to United Fruit in the 1930s, via his law firm Sullivan & Cromwell. Under President Eisenhower he was US secretary of state, while his brother Allen was on the United Fruit board and director of the CIA.
11 Melo's father, a largely forgotten grassroots organizer, led the first successful peasant land occupation which thwarted a backroom deal between United Fruit and an ambitious local landowner. He was murdered not far from El Progreso in 1974. No one was prosecuted.
12 The two-time president was eventually forced out in 1975, on the back of a corruption scandal linked to a hefty bribe from United Brands to reduce fruit export taxes.
13 The US coordinated the Contra war in Nicaragua and supported military death squads in El Salvador and Guatemala from Honduras. The Honduran military received training in repressive techniques by the CIA and special forces, the Argentine junta and Pinochet's Chilean squads.
14 North was convicted over the Iran-Contra affair, but the conviction was reversed and charges dismissed in 1991. He was named president of the powerful gun lobby, the National Rifle Association, in 2018.

15 In 1983, when Álvarez's oppressive methods were well known to the US embassy, the Reagan administration awarded him the Legion of Merit for 'encouraging the success of democratic processes in Honduras'.

16 The training provided by Argentine and Chilean death squads, who had already perfected the art of political abduction and murder, was facilitated by the US and proved indispensable to Central American military dictatorships.

17 The case upended the pervasive culture of denial by repressive Latin American governments. The IACHR declared forced disappearances illegal on multiple grounds, and as long as a person remains disappeared, the crime stands.

18 Salvadoran Archbishop Óscar Romero, who spoke out against poverty, social injustice and state repression, was shot by a sniper while saying mass on 24 March 1980. Though the assassination was carried out by a military death squad, neither perpetrators nor instigators faced justice. Romero was made a saint in 2018. Bishop Juan Gerardi was murdered in a military operation in April 1998, two days after the publication of the truth commission report *Guatemala: Nunca más*.

19 Including General Álvarez, Captain Billy Joya Soto, and future army chief Romeo Vásquez Velásquez, who greenlighted the 2009 coup.

20 Álvarez was deposed by his own men in 1984, accused of making a power grab and stealing excessive sums of money. In exile the former death squad commander became a consultant to the Pentagon and reinvented himself as an evangelical pastor. He returned home pledging to preach, only to be gunned down in a well-planned, professional hit that Battalion 3-16 would have been proud of.

21 Dr Almendarez founded the Central American anti-torture and human rights organization, CPTRT.

22 Ronald Reagan famously said that another evangelical, the Guatemalan dictator General Efraín Ríos Montt, was simply misunderstood. Ríos Montt was found guilty of genocide and crimes against humanity in 2013. The verdict was then corruptly returned to trial, and he died aged ninety-one in 2018 in the middle of a new trial.

2. The Criminal State

1 The Zapatistas today are part of a global indigenous movement that rejects capitalism and globalization.
2 At least according to the early chronicles of the Spanish conquest by the official, some say discredited, historian Antonio Herrera y Tordesillas (1549–1626).
3 Miriam Miranda is coordinator of OFRANEH (Honduran Black Fraternal Organization), the country's first grassroots ethnic minority rights group founded in 1978.
4 Palmerola, official name Soto Cano Air Base, is located between Siguatepeque and Tegucigalpa, five miles south of Comayagua.
5 The nationalist Callejas is credited with unleashing neo-liberalism on Honduras between 1990 and 1994, by promoting the privatization of natural resources and lands occupied by untitled indigenous and campesino communities.
6 This office was the Fiscalía Especial de Etnias y Patrimonio Cultural.
7 The right to unionize is recognized in the Central American Free Trade Agreement (CAFTA) and the Constitution, but most maquila workers are poor young women. Some do not know their rights, others are actively discouraged from joining or forming trade unions and the names of those who do are often shared with other factories, effectively blacklisting them as troublemakers. See waronwant.org/women-factory-workers-honduras.
8 Berta met the pontiff at the first World Meeting of Popular Movements, where he assured delegates that their joint calls for 'land, housing, and work' would have a place in his then-forthcoming encyclical on the environment.
9 In 2017, Olivia was elected to Congress representing the Libre party.
10 I visited Vallecito in August 2017, the morning after a two-day Agrarian Platform assembly. The platform is a collective of campesino organizations campaigning for land rights. Living conditions in Vallecito were very basic for the dozen or so families trying to put down roots.
11 Miriam was detained by police in Tela, Atlántida, in March 2011 while protesting peacefully in support of a teachers' strike.

3. The Neo-liberal Experiment

1 Berta collaborated closely with Grahame Russell and Annie Bird from Rights Action on everything from grassroots education to community resistance and international legal battles.
2 Vicente Fox, president from 2000 to 2006, officially launched PPP in El Salvador in June 2001, and was its most prestigious advocate.
3 See geocomunes.org for more detail.
4 It was only four years since the peace accords in Guatemala, the last civil war to end in Central America.
5 In 2017 Honduras was ranked the most unequal country in Latin America and the third most unequal globally (using the Gini coefficient).
6 In 2018, the official minimum wage covered only two-thirds of a basket of basic goods (*canasta básica*), while remittances, mainly from undocumented migrants in the US, account for a fifth of GDP and supply the only explanation for the vast number of thriving shopping malls.
7 Tanya M. Kerssen, *Grabbing Power: The New Struggles for Land, Food and Democracy in Northern Honduras*, Food First Books, 2013.
8 By 1920, 0.5 per cent of the population were Palestinian migrants, according to the census; now, there are about 250,000 descendants, with most identifying as various denominations of Christian.
9 As the competition intensified, in 1924 the Arabs donated a towering statue of Lempira on Independence Day to prove their patriotism. The monument – Lempira decked in feathers, with two lions – still stands on Lempira Boulevard in San Pedro Sula.
10 The last three presidents – Juan Orlando Hernández, Pepe Lobo and Mel Zelaya – are from landowning stock, and governed thanks to the wealth and influence of the transnational elites.
11 Dinant was founded in 1960 to manufacture soaps and detergents, before diversifying into processed snacks and agriculture and going on to conquer markets across the region. It trades as Corporación Dinant SA de CV.
12 Facussé was the son of Palestinian Christians who migrated to Honduras in the early 1900s; he was vice-president of APROH until at least 2011; his nephew Carlos Flores Facussé served as president of Honduras from 1998 to 2002.
13 The IMF/World Bank-sponsored programme was supposedly aimed at attracting foreign investment, but resulted in the state absorbing millions of dollars owed by Dinant and other private enterprises.

14 In the early 80s, the oligarchs delivered a policy wish-list known as the Facussé Memorandum to the government, and US officials delivered a complementary policy document that anticipated the future Washington Consensus.
15 The African palm plan was well under way in the 1990s: an Organization of American States (OAS) study in 1964 discussed turning over 150,000 acres in the Aguán to palms, considered a more stable crop than bananas. In the 1990s the INA encouraged the fledgling cooperatives to plant seedlings it supplied, but without revealing key details which would later work against the campesinos: African palms grow up to twenty metres, with invasive roots which deplete the soil, and need twenty litres of water per day – a huge environmental cost in a country vulnerable to drought.
16 The municipal law contradicted the agrarian law, which according to the Constitution has superior authority. The agrarian law stipulates that no one can own more than 250,000 hectares of land.
17 The forced evictions led to the creation of MUCA (Unified Peasant Movement of Aguán) and then MARCA (Authentic Campesino Claimant Movement) with the objective of recuperating the lost farms. First, they tried the courts; then, land occupations after the coup; then, negotiating with the palm magnates to buy back their stolen land; and then more land occupations.

4. The Dream and the Coup

1 The troops were deployed from the 1st Battalion in Tegucigalpa, where US special forces were conducting training at the time: see securityassistance.org.
2 US embassy cables suggest the cardinal and Ambassador Charles Ford bitched about Zelaya to each other. Zelaya cut a 100,000-Lempiras monthly tax-funded stipend to the cardinal initiated by President Carlos Flores. The cardinal received $41,600 per month from the Catholic university. See espresso.repubblica.it.
3 The armed forces refused to hand over firearms used that day to test against the bullets found at the crime scene. General Vásquez claimed his troops only fired into the air, and that Isis Obed was killed with a .38, not a military weapon.
4 In a December 2005 cable profiling the newly elected Zelaya,

Ford wrote: 'Allegations of involvement with drug trafficking and other forms of illicit enrichment have cropped up periodically since at least 1988, but there is no reporting to substantiate such allegations ... The overall arc of his career shows him to be flawed within the range of normal for Honduran politicians, but basically well-meaning.'

5 Unlike most of his predecessors, Zelaya was not college-educated and spoke little English.

6 US interference in Honduran politics is well documented. In 1994, soon after Hugo Noé Pino was named president of the Central Bank, a USAID functionary hand-delivered a document, a white paper of sorts, which made clear that any change to the exchange rate regime would be unacceptable. 'I ignored him and made the changes we saw fit, but it demonstrated the influence the US and international funds expected in Honduras, an influence which almost always benefits the elites,' said Pino.

7 Zelaya's version is contradicted in a 15 May 2008 cable, in which Ford wrote: 'While Zelaya was open to our point of view on the selection of key members of his Cabinet, he was absolutely closed to listening to us on his appointment of his ambassador to the OAS and to his appointment of Jorge Arturo Reina as ambassador to the UN. The Honduran voting record in the UN in terms of coincidence with US positions is at the lowest point in decades.'

8 The first Zelayas arrived in Honduras from northern Spain more than 400 years ago. The family are traditional landowners on the second tier of the economic and social structure, below the transnational oligarchy. Zelaya left university without graduating to take over the family ranching and logging enterprises in Olancho after his father's conviction for the Los Horcones massacre. He had stints as director of COHEP (the big business club, which later plotted against him) and the loggers' association. The father of his wife Xiomara Castro was a prominent commercial lawyer whose clients included Miguel Facussé and former president Rafael Callejas. The 2006 wedding of their son Héctor to Marcela Kafati, daughter of coffee baron Jesús Kafati, was attended by the cream of Honduran politics and business.

9 In 2005, Honduras, the second poorest country in Latin America after Haiti, spent $833m on imported fossil fuels, rising to $1.6bn in 2010 as a result of rising costs and consumption.

10 Launched in June 2005, Petrocaribe allowed Caribbean states to buy oil from Venezuela under preferential terms, such as paying 50 per cent up front and the rest over two decades. Alternatively, the debt could be paid by supplying Venezuela with services or

products it needed, from doctors and teachers to bananas, sugar and beef.
11 The bidding war was partially won by US firm ConocoPhillips but was mired in allegations of political grandstanding, incompetence, corruption and sabotage, with boycotts and price hikes by storage facilities in Honduras which rendered the cheaper fuel deal unworkable. In the end, Honduras became the seventeenth and final country to join Petrocaribe in December 2007, and the first to leave – straight after the coup. It returned to the Petrocaribe fold in May 2012, when crude oil reached $110 a barrel.
12 The Bolivarian Alliance for the Americas (ALBA) is a trade agreement based on cooperation and social welfare rather than free market principles. It was created by Chávez and Fidel Castro in 2004 as an alternative to the US-promoted Free Trade Area of the Americas (FTAA, in Spanish ALCA). Honduras become the sixth country to join in August 2008.
13 When Zelaya took power, the country's largest public company was losing 3m Lempiras, about $120,000 every day, and wasting a quarter of its energy stocks through thefts and leaks. Fossil fuel plants provided two-thirds of the country's electricity; the rest mostly came from the state-owned 300-megawatt El Cajón dam on the Comayagua River, near San Pedro Sula.
14 The inflated contract for billings, metre readings, payments, cuts and re-connections was held by a company linked to political chameleon Arturo Corrales, whose past posts have included security minister and foreign minister. In a US embassy cable profiling the post-coup movers and shakers, Corrales was ranked alongside former presidents Carlos Flores and Rafael Callejas as an influential political broker. He was a post-coup negotiator for the interim president, Roberto Micheletti, and security minister under Pepe Lobo.
15 Enrique Reina, Zelaya's private security officer at the time, said it was because Zelaya trusted Defence Minister Mejía. Despite the army's authoritarian roots, it is widely considered the country's most professional institution, with highly skilled officers who were underemployed.
16 Berta was granted protective measures by the IACHR in 2009.
17 In 2013, Hernández was president of Congress and standing for president; Pacheco was his security adviser.
18 Moncada, a lawyer by profession, was appointed labour minister by Zelaya in 2006. She was part of Zelaya's inner circle, exiled after the coup due to arrest warrants which Interpol ruled were politically motivated and refused to execute.

19 See audit tsc.gob.hn. The sales violated the State Contracting Law, which prohibits government institutions from contracting with companies owned by officials or employees who could influence or participate in the selection of companies.
20 In Brazil, where at least $350m was paid out through the company's dedicated bribery department by 2018, a third of President Michel Temer's ministers were under investigation, according to the US Justice Department. Other senior politicians linked to the scandal include four ex-presidents of Peru and the vice-president of Ecuador, Jorge Glas, sentenced in December 2017 to six years in jail. See US Department of Justice, 'Odebrecht and Braskem Plead Guilty and Agree to Pay at least $3.5 billion in Global Penalties to Resolve Largest Foreign Bribery Case in History', justice.gov, 21 December 2016.
21 As part of this ministerial post, Zelaya created the Nuestras Raíces (Our Roots) programme to finance local projects such as bridges, clinics and kindergartens in marginalized communities.
22 There are three vice-presidents, known as *designados presidenciales*, or presidential designates.
23 Rallies were held after the government failed to respond to twelve demands by the Bloque Popular, exhorting the state to protect public services and natural resources. The protests were repressed by presidents Ricardo Maduro and Manuel Zelaya.
24 The independents easily surpassed the 45,000 signatures needed to qualify as candidates; Zelaya and Rafael Callejas both signed. At the time of the coup, the polls put Liberal candidate Elvin Santos in front, the National Party's Pepe Lobo was down and out, and the Reyes camp was doing remarkably well for independents.
25 Revising constitutions is not uncommon in Latin America.
26 Llorens replaced Ford in September 2008. Ford went to the US Southern Command as an adviser on public–private partnerships.
27 Born in 1943 in El Progreso, Micheletti is an old-school, anticommunist, power-hungry networker who in 2005 failed for the second time to win the Liberal nomination for president.
28 Vásquez retired in 2010, and was appointed head of state-owned communicaions company Hondutel by Lobo. He stepped down to enter politics and founded the Honduran Patriotic Alliance party in 2011, standing for president in 2013 and 2017. He plans to stand again in 2021.
29 Liberal presidential candidate in 2009, supported by Flores and Micheletti.

30 Vásquez said he was summoned to the Supreme Court at 9 p.m., and handed an order to detain the president and remove him from the country; others claim this court order was produced retrospectively.
31 At the time of the coup, the National Party was trailing 10 points in the polls.
32 Emails from her private server published by WikiLeaks show how US officials pressured the OAS to sideline Zelaya and push for new elections, even after the organization voted to suspend Honduras.

5. The Aftermath

1 Sotero was forcibly recruited as a teenager when the army came to his village to round up young boys. He served five years (instead of the obligatory two), but left after being ordered to punish Salvadoran rebels. Forced conscription was outlawed in 1994.
2 Agustina pressed multiple charges including torture against the officers, which over the years were dismissed one by one until just two female officers were charged with abuse. She resisted pressure from the judge to accept compensation and a public apology, and after long delays the trial was scheduled for 26 September 2018 – but suspended at the last minute, after judges claimed more urgent cases had cropped up. 'They want me to get tired and drop the case. Never!' she said.
3 The post-coup government restored the fuel tariff and took out high interest loans from local banks, some owned by coup backers, and a decade later these debts are still crippling the country: in 2017 one in every four tax dollars was used to service the public debt, compared to one in every $10 in 2010. In real life terms this means more than double as much money is now spent on debt than on health.
4 The PPP-inspired regional energy corridor enabled the power harnessed by dams, wind turbines, geothermal and solar plants to be stored and transported to meet faraway consumer and industrial demands.
5 In October 1998, Hurricane Mitch caused devastating flooding on the north coast, leaving at least 7,000 dead, and thousands more homeless and destitute. While families and emergency workers searched for bodies washed away by the floods, Congress

introduced a law allowing open pit mines, without any warning or consultation (they were banned again in 2006).
6 Hernández served as president of Congress and the National Party between 2010 and 2013.
7 The US cut security, economic and development assistance programmes in Honduras worth almost $36m, according to the US government accountability office. In March 2010, Clinton authorized aid to resume.
8 The Liberal deputies elected were aligned with the coup and voted with the government.
9 The multiple incentives to attract extractive industries were very similar to those given to the banana companies, maquila owners and franchisers in previous decades. A month after the conference, Honduras was allowed back into the OAS.
10 The list of specific promises included money for community-led renewable energy projects and access to carbon credit schemes; museums and cultural projects in fifteen historically important Lenca sites; and a working group to agree national legislation to reflect ILO 169 and UN conventions. COPINH's women's refuge in La Esperanza was built thanks to money pledged in this meeting, but most other promises were broken.
11 Hernández claimed the four judges were unseated because days earlier they rejected a police corruption measure. In fact, they had argued that the polygraph test was not scientifically robust, which meant using it to assess honesty would violate police officers' constitutional rights. In October 2018, the IACHR accepted their legal challenge to the removal.
12 Two of the four sacked for political participation, Tirza del Carmen Flores Lanza, an Appeals Court judge, and Guillermo López Lone, a Criminal Court justice and president of the judges' association, were finally reinstated in 2018 after an international campaign and 2015 IACrtHR ruling. The other two accepted financial compensation in 2015.
13 The company was created by Roberto and Geovanny Abate Ponce, brothers who worked for Castillo's Digicom company. Castillo was officially named president in November 2011, but in 2019 anti-corruption prosecutors alleged that he was the de facto company rep from the start.
14 ENEE studied multiple locations on the Gualcarque River from 2003, and had identified a feasible location for a hydroelectric project – the same place proposed by DESA.
15 DESA got permission to do the feasibility study on 14 December 2009, and submitted it on 16 December 2009, but it was dated 8

December 2009.
16 In the 'Gualcarque Fraud' indictment hearing in March/April 2019, prosecutors alleged that David Castillo and Carolina Castillo colluded to use ENEE's studies to develop DESA's own request to build a hydroelectric project at the same location.
17 A 14.5-megawatt dam was approved by SERNA's deputy minister Jonathan Laínez on 25 March 2011, by which time ENEE and Congress had already committed to buying energy from DESA.
18 The study was put together by the National Institute of Forest Conservation and Development (ICF).
19 The outcome of the vote, attended by COPINH leaders Salvador Zúñiga and Sotero Chavarría, was recorded in the community's official book of acts.
20 Domínguez was charged on 15 April 2013, making Honduras the first country to bring criminal charges for ILO 169 violations.
21 Laínez was charged in August 2013, and again in July 2016 with the same offence linked to Aurora II in Santa Elena, La Paz (one of several dams on Lenca territory linked to nationalist politician Gladis López). Roberto Cardona, the vice-minister who expanded the dam's capacity, was charged in November 2016.
22 The consortium comprised FMO, FinnFund and the Central American Bank for Economic Integration (BCIE).
23 In 2018, Berta's family launched legal action against FMO in the Netherlands. FMO and its partner FinnFund withdrew in mid-2016.
24 See worldbank.org.
25 Inversiones Las Jacarandas was founded in 1986 by Pedro Atala Simón and his family, including sons Jacobo and José Eduardo Atala Zablah. The company is now owned by his six children, cousins to Camilo Atala Faraj.
26 The IFC does business with the Panama bank but is not an equity holder.
27 In 2012, DESA got a $5m loan from Banco Ficensa, a separate Honduran bank founded by General Oswaldo López Arellano, which later received IFC loans worth $18m. The IFC's own rules require it to consider whether a bank is involved in harmful projects before lending it money.
28 Ficohsa responded via US law firm Mishcon de Reya.
29 Earth Rights International, a US legal group, is suing the IFC on behalf of Aguán farmers who asked to remain anonymous because they fear reprisals. See earthrights.org, Human Rights Watch, and hrw.org.

Notes for Pages 99–105

30 Former president Ricardo Maduro also invested in the resort. Camilo Atala served as his investment minister between 2002 and 2006.

31 In 2015, the IACrtHR ruled that the State of Honduras had denied the community's right to consultation when agreeing tourism projects on Garifuna land.

32 PEMSA Panama is a 33 per cent shareholder of DESA; the anonymity of shareholders/owners is protected in Panama. Castillo created PEMSA Honduras in 2015. Until his arrest in 2018, he was the president of PEMSA Honduras, PEMSA Panama, DESA and Concasa, companies created to execute Agua Zarca. DESA is the company with Agua Zarca contracts; PEMSA the administrator; Concasa subcontracted for construction.

33 The price is fixed at $0.18 per kilowatt hour until 2024; in 2018, the market price was $0.08. SEE Social Forum on External Debt and Development of Honduras (FOSDEH).

34 In 2016 there were 334 energy-generating projects in Honduras (177 hydroelectric, 60 solar, 39 wind, 27 thermal energy, 26 biomass, 4 geothermal, 1 unspecified); and 538 mining projects, 267 exploiting minerals, 188 in the exploration phase, and 83 unspecified: Observatory of Natural Goods and Human Rights by CEHPRODEC.

35 Largely thanks to renegotiated contracts with the suppliers and distributors.

36 In 2010, the government spent 33 per cent on education, compared to 20 per cent in 2018; health spending fell from 15 to 11 per cent, and environmental protection from 1.1 to 0.4 per cent over the same period. Meanwhile the defence and security budget increased from 12 to 14 per cent, excluding the new secret security tax. Source: ICEFI.

37 The two-time president Oswaldo López Arellano, of Bananagate fame, was her uncle.

38 No one was ever prosecuted. Instead, the implicated police chiefs launched spurious counter-allegations against the journalists which were eventually thrown out.

39 Bonilla served as security minister under Lobo when police chiefs allegedly executed the anti-drug czar Arístides González, and Honduras was the world's most murderous country

40 'EEUU Les cancela las visas a nueve involucrados en caso Arca Arbietta', Laprensa.hn, 3 February 2019.

41 See 'Report to Congress on Corruption in El Savador, Guatemala, and Honduras', insightcrime.org, May 2019.

42 In 1982, during the bloodiest period of the civil war, 400 people were killed to make way for a World Bank and Inter-American Development Bank-backed mega dam.

43 The IACHR has issued three rulings, including one in Honduras involving the Garifuna, which confirms indigenous people's right to decide their own development priorities – their self-determination – as a key element of ILO 169-compliant consultations. A consultation must be free, prior and informed, and ongoing during the implementation of a project, so that changes such as enlargement of a dam or mine are not authorized without community consent and compensation. Communities have the right to say no.

44 The ILO is a UN tripartite organization made up of states (labour ministries), employers (industry reps) and workers (unions) to set labour standards, develop policies and devise programmes promoting decent work conditions. Indigenous communities do not have a seat at the table, except through the unions. The ILO position is that communities cannot veto government economic development plans, yet the international legal rulings have in contrast confirmed the legal right to self-determination.

45 Socialization is not a term or process recognized legally in the ILO or UN Convention. 'It is urgent for the Honduran Congress to develop a law on free, prior and informed consent and consultation for indigenous peoples and other communities in line with international standards. The practice of "socialisation" of projects is not equal to meaningful consultation,' said the UN human rights and business delegation in 2019. See ohchr.org.

46 Sánchez says he was offered 25,000 Lempiras. Tomás García was offered 20,000, shortly before he was shot dead at the dam encampment.

47 CONGEDISBA (Consejo de Gestión y Desarrollo de las Comunidades, Council for Communities Management and Development), which DESA promoted as an alternative to COPINH.

6. The Criminal State

1 Bustillo, engineer Francisco Rivas and the environment and community manager, Sergio Rodríguez, testified against the three COPINH leaders on 13 September 2013.
2 Interview with Bustillo in Tamara prison in August 2017.
3 One of Atala's mobile phones was seized by prosecutors after the murder, and the data extracted were admitted as evidence by the court.

Notes for Pages 113–20

4 In 2001, the SOA was renamed the Western Hemisphere Institute for Security Cooperation.
5 The charge was dismissed, then reinstated, and then finally dismissed in 2014 with a conciliation agreement in which the state recognized that Berta was defending the rights of the Lenca people.
6 A few months later, the weapons charge was used to justify the arrest warrant for Berta under the new 'two strikes and you're off the street' rule.
7 Mejía was appointed to the OAS in 2017 and then retired in January 2018 after being passed over for the post of national police chief.
8 Tomás was the first murder victim; but on 23 April 2013, Paula González, a thirty-three-year-old mother of six, died after the car taking the environment minister to the riverbank (to assess crop damage caused by dam construction) upended, hitting several people. Her aunt Rosalinda Domínguez suffered back and shoulder injuries, and her nine-year-old son a head injury. A helicopter was sent for the minister and driver, but the community members were left to make their own way to San Pedro Sula. Paula died of multiple internal injuries.
9 Chinese construction company Sinohydro withdrew after Tomás was killed, and the dam project was temporarily suspended.
10 In September 2017, Allan and his partner had a little girl whom they named Bertita. If it had been a boy, they would have called him Tomasito.
11 William Rodríguez, an active young COPINH member, was accused by the family but never prosecuted. He was killed in murky circumstances at a party in May 2015. Informant Salvador Sánchez was present.
12 The Madrid family obtained individual titles for numerous plots of communal Lenca land through the Intibucá mayor's office from *circa* 2006 onwards – around the same time government technicians from the national energy company (ENEE) started conducting studies to see *if* a dam was feasible on the Gualcarque. Several Madrids got low-skilled work with DESA as drivers or security.
13 See rightsaction.org/sites/default/files/Rpt_131001_RioBlanco_Final.pdf.
14 See insightcrime.org/investigations/honduras-elites-organized-crime-juan-matta-ballesteros/.
15 See presidency.ucsb.edu.
16 As the Iron Curtain fell, the US tried to clean up in Central

America. In 1988, US marshals working with rogue Honduran military officers ambushed Matta on his morning run, in what was essentially an illegal rendition.

17 The case appeared to be blocked by the attorney general, Leonidas Rosa Bautista, although he had pledged to tackle corruption when he was appointed in 2005 to replace Ovidio Navarro – who himself had been accused of stonewalling charges against Callejas and other senior party members. Both were accused of conflict of interest: Navaro was Callejas's personal lawyer before becoming attorney general; Battista was a Nationalist deputy when elected by Congress as AG – a move forbidden by the minister's own rules.

18 Jari Dixon was elected to Congress with the Libre party in 2013.

19 Following the hunger strike, Fernández resigned as public prosecutor and with his brother Martín formed MADJ (Movimiento Amplio por la Dignidad y la Justicia) a legal and social collective representing communities resisting extractive mega-projects, mostly in the country's north.

20 At least $350m was pilfered from the national insurance system which provided decent affordable healthcare for ordinary people in the formal labour market.

21 By mid-2019, fifteen people had been sentenced, including functionaries but no elected politicians, over thirty others charged or on the lam. More than 300 people could have benefited from the scam, according to the Christian anti-graft group Association for a More Just Society (Spanish abbreviation ASJ).

22 Hilda reportedly died in a helicopter crash in December 2017. The following year she was named as a key figure in the Pandora's Box scam, which prosecutors said used two front NGOs to embezzle around $12m earmarked for agricultural projects. Most of the money ended up in the 2013 election campaign funds for the National and Liberal parties. This turned out to be the tip of the iceberg: over the past decade at least $70m had been funnelled to politicians and political parties using dozens of shell NGOs and to a secretive slush fund controlled by the presidency which ballooned after the coup. See Jeff Ernst, 'Exclusive: A Pandora's Box of Corruption in Honduras', pulitzercenter.org, 6 August 2019.

23 See 'Alrededor de tres mil personas han muerto por desfalco al IHSS', criterio.hn, 28 May 2015.

24 In September 2018, as Berta's murder trial approached, the privatized kidney dialysis company threatened to cut off services to more than 3,000 patients on account of $12.5m in bills unpaid by the health ministry. Where did the money go?

25 The OAS-backed MACCIH (Mission to Support the Fight against Corruption and Impunity in Honduras) was created in 2016. This concession by Juan Orlando Hernández was enough to calm the protests and keep the US aid tap running.
26 See US Justice Department, 'Martinez Turcios Indictment', justice.gov.
27 In his testimony, Maradiaga said they transported more than twenty tons of cocaine within Honduras between 2009 and 2013, and informed Fabio Lobo, Pepe Lobo's son, of five to eight incoming cocaine shipments in advance.
28 Tony Hernández was a Nationalist deputy between 2013 and 2017, labelled by the US embassy as a 'person of interest' in 2016. This call with Tony was one of multiple revealing conversations recorded by the collaborator Leonel.
29 In testimony, when asked what other protection Pepe Lobo mentioned, Leonel said they were told not to worry – 'if anything were to happen, we should talk to Juan Gómez, Juan Gómez in turn would talk to Fabio, who would contact General Pacheco Tinoco.'
30 Fabio Lobo's relationship with Los Cachiros wasn't exclusive. For example, he also worked with gangsters Los Valles, another family syndicate, who controlled the border with Guatemala. This deal, according to a US federal indictment, included high-ranking customs officials, Liberal Party deputy Fredy Nájera, and El Chapo's Sinaloa cartel in Mexico. Fabio pleaded guilty to one drug trafficking charge and was sentenced to twenty-four years. Fredy handed himself over to the US justice system in late 2018 and pleaded guilty to conspiring to import cocaine into the United States and possessing machine guns and destructive devices – a plea he later tried to withdraw.
31 Including building contracts for housing, offices, a school, restaurant and health clinic for the publicly owned Patuca III dam in Olancho.
32 See 'Cachiros Lavaron L203.7 millones a través de Enee', laprensa.hn, 2 April 2017.
33 A few days later, the embassy added Santos Rodríguez Orellana, an army captain stationed in La Mosquitia. Soon after, Rodríguez told Univisión that his life had been ruined after he impounded a drug-ferrying helicopter allegedly owned by Tony Hernández and his cousin Samuel Reyes, the defence minister. (The claims were denied by the cousins.) Orellana was given a dishonourable discharge in October 2018.
34 In 2009, Jaime transferred a plot of land to one of the Cachiro

brothers in the hope of getting 'below market rate' cattle prices, according to a document included in the case file against Tony Hernández in 2019. The land was used for African palms and hosted an airstrip for drug planes. See Steven Dudley, 'Epílogo: cómo élites y narcos hacen negocios y política en Honduras', *Insight Crime*, 9 October 2019, es.insightcrime.org.

35 In 2017, a MACCIH-led corruption investigation was opened into the seized property management office (OABI) following years of allegations of incompetence and wrongdoing. By 2019, OABI was estimated to have overseen asset seizures worth a billion dollars which its registers were unable to adequately track.

36 Miguel Facussé died aged ninety without ever being charged with drug trafficking, organized crime or any crime related to the slaying of campesinos in the Aguán – not even those killed by Dinant security guards, or those buried on his plantations. He never denied that drug planes landed on his property, but claimed he was a victim of organized crime.

37 In February 2005, less than a year after the cable about the burnt-out drug plane, the embassy's economic attaché attended a meeting of Honduran business heavyweights, including Facussé, his combative relative Adolfo Facussé and representatives of banana kings Dole and Chiquita. They discussed how to derail new government levies and costly security measures to Puerto Cortés, a big port near the Guatemalan border.

38 For DESA to move the planned dam to the other side of the river in San Francisco de Ojuera, land and support in Valle de Ángeles would have been needed.

7. The Threats

1 Taken from Rodríguez's court testimony of November 2018.
2 Coordinadora Indígena del Poder Popular de Honduras (CINPH).
3 Karla Lara, Yessica Trinidad, Daysie Flores and Melissa Condesa.
4 Seven of the ten countries with the highest femicide rates are in Latin America.
5 There are specific laws targeting violence against women, and special courts and prosecutors to deal with femicides or gender-based hate crimes. But strong laws have not translated into strong actions: Honduras classified femicide as a hate crime in 2013, but by 2018 only seventeen cases had been brought.

Notes for Pages 147–55

6 Machismo is more complex, deep-rooted and structural than sexism. That's why women privileged by ethnicity, wealth, education or class can be just as invested in maintaining the power structures of machismo.

7 Criminal and civil suits, survivor testimonies, declassified US documents, and truth commission reports have detailed how, why and when hit lists were used in Chile, Argentina, Peru, Colombia, El Salvador, Honduras and Guatemala among others.

8 Panamanian-born Maduro is a Stamford-educated economist and former Central Bank governor who entered politics after the kidnapping and murder of his twenty-five-year-old son. He was elected despite a constitutional ban on foreign-born presidents.

9 The Barrio 18 and Mara Salvatrucha 13 are the biggest and most infamous maras across the Northern Triangle countries, with the largest numbers in El Salvador. They were created in poor LA neighbourhoods during the 1980s by teenage children of Salvadoran civil war refugees, and exported back home by gang leaders jailed and then deported. Since then they have evolved.

10 The nephew of the 3-16 death squad commander, Álvarez was accused alongside Gladis López in the fake NGO Planeta Verde case, but a judge dismissed the charge against him.

11 Social cleansing is a misleading term, as not every gang was a target. The anti-gang rhetoric appears to be a perverse ruse, sometimes at least, for crushing one group to replace it with another depending on who the cops were working with. None of the officers named by Borjas faced justice for the crimes alleged in the report. She was elected to Congress representing the Libre party in December 2017.

12 In November 2013, Libre participated in the general elections with Xiomara Castro as its presidential candidate, her husband Mel Zelaya at the helm behind the scenes. She lost to Hernández amid allegations of fraud.

13 The base was upgraded thanks to US tax dollars. See rightsaction.org.

14 By 2005, only fourteen of the original eighty-four cooperatives were still controlled by campesinos, and MUCA's legal claims had failed due to violence and bribes targeting farmers and lawyers.

15 Celio is married to the daughter of veteran campesino leader-turned-Libre deputy Rafael Alegría, who was repeatedly told about his role as mastermind killer, but did nothing.

16 The IACHR ordered precautionary measures for 123 campesinos in May 2014, but they were never implemented. The commission ordered protection for a further thirty-one farmers in December

2016 after MUCA president José Ángel Flores was shot dead. By mid-2018 over 150 campesinos were dead, three disappeared and the remains of several were found buried on Miguel Facussé's Dinant plantations.
17 In a 2012 interview with the LA Times, Facussé said: 'I probably had reasons to kill him [Trejo], but I'm not a killer.'
18 Perdomo is with the Technical Agency for Criminal Investigation (ATIC), a US-vetted specialized unit of the Public Prosecutor's office set up in 2015 to investigate serious crimes like murder, rape, human trafficking, illicit association, extortion and counterfeit currency.
19 Celio Rodríguez Ponce and La Ardilla feature on the 2018 most wanted list of criminals, under Multiple Homicides.
20 The Honduran Council of Private Enterprise, uniting some seventy business groups, describes itself as the political and technical arm of the sector.
21 OFRANEH's protests won a few concessions, but the law was approved with only a handful of dissenters from Libre – a party born out of the post-coup grassroots movement, that counts on political support from indigenous communities most likely to bear the brunt of the law.

8. Resistance and Repression

1 An Argentine alternative news channel, on the lines of *Democracy Now!*
2 Juan Galindo was murdered in 2014 in the Bajo Aguán; Michael Rodríguez, aged about fourteen, disappeared on 26 October of that year; his body was found in the river four days later. His brother William, an active COPINH member, was killed in suspicious circumstances in May 2015.
3 Extracts from an April 2016 interview with the *New York Daily News*.
4 The Kawas ruling by the IACHR in 2009 was the first ever regarding an environmental defender. It required states to protect those at risk from human rights violations.
5 Margarita Murillo was a founding member of the Liberty and Refoundation Party (Libre); her murder remained unsolved in 2018.
6 Source: a retrospective study conducted in 2017 by Just Associates (JASS) in Honduras.

7 'En Ingles los abogados mueren porque', hondurasinmiedo.org, September 2016.
8 See 'Centro de Monitores de Medios', cattrachas.org.
9 The Human Rights Defenders, Journalists, Social Communicators and Justice Operators law was approved in April 2015 amid international outrage at the targeted killings. The protection mechanism is administered by the security ministry. The security minister, Julián Pacheco when Berta was killed, also holds political responsibility for the IACHR's protective measures.
10 See ciprodeh.org.hn.
11 Juan Galindo and Margarita Murillo were also assigned protective measures after the coup, but these were not implemented before they were killed.
12 Castellanos served two terms, from 2009 to 2018.
13 On 8 September 2017, 500 police were deployed to evict students occupying campus buildings. Tommy was among those beaten, pepper-sprayed and arbitrarily detained; she was accused of cover-up (*encubrimiento*) and threatening state security (*atentado contra la seguridad del Estado*). In 2018, after several months in hiding, she was granted political asylum and left Honduras.
14 Traffickers turned to the Mexico–Central America corridor after Caribbean routes were shut down by international law enforcement. By 2018, most cocaine smuggling was maritime, and seizures suggest an overall fall, but Honduras remains a major transit route and is becoming a producer country, with mounting evidence that protected forests are being decimated to cultivate coca.
15 In 2017, the Association for a Fairer Society (ASJ) identified sixteen former mayors from all political parties who had been charged with crimes including murder, arms trafficking, corruption and extortion.
16 Steven Dudley and Felipe Puerta, 'A Honduras Political Clan and Its Criminal Fiefdom', insightcrime.org, 19 October 2017.
17 See US Department of Justice, 'Urbina Soto Indictment', Justice.gov.
18 See Jeff Ernst, 'Witness Directly Involves the President of Honduras in the Use of Drug Money for His Campaigns', univision.com, 8 October 2019.
19 Before the coup, thirty-five children and young people were murdered on average every month. This rate spiked to seventy-one during Lobo's presidency, then dropped to sixty-three during Hernández's first term, according to the UNAH Violence Observatory.

20 René Ponce, appointed head of the armed forces after the 2017 election violence, led military police training and ops in San Pedro Sula while regional military commander, before becoming head of the inter-agency force FUSINA (in which military police are deployed). His US record includes attendance at the School of the Americas and anti-terrorism training at the Joint Special Operations University at MacDill Air Force Base in Florida.

21 Corruption costs the state 30bn Lempiras ($1.23bn) annually, according to the National Anti-Corruption Council.

22 A growing number of women are crossing borders to escape violence and poverty in a global trend known as the feminization of migration. In Mexico, one in four undocumented Central American migrants apprehended by immigration agents in 2017 were female, compared to only one in seven in 2011. While rising numbers flee a deadly mix of gang violence, organized crime and abuses by security forces, home remains the most dangerous place for women and girls.

23 There are some seventy migrant shelters in Mexico along the tracks used by freight trains known as La Bestia, the Beast, which have carried hundreds of thousands of hopeful Central Americans north since Hurricane Mitch in 1998. The shelters are increasingly full of asylum seekers now that Mexico has become a 'destination country', as it was during the Latin American dictatorships. Around 29,300 people, almost half of them Hondurans, applied for asylum in Mexico in 2018, compared to 2,136 in 2012. In 2017, the UN Refugee Agency reported 74,213 Honduran refugees and asylum seekers worldwide, up from 3,424 in 2012.

24 The murder rate across the Northern Triangle makes it the most dangerous region in the world outside Syria. See sas-space.sas.ac.uk.

25 Trump was not the first president to greenlight family separations, just the first to do so openly. Similarly, the 2018 migrant caravans were not the first: travelling in big groups has become increasingly common as the demographic of migration has shifted from single males to families and children who hope for safety in numbers.

26 Details are secret on grounds of 'national security'. Most decisions are made by a committee led by the president which includes leaders of the Supreme Court and Congress, plus the attorney general, the head of intelligence and the foreign, defence and public security ministers. 'It's like a parallel cabinet and makes a mockery of the separation of powers,' Victor Meza said.

27 The purge cost over 800m Lempiras ($35m) in compensation

payouts, and few ousted cops faced charges. The purge committee appointed by Hernández comprised Vilma Morales, the Supreme Court president at the time of the coup, Alberto Solórzano, an evangelical pastor, and Omar Rivera, the co-director of ASJ, the evangelical justice watchdog. The plan is to expand the police force to 26,000 by 2022, representing a 70 per cent increase from 2016, in addition to the 5,000 new military police.

28 Forensic teams cover only the big cities, which means murders can be missed or wrongly classified.

29 Remittances topped $4.5bn in 2018, accounting for 20 per cent of GDP and the main source of foreign income.

30 From 2008, US Special Operations Forces switched attention from Latin America (Colombia mainly) to Central America after describing the region as 'increasingly plagued with violence and illicit trafficking'. Four training ops were conducted in 2009, the year of the coup; but most took place between 2011 and 2014. See wola.org/analysis/u-s-special-operations.

31 See 'A Special Joint Review of Post-Incident Responses' by the Department of State and Drug Enforcement Administration to Three Deadly Force Incidents in Honduras at oig.justice.gov.

32 The drug bust was part of an ill-fated militarized DEA programme imported from Iraq, abandoned long before the investigation was published in 2017.

33 Richard Dobrich was suspended in 2018, accused of using government resources to procure sex workers, but was later cleared.

34 Berta was the second Goldman Prize winner murdered since the award's inception in 1989. Nigerian Ken Saro-Wiwa, who defended the rights of his Ogoni people against multinational oil companies, was jailed and executed by the government in 1995 shortly after being announced a winner. In January 2017, the Tarahumara farmer Isidro Baldenegro, awarded the prize a decade earlier for fighting illegal logging in Mexico's Sierra Madre, was shot dead.

9. The Investigation

1 Sub-Commissioner Juárez was the local officer in charge of Berta's IACHR protective measures.
2 The inspector general investigates internal police affairs and answers directly to the minister of security.

3 She'd been working on borrowed laptops since 4 November 2015, when her own was stolen by an unknown man let into Doña Austra's house by the domestic worker.
4 Under Honduran law, victims and witnesses – Gustavo qualified as both – cannot be prevented from leaving the country. In addition, a bilateral treaty meant Gustavo could have collaborated in the murder investigation from Mexico.
5 Gustavo's personal belongings were returned in October 2017. He was never called upon to give another statement or identify his assailant.
6 Lemus was never questioned under caution about his false testimony.
7 In June 2018, Villanueva reported death threats after publicly denouncing ATIC investigators who allegedly altered the crime scene of their murdered colleague Sherill Yubissa, obstructed forensic experts, and declared her death a suicide. Villanueva was sacked in December 2018.
8 The information was shared on the WhatsApp group Committee PHAZ (Project Hydroelectric Agua Zarca) created by David Castillo on 7 October 2015. It included Rodríguez, Ávila (security chief), Pedro Atala Zablah (shareholder and board member who shared my *Guardian* story with the group), José Eduardo Atala Zablah (shareholder and board member), finance manager Daniel Atala, project manager José Manuel Penabad Pages, Roque Galo (PR) and Jesús Beorlegui Díaz (PR).
9 Several communities whom Penabad wanted to involve refused. Information seized as part of the murder case showed Rodríguez previously paid locals 200 Lempiras a day, a good wage in the region, to counter a COPINH mobilization.
10 Elite soldiers from the interagency taskforce FUSINA and ordinary police were deployed.
11 The PR team comprised Roque Galo and Spanish national Jesús Beorlegui Díaz. Díaz, a specialist in corporate communications, on 20 February 2016 encouraged his group to aggravate damage to nail a criminal charge against COPINH. 'I suggest if they hardly broke anything, better to change it, just break it and take pictures. Do I make myself clear?' 'Copied,' responded Sergio, in the security PHAZ chat. In July 2013, after Tomás García was murdered, Castillo and Rodríguez had discussed paying a weekly 1,000 Lempiras to an HCH TV journalist, who on 15 April 2016 was driven to the river by DESA staff.
12 A camera drone was deployed in the hope of gathering evidence of damaged company property to send to its international

financiers, international media and prosecutors. DESA had a private lawyer on the scene ready to file criminal complaints.

13 The team was thrown out by the Mexican government after it blew apart the official version of events and uncovered clues linking the military and a drug trafficking cartel to the crime.

14 Celeste Cerrato and Jair López, former public prosecutors, were retained by DESA after the murder and accompanied Sergio and Jorge Ávila when they gave voluntary statements in March. Lead prosecutor Ingrid Figueroa warned Jair of the raids in advance.

15 The criminal justice system is based on the Spanish model. Since Berta's children and mother qualified as victims, each had the right to instruct private prosecutors and to access the investigation and the evidence obtained by the state (Article 16 of the Penal Code).

16 Rodrigo Cruz is a false name to protect him and his family.

17 The sixteen were picked from over 200 recruits and integrated into the 7th military police battalion in San Pedro Sula in May 2015.

18 In Cascabel, Cruz said foreign instructors (whose fatigues were different) supervised the Honduran trainers, but never spoke directly to the soldiers, and kept their faces covered. In Tesón, Cruz identified military instructors from Panama and Colombia, among others who spoke English and a foreign language which Cruz didn't recognize. The retired general Romeo Vásquez confirmed that Israeli trainers (and equipment) are common in Honduras.

19 Injections were administered every twenty-four to thirty-six hours by an army nurse to all sixteen members of the unit, and blood samples were taken between doses. 'I didn't feel tired or hungry, no fear, no pain, I didn't feel anything for the people in front of me,' said Cruz. They were also given amphetamine tablets to help with energy and motivation. After deserting, Cruz suffered mood swings, memory problems and stomach complaints for over a year.

20 The Xatruch battalion was created by President Maduro for deployment to Iraq.

21 Cruz was promoted to First Sergeant a month after joining Xatruch, after completing Tesón.

22 For the background to Celio and the land struggles, see Chapter 7. Cruz recognized him from photographs.

23 Galindo was president of the Rigores farm in the Aguán, part of the MUCA cooperative, and a Libre party activist. He continued to be harassed by security forces despite IACHR protective measures, so went to El Salvador for some respite, but returned in May

2014 to see his family. Juan Galindo was shot dead on his way to church on 11 November 2014, eyewitnesses said by men in police uniforms.
24 Samuel Reyes is President Hernández's cousin. The president's brother, retired colonel Amílcar Hernández, wheelchair-bound from a parachuting accident, plays a crucial though unofficial role in defence.
25 His request for a face-to-face meeting with *Guardian* editors was refused, and the ambassador was asked to submit his complaint to the Readers' Editor as per *Guardian* policy.
26 There are press reports with photos of the 13 May 2015 press conference. Members of Congress wrote to the State Department raising concerns about the US training a force linked to human rights abuses; the department never wrote back saying the training didn't take place.
27 A retired homicide detective and former federal prosecutor helped Honduran investigators and provided technical assistance. Nealon discussed the case at his weekly meetings with the attorney general.
28 Torres had been detained for illicit association six days earlier, but was released after the judge ruled prosecutors had insufficient evidence to pursue the charge.
29 The SOA trained hundreds of Latin American officers who later committed human rights abuses.
30 Díaz participated in several counterinsurgency courses at the 1st and 15th special forces battalions, on dates which coincided with some US special forces training missions. Xatruch is based at the 15th Battalion, but army deserter First Sergeant Cruz's elite unit mainly operated out of the Tacoa barracks.
31 Díaz said he was assigned to FUSINA between March and June 2015 as the regional boss of the department of Comayagua, but it does not appear on his military record.
32 Pacheco Reyes is involved in multiple energy companies including PEMSA and Proderssa. I hand-delivered a letter requesting an interview in March 2018, but he didn't respond.
33 Prison governors are military personnel, while prison guards are police.
34 Díaz was transferred from high security (*máximo*) to low security (*diagnóstico*) by the previous governor, Lieutenant Colonel César Nájera, who was suspended after twenty-two alleged Barrio 18 gang members escaped in May 2017.
35 Rodríguez is a biology graduate with a master's in geo-environmental studies.

Notes for Pages 207–18

36 He was employed directly by DESA via Pro-Tec security and control; Ávila, his replacement in 2015, was employed by Sepsa.
37 Claudia Erazo was Sergio's deputy, whom he spoke to before speaking to Bustillo on 3 March 2016, but she was never questioned by prosecutors.
38 There are an estimated one million unregistered guns circulating in Honduras.
39 Tattoos have been used to allege and indicate gang membership. Torres said he was frequently stopped and searched because of his tattoos and Nike Cortez trainers, which are also associated with gangs.
40 We met several times, sometimes with her family, always with the armed bodyguard provided by the state. We also spoke by phone, and I saw some of her witness statements.
41 Rigoberto Rodríguez, a.ka. El Negro, who worked for Orion Security, is serving thirty-one years for murdering Catarino López and José Luis Lemus in November 2011. Press reports incorrectly referred to him as chief of security, but according to Juan, 'He was an ordinary guard who passed us information about raids and operations against campesinos.'
42 Hernández 'confessed' to ATIC agent Jesús Perdomo without a lawyer present, again during his initial court testimony, and to GAIPE investigators.
43 Borjas revealed that parallel structures in the police and army were carrying out extrajudicial executions for business leaders, rival criminal gangs and politicians. She was elected to Congress representing Libre in December 2017. See Chapter 7.
44 Pacheco retired from the armed forces before taking up the appointment in January 2015, after a backlash by civil rights groups.
45 Top-ranking National Party politicians named in the IG report included Gladis López and her husband Arnold Castro, David Castillo, Roberto Pacheco Reyes and members of the Atala clan.
46 The international expert advisory group (Spanish acronym GAIPE) included Roxanna Marie Altholz from the University of California, Berkeley; Daniel R. Saxon from Leiden University; Miguel Ángel Urbina Martínez, a Guatemalan expert in Latin American criminal law; and Colombian litigators Jorge E. Molano Rodríguez and Liliana María Uribe Tirado. During four trips to Honduras they interviewed over thirty individuals and reviewed legal documents and evidence seized by the Public Prosecutor's Office, including 40,000 pages of phone messages.
47 At the time of the report's publication, none of the shareholders

or Daniel Atala had been interviewed under caution.
48 Castillo's wife Tania is a US citizen.
49 The Berta Cáceres Act was introduced by Rep. Hank Johnson on 2 March 2017 and co-sponsored by sixty other members of the House of Representatives. The bill states: 'The Honduran police are widely established to be deeply corrupt and to commit human rights abuses, including torture, rape, illegal detention, and murder, with impunity', and that the military has committed violations of human rights. Therefore, the bill asks that the United States suspend all 'security assistance to Honduran military and police until such time as human rights violations by Honduran state security forces cease and their perpetrators are brought to justice'.
50 Ávila enlisted through the armed forces, the Fuerza de Seguridad Pública, which was responsible for public security until 1996. The security guards accused him of keeping money meant for everyone's food and petrol.
51 I interviewed Tania in April and November 2018. In November 2017, Tania stood for Congress representing the Patriotic Alliance party founded by the coup general, Romeo Vásquez. She lost.
52 Sixty-five negative repercussions were identified in the SERNA environment impact study.
53 Xon was an expert witness for the victims (COPINH).
54 The report was sent by London-based Pagefield Global, a reputation management firm. Soon after, Elizabeth Schaeffer Brown, director of New York-based PR firm Uncommon Union, contacted university professors and NGO lawyers using a private email address about organizing observers for the murder trial. (An international observer mission of lawyers had already been organized.) I asked ESB to clarify if she was acting as a private citizen or on behalf of a client, but she never responded.
55 Prisoners held on remand should be tried within two years, though in special circumstances the court can extend pre-trial detention by six months.
56 Ten USB sticks, three cameras, four tablets, seven SIM cards and three computers had not yet been tested; the technicians were only given mobile phones, no other digital devices, apart from some of Berta's devices.
57 Apart from confirming the number of the chip in the phone that had been wiretapped.
58 Víctor Fernández and Rodil Vásquez representing Berta's three daughters and Doña Austra; Omar Mejivar and Ariel Madrid representing Berta's son Salvador Zúñiga Cáceres; Kenia Oliva and Edy Tábora for Gustavo Castro.

59 Their father Pedro Atala Simón founded Inversiones Las Jacarandas, and was the paternal uncle of Camilo Atala Faraj.
60 Evidence rejected for Sergio Rodríguez's defence included videos of Berta at protests, WhatsApp chats between Berta and Castillo, and a psychological evaluation which concluded Sergio was not capable of masterminding a murder.
61 The memorandum of understanding between USAID and DESA was signed on 15 December 2015, as security forces were being deployed to repress Berta's renewed opposition to the newly designed Agua Zarca dam. Photos of school children with DESA rucksacks and Sergio Rodríguez signing the contract were circulated in a glossy press pack. The agreement pledged US taxpayer dollars for technical farming assistance and increased crop diversity in ten communities near the dam. The beneficiaries were to be determined by DESA.
62 Juárez couldn't be located. In June 2016 he was purged from the police for alleged links to organized crime, specifically helping Joaquín 'El Chapo' Guzmán deliver a bullet-proof SUV to a government security official in 2005. The case against him was never prosecuted.
63 Experts proposed by the victims who were rejected included Harald Waxenecker, a specialist in Central American criminal networks, and Efrén Sánchez Javela, a forensic systems engineer, who together would have testified on the roles, responsibilities and connections between the defendants, and outlined a bigger alleged criminal structure.
64 The family lawyers appealed the results of the evidence hearing, arguing that the decisions were arbitrary and violated the victims' right to present an independent argument and hypothesis about the crime. They also appealed the decision to reject COPINH as a victim and the ban on video transmission. The appeals were quashed the day before the verdict.
65 Testimony on the social, political, racist, economic and historical context of Berta's murder by Guatemalan experts was rejected.
66 The recusal petition cited the court's failure to sanction the Public Prosecutor's Office for repeatedly ignoring orders to share evidence, as well as its decision to deny COPINH victim status and ban video transmission of the hearing.
67 Ardilla and his *compadre*, former military man Celio Bautista Rodríguez Ponce, were put on the country's most wanted list in April 2018. Arrested in Mexico, supposedly trying to reach the US, Adrilla was extradited to the Trujillo prison where one of his brothers was also being held for murder.

68 By 2018, only six out of seventy-five cases of murdered Honduran journalists had been solved.
69 Alfaro offered Yoni a meeting and financial help via a local journalist. 'If Alfaro wants to help me, he should capture killers in the paramilitary group he created,' Yoni told the journalist. Alfaro was commander of Xatruch in the Aguán between late 2012 and early 2014, when the paramilitary group led by Celio and Ardilla was created.
70 By law, the ruling should be made within seventy-two hours of receiving the written petition.
71 It was the third time the victims' lawyers did not attend in person, on the grounds that the pending appeal meant the judges were still recused and any hearing was therefore illegal. Failing to give the lawyers the opportunity to defend themselves was likewise illegal.
72 The victims had filed several criminal complaints against the Public Prosecutor's Office for its failure to diligently investigate the case, abuse of authority and violating their right to participate in the investigation and trial.

10. The Trial

1 Each defendant had two lawyers, apart from the twins who shared. Rodríguez, Díaz, Hernández and Bustillo had private lawyers, the other four public defenders. Rodríguez had a third, DESA's legal representative, who couldn't address the court.
2 The court is comprised of four judges. In each case, one is designated as president, and one as the supplement. Esther Flores was president, Jocelyn Doñaire the supplement, and the others were José Orellana and Delia Villatoro.
3 The prosecutors were Ingrid Figueroa, Melissa Aguilar, Javier Núñez and David Salgado.
4 Dr Hernández stayed with the body until it was collected at 6 a.m., by which time uniformed cops, detectives, prosecutors and members of COPINH had entered the house.
5 The projector bore a large USAID sticker.
6 To keep the defendants in custody legally for over thirty months, prosecutors had to prove defence teams had caused unjustified delays, like appealing a ruling which was rejected. The legal wrangling took up a whole day, but they stayed in jail, and the trial continued for another month.
7 The gun was discovered without a family witness, as the twins'

mother Diana was at that moment with the second inspection team in Edilson's house next door. This violates procedural rules.
8 Two of the bullets were so damaged they were untestable.
9 He was unnecessarily vague at times; the prosecution's questions were poorly formulated.
10 After being fired from DESA on 31 July 2015, Bustillo worked as security chief for PCI Inc. until he was fired by the US firm in December 2015.
11 Hernández alluded to this in his earlier testimony.
12 At the trial, through his defence lawyer, Torres said he was deported by Mexican immigration, one of 54,000 Hondurans deported from Mexico in 2016.
13 Gustavo offered to return to Honduras in 2017 to identify his assailant and testify to the court, but the paperwork was stalled by the Attorney General's Office.
14 They did exchange seven WhatsApp messages in January 2016.
15 His testimony in favour of Rodríguez from the initial hearing on 6 May 2017 was admitted as evidence; he was contracted in September 2015 and left the country in July 2016, after the project was suspended.
16 Community leader Chico Sánchez was at the old oak tree back in April 2013, when Berta warned that opposing the dam would trigger violence and divisions.
17 On top of the 2,200 Lempiras ($80) a month in cash, the phone chats show that Rodríguez frequently topped up Salvador's phone credit. The victims' lawyers had intended to play back several calls between Sergio and Salvador recorded after the murder, something the prosecutors didn't do.
18 DESA paid Doña Pineda 25,000 ($1,000) and her mother 85,000 ($3,500) damages, and kept the land.
19 It was submitted to the court after the victims' lawyers were ousted, so they didn't get a copy.
20 Banco Ficohsa refused to supply the bank and credit account details requested by the accountant. She didn't obtain the company register or filings for either DESA or Concasa.
21 DESA has the Agua Zarca contracts; PEMSA is an administrator; Concasa subcontracted for construction. All are located at the same offices in Tegucigalpa, and various executives, managers and lawyers overlap.
22 Rodríguez also worked as an independent environmental consultant and via his consultancy firm Ecología y Servicio. Clients included the World Bank and mining companies. In 2016

Rodríguez started working on other PEMSA energy projects, including the Proderssa solar plant in Choluteca where Bustillo was promised a security job.
23 Locals were paid 200 Lempiras a day.
24 The six-year, $30m EU Justice project launched in 2013 was mainly funded by Spanish aid. The EU spent several million on equipment like computers and scanners, much of which was left in storage for months.
25 Mora eventually told me to request the missing information from the court clerk. I did, twice, but never got it. My requests to interview head prosecutor Ingrid Figueroa were also unsuccessful.
26 After the victims' lawyers were expelled, Berta's family and friends held a press conference with signs that read: 'The *ministerio público* [public prosecutor] doesn't represent me'.
27 I posted regular summaries from the trial on Twitter in English, to ensure there was public record of the evidence, proceedings and controversies, and because it helped me digest the evidence and identify gaps that I needed to investigate further.
28 Elsia Paz is involved in various energy projects, including a dam in La Esperanza which she routinely cites as evidence that Berta's mother and the Lenca people adore her.
29 See *La Jornada*, 13 November 2018, jornada.com.
30 His lawyers also unsuccessfully objected to the presentation of Castillo's phone data on the grounds that he was not on trial.
31 Phone data can be retrieved manually or using forensic software, the quality and age of which determine what data can or cannot be extracted. PIN numbers can also prevent access. The content of phone calls can only be retrieved retrospectively by using phone taps.
32 Castillo's number was registered in the name of a Standard Fruit manager.
33 This was one of the group chats used to share information about COPINH activities and Berta's movements, and the company's response to them. Some included consultants and contractors, others were limited to company managers, shareholders, security and comms people.
34 According to Berta's WhatsApp messages extracted and published by DESA's international lawyers (not admitted as evidence), Castillo arranged the medical appointment for Doña Austra with a specialist recommended by his wife, and claimed to have paid the bill. She asked him on WhatsApp to help get her a quote for the subsequent surgery. But Berta's father told me he loaned her the money for the operation.

35 Bustillo also communicated with Castillo and Hernández during this period, but we don't know what about as their phones were not tapped.
36 The company security group prepared a file of photos and testimonies with the help of a notary and filed the criminal complaint on 22 February 2016, which they scanned and shared.
37 After the murder, he closely monitored press coverage regarding the investigation and who was being blamed.
38 On 21 February Díaz and Bustillo met in Siguatepeque, after which Bustillo's phone was captured in La Esperanza when he communicated with contact Díaz 2, while Díaz's other phone was inactive. The same occurred on 27 February. Barahona surmised that Díaz was in La Esperanza with Bustillo on those two occasions.
39 On 2 March, Hernández and Bustillo messaged fifty-five times and spoke twenty-six times; Edilson Duarte spoke to Torres eleven times and Hernández thirty times; Hernández spoke to Rápalo four times; Bustillo to Díaz three times.
40 Hernández's phones were registered in La Esperanza from 3:54 to 11:38 p.m.; Rápalo's from 5:27 to 8:29 p.m.; Duarte's from 6:05 to 11:38 p.m.; and Torres's from 6:28 to 11:43 p.m.
41 Two were registered to Henrry Hernández.
42 They texted at 10:56, then again at 11:55 p.m.
43 On 3 March Bustillo called Castillo four times, they spoke once (five plus messages); Hernández five times (four messages); Rápalo eight times (thirty-six messages).
44 This was when DESA retained Jair López and Celeste Cerrato.
45 Cuéllar was the SERNA minister when DESA obtained the Agua Zarca licences; his two vice-ministers were charged with abuse of authority. Cuellar and his wife have been implicated in the IHSS fraud, but they have not been prosecuted and Honduran authorities reportedly refused to cooperate with connected investigations in Costa Rica and Colombia. See 'Ministerio Público protege al exfiscal Cuéllar para no mandarlo a la cárcel por corrupción', confidencial.hn, 27 March 2019.
46 Amsterdam & Partners LLP, 'War on Development: Exposing the COPINH Disinformation Campaign Surrounding the Berta Cáceres Case', casocaceres.com, 15 November 2018. A petition by Rodríguez's lawyers for the WhatsApp chats to be extracted by Barahona and admitted into evidence was rejected, because the court had previously sworn in a defence expert to do this, but the report was not correctly submitted.
47 This was Castillo's defence at his initial hearing and what he told me in Tamara prison.

48 Castillo's answer was that Corea was in the analysis wing of C2 (command and control), covering strikes, protests and the presidential palace, with no link to COPINH or Sinohydro, the Chinese dam construction company, and the vehicle was loaned to the armed forces by the company to provide security to the Patuca III dam.

49 After the criminal charges against Berta were dropped in early 2014, the situation in Río Blanco grew less tense and conflictive. COPINH members were still sporadically attacked (Michael and William Domínguez; Don Justino; María Santos Domínguez), and Olvin García's violent group became a problem, but clashes were not as constant or visible since security forces and guards were less present. The community was still in resistance, but there was no construction and no information; DESA was secretly obtaining permits and redesigning the project from the Ojuera side of the river, but the community was unaware.

50 The message count jumped from 1,104 to 1,192, suggesting eighty-eight messages sent or received between 16 October and 25 December were not published.

51 'Vamos a arreglar las cosas con Berta por las buenas o las malas.'

52 Trejo was head of the 7th regional public security commando which until 1998 was part of the armed forces. He, alongside death squad Battalion 3-16 officer Billy Joya and others, were accused of the illegal detention, torture and attempted murder of six students in Tegucigalpa in 1982. They fled Honduras for Spain after arrest warrants were issued in September 1995. See derechos.org.

53 The officers were deployed on 3 March from Tegucigalpa to La Esperanza, where they spent several weeks investigating the crimes, concurrently with ATIC.

54 Ávila's wife told me she had documents incriminating DESA managers and execs, but wanted to claim asylum before sharing them.

55 Rodríguez said the roadblock was a response to the failure by Chinese construction company Sinohydro to deliver projects, a failure due to language/communication problems, and that it was Berta and COPINH who suddenly appeared and changed the agenda. But some Río Blanco locals joined COPINH as far back as 2004; in 2011 they detained a tractor to oppose road construction and although frightened when the mayor threatened them with jail, they still overwhelmingly voted against the dam. In 2012, Brigitte Gynther went with Berta to the community to talk about ILO 169: 'People were very worried about

their river, and wanted to stop the dam, but were scared and didn't know how.'

56 The presidents of the *patronato*, Donald Madrid, and of the water committee, Fausto Benítez, did switch from ardent opponents to supporters, and Donald was removed as president. That's when Chico Sánchez and Tomás Gómez were offered bribes to flip (25,000 and 20,000 respectively) but refused. This is socialization: targeting individual community leaders rather than reaching agreement with the whole community.

57 DESA appealed the dismissal to the Constitutional Court, describing the alleged criminal damage and invasion as anarchic acts against a private company that were unprecedented in Honduras until the destabilizing presidency of Manuel Zelaya and that were influenced by powerful national and international interests including Venezuela and Cuba. The case was dismissed *after* Berta's death.

58 Rodríguez said there were strict instructions to avoid repression and a repeat of 2013, and those was part of the agreement with investors. But we know from the phone data that local thugs were encouraged to attend protests and events.

59 In this period from October 2015, DESA officials met with the security minister and communicated with high-ranking police chiefs to ensure protests were heavily policed; submitted criminal complaints helped by a contracted notary and local prosecutors whose transport was paid; paid local people to hold counter-protests; paid informants and discussed adding new informants.

60 Rodríguez was caught out in a lie of his own. At an earlier hearing he claimed to have had no contact with Bustillo after he left DESA in July 2015, when in fact they communicated regularly for the rest of that year, and exchanged WhatsApp messages and emails in early 2016. When asked about this contradiction by the prosecution, Rodríguez said he'd forgotten. Rodríguez also alleged that Barahona purposefully said he sent the picture of Berta's body, rather than received it, and said his phone was captured in La Ceiba in order to wrongly link him to the *sicarios*.

61 Díaz, Bustillo and Rodríguez found not guilty as the crime against Gustavo wasn't premeditated, judged ruled.

Afterword

1 At least $32bn in remittances were sent to Honduras between 2010 and 2018, double the amount sent over the previous nine years. They now account for 20 per cent of the GDP. A handful of oligarchs control and own the banks, meat and dairy plants, supermarkets, malls, fast-food joints, energy companies and media outlets. See World Bank, 'Personal Remittances, Received (Current US$) – Honduras', worldbank.org.
2 Some of Tony Hernández's Colombian cocaine bore his initials – a detail inspired by the Tommy Hilfiger logo. The jury were also shown a machine gun belonging to him embossed with his brother's name and job title: president of the republic of Honduras.
3 See 'Las preocupaciones de Santos', Criterio.hn, 31 July 2018.
4 United Nations Office of the High Commissioner on Human Rights, 'Honduras Government and Businesses Must Ensure Protection of Rights of People Affected by Development Projects, Say UN Experts', ohchr.org, 29 August 2019.
5 Michel Forst, 'Report of the Special Rapporteur on the Situation of Human Rights Defenders', United Nations General Assembly, 15 July 2019, undocs.org/en/A/74/159.
6 Nina Lakhani, 'Family of Slain Honduran Activist Appeal to US Court for Help in Her Murder Trial', *Guardian*, 31 August 2019.

Acknowledgements

Thank you first and foremost to Berta's family, friends, and COPINH colleagues, and especially the people of Río Blanco whose dignity and resolve was truly inspiring.

Thanks to Annie Bird for her invaluable help early on, and Brigitte Gynther for her attention to detail, patience and doggedness throughout. Miguel Urbina, Victor Fernandez, and the rest of the gang of abogados who helped me navigate the legal process. Thank you to Miguel Gillard for his brutally honest edits, Louis Charalambous for lawyering the manuscript, to Daniel Langmeier for help fact-checking, and to Lorna Scott Fox who was an excellent copy editor.

Thanks to Michael McClintock and Rolando for the writing oasis in Malinalco, Elizabeth Kennedy for a safe place to stay in Tegucigalpa, and Yoni Rivas for cooking delicious campesino breakfasts despite no running water.

This book would not have been possible without the help, trust and time of so many people who loved, admired and respected Berta Cáceres. She was taken too soon.

Index

Agua Zarca Hydroelectric Project, 4, 12, 28, 42, 43, 54, 63, 73, 89, 91–9, 105, 106, 109, 111, 112, 115, 122, 123, 125, 137, 139, 142, 144, 147, 192, 206, 216, 222, 239, 243–5, 247, 248, 254, 256, 271, 273, 275, 276, 280, 297, 308, 313, 316, 317
Al Jazeera, 196
ALBA (Bolivarian Alliance for the Americas), 71, 72, 292
ALCA (Free Trade Area of the Americas), 51, 292
Alberto, Carlos, 16–18, 31, 33
Alberto, Kenny, 209
Alfaro, Germán, 153, 155, 156, 230, 314
Almendarez, Juan, 33, 287
Alvarado, Leonardo, 105
Alvarado, Sarai, 191
Álvarez Martínez, Gustavo, 25, 33, 34, 60, 287, 303
Álvarez, Óscar, 149
Álvarez, Vitalino 'Chino', 151–3, 155–7, 198, 229, 230
Amaya, Carlos, 77
Amaya, Milton, 112
Amaya, Ramon, 77
Amin, Samir, 158
Amnesty International, 25, 32, 103, 109, 229
Andrés Tamayo, José, 163
Ángel, Mario, 169, 170
Ángel, Miguel, 169, 170, 311
Antúnez, Ritza, 251
Árbenz Guzmán, Jacobo, 22
Ardilla, La, 156–158, 227, 304, 314; *see also* Caballero Santamaría, Osvin, 156, 227
Ardón Soriano, Amílcar Alexander, 169, 170, 278, 320
Argentine Anti-communist Alliance (AAA), 33
Arístides González, Julián, 129, 298
Arriaga, Herzog, 251

Arzú, Aurelia 'La Patrona', 48, 148
Atala Faraj, Camilo, 96, 216, 296, 297, 313
Atala Midence, Daniel, 29, 97, 106, 111, 114, 116, 129, 136, 189, 217, 225, 248–50, 252–4, 255, 265, 299, 308, 312
Atala Zablah, Jacobo, 114, 266, 296
Atala Zablah, José Eduardo, 97, 114, 129, 217, 225, 256, 266, 296, 308
Atala Zablah, Pedro, 114, 115, 189, 256, 308
ATIC (Agencia Técnica de Investigación Criminal/Technical Agency of Criminal Investigation), 168, 185, 188, 209, 210, 218, 238, 240, 266, 304, 308, 311, 319
Ávila, Jorge, 3, 5, 114, 136, 137, 143, 192, 193, 217, 220–2, 226, 243, 256, 263, 265, 270, 308, 309, 311, 312, 319

Banco Continental, 130–2
Banco Ficensa, 97, 297
Banco Ficohsa, 96, 97–9, 217, 316
Barahona, Brenda, 254, 255, 258, 259, 261–4, 266, 267, 269, 271, 272, 317, 318, 320
Barahona, Marvin, 44, 89
BBC, 32, 190
Berta Vive (Berta Lives), 192, 193, 243, 266, 274
Big Three, 151
Bird, Annie, 54, 153, 155, 170, 177, 230, 289
Blanco Ruíz, Wilter Neptalí, 129
Bloomberg, 96
Bloque Popular, 77, 78, 85, 293
Bodden, Rose, 240, 255
Bonilla de Lobo, Rosa Elena, 279
Borjas, Maria Luisa, 149, 215, 216, 270, 303, 311
Bovadilla, Edna, 109, 112, 113, 212
Bush, George W., 70, 71, 83
Bustillo, David, 135
Bustillo, Douglas Geovanny, 2, 28, 29, 110,

114, 116, 118, 142, 143, 194, 195, 202–5, 207, 208, 215, 221, 231, 233, 239, 241, 249, 252, 253, 255, 257–9, 260–5, 269, 271, 272, 274–6, 282, 299, 311, 314–17, 319, 320

Caballero Santamaría, Osvin, 156, 227; see also Ardilla, La, 156–8, 227, 304, 314
Cabrera, Jaime, 198
Cáceres, Gustavo, 75
Cáceres Flores, Agustina, 1
Cáceres Flores, Berta Isabel, ('Laura', 'Laurita), 1–11, 13–16, 18, 19, 28–35, 37–41, 44–7, 49–58, 65–7, 72, 73, 75–8, 82, 85–8, 90–2, 94–9, 101, 103, 105, 106, 109–18, 121–5, 127, 133–5, 137, 139–51, 153, 156, 157, 159–65, 167, 171, 177, 179–81, 183–96, 198, 199, 201, 202, 203–7, 209–13, 215, 216, 218–20, 223–6, 228, 229, 231–46, 248–58, 260–77, 280, 282, 283, 285, 288, 289, 293, 299, 301, 305, 307–9, 312, 313, 315–21
Cáceres Molina, José, 18, 188
Cachiros, Los, 73, 100, 125–31, 135, 152, 157, 158, 168, 169, 202, 275, 278, 280, 301, 320
CAFTA (Central American Free Trade Agreement), 52, 288
Callejas, Rafael Leonardo, 41, 43, 62, 121, 288, 291–3, 300
CAMIF (Central American Mezzanine Infrastructure Fund), 96, 97
Camosa, 225
Canales, Reynaldo, 63
Carasik, Lauren 111
Cardona, Roberto, 94, 95, 296
Carías Andino, Tiburcio, 16
Carnegie Endowment, 122
Casa Alianza, 171, 172
Casco Torres, José Rolando, 114, 115, 187, 225, 226
Castellanos, Julieta, 167, 168, 305
Castillo, Carolina, 93, 114, 225, 250, 296
Castillo, Dayanara, 167
Castillo Mejía, David Roberto, 4, 28, 29, 73, 74, 93, 97, 100, 110, 113, 114, 116, 129, 136, 137, 142, 143, 167, 189, 193, 203, 205, 207, 217–21, 223, 242, 245, 246, 248, 255–7, 259, 261, 263–9, 271, 272, 274, 282, 283, 295–7, 308, 309, 311–13, 316–18
Castro, Arnold, 101–4, 311
Castro, Fidel, 51, 83, 292
Castro, Gustavo, 4, 5, 7, 8, 9, 10, 52–6, 88, 145, 151, 183–9, 201, 212, 213, 231, 233, 235, 237, 240, 251, 255, 264, 272, 276, 282, 308, 313, 314, 315, 320
Castro, Xiomara, 66, 67, 163, 291, 303
Castro López, Gracia Maria, 102
Cattrachas, 165, 305
CEHPRODEC (Honduran Centre for the Promotion of Community Development), 89, 297

Centre for Women's Studies (CEM-H), 143
Central American Institute of Fiscal Studies (ICEFI), 159, 297
Cerrato, Celeste, 254, 266, 309, 317
Centro Regional Entrenamiento Militar (CREM), 27, 28
Chavarría, Sotero, 5, 6, 86, 145, 185, 193, 206, 245, 294, 296
Chávez, Hugo, 67, 69, 70–2, 81–4, 86, 292
Chayes, Sarah, 122
Chelito, 215
Cheney, Dick, 70
Chico (Antonio Montes), 32, 33
Chinchilla, Óscar, 91, 92
Chiquita, 21, 302
CIA, 22, 24, 26, 34, 86, 120, 286
Cienfuegos, Fermán, 34, 38
Cinchoneros, Los (Popular Liberation Movement), 18
Citigroup, 96
Clinton, Hillary, 82–84, 86, 88, 162, 166, 295
Cobras, 172, 192, 194
Coca, 210, 211, 215, 240; see also Torres, Óscar Aroldo, 201, 210, 212
COFADEH (Committee of Relatives of the Disappeared in Honduras), 26, 199
COHEP (Consejo Hondureño de la Empresa Privada/Honduran Council of Private Enterprise), 160, 291
Committee for Free Expression (C-Libre), 229
Committee to Protect Journalists (CPJ), 229
Communist Party, 18, 285, 286
COMSSA (Consultorias Mantenimientos y Servicios), 128
CONADEH (National Human Rights Commission), 165
Concasa, 248, 297, 316
Confianza, La, 154, 155, 157, 197, 229
CONGEDISBA (Council for Communities Management and Development), 114, 134, 298
Constitutional Court, 91, 231, 319
Contra, 18, 24, 33, 35, 61, 120, 286
Constructora Norberto Odebrecht, 74
Convergence of Movements of Peoples of the Americas (COMPA), 53, 56, 57
Corea Munguía, Elvin Noé, 267, 318
Corrales, Arturo, 116, 292
Council of Popular and Indigenous Organizations (COPINH), 1–6, 13, 14, 29, 38, 39, 41, 43, 45, 46, 55–8, 60, 73, 75, 77, 86, 88, 91, 99, 102, 103, 109–15, 118, 121, 122, 124, 133–5, 139, 141–6, 150, 153, 162, 181, 184–7, 189, 192, 193, 206, 218, 221, 223, 225, 226, 229, 234, 238, 241, 243–5, 248, 251–6, 261, 267, 271, 274, 275, 277, 282, 283, 295, 296, 298, 299, 304, 308, 312–15, 317–19
Council of Hemispheric Affairs, 90
Counter-Intelligence Department, 73
Cruz, Juan Carlos, 270

Index

Cruz, Rodrigo, 196–200, 229, 251, 309, 310
Cuarta Urna, 77–80, 83
Cuéllar, Rigoberto, 266, 317, 318
Darr, Nadia, 98
de Jesús Trejo, Manuel, 270, 318
de Torre, Julie, 200
Dedos, Los, 258, 260
Del Cid, Jany, 95, 105, 119, 150, 185, 207
Democracy Now, 304, 305
DESA (Desarrollos Energéticos SA), 1–4, 13, 14, 28, 29, 63, 92, 93, 94, 96–8, 100, 101, 106, 107, 109–19, 121, 122, 124, 129, 134–7, 142, 187, 189, 191–5, 203, 204, 206, 207, 217, 218, 220–3, 225, 233, 239, 241–7, 249–52, 254–7, 263, 265–9, 271, 272, 275, 296–8, 300, 302, 309, 311, 313–19
Díaz Chávez, Mariano, 194, 195, 202–6, 215, 224, 231, 233, 237, 241, 249, 251, 255, 258–63, 265, 269, 270, 272, 274–6, 282, 310, 311, 314, 317, 320
Díaz de Terán, Luis, 226
DiCaprio, Leonardo, 218
Digital Communications SA (Digicom) 74, 295
Dinant Chemicals, 60, 99, 152, 197, 203, 289, 302, 304
Dixon, Jari, 121, 300
DNI (Dirección Nacional de Investigación), 17, 26, 34
DNIC (Dirección Nacional de Investigación Criminal/Directorate of Criminal Investigation), 185
Dobrich, Richard, 178, 307
Domínguez, Aureliano, 253
Domínguez, Briselda, 116
Domínguez, Martiniano, 13, 94, 95, 222, 223, 296
Domínguez, Rosalina, 117, 188, 192, 299
Drug Enforcement Administration (DEA), 73, 120, 124, 127, 162, 173,177–9, 307, 327
Duarte Meza, Edilson, 194, 195, 208–11, 213, 214, 231, 233, 237, 239, 240, 241, 255, 262, 263, 264, 272, 274, 276, 282, 315, 317
Duarte Meza, Emerson, 195, 208– 11, 215, 231, 233, 234, 237, 240, 255, 264, 272, 274, 276

Earth Rights International, 99, 297
Eddy, Don, 266
Encinos, Los, 43, 103, 105
ENEE (Empresa Nacional de Energia Electric/National Electric Energy Company), 13, 72–4, 77, 93, 94, 100, 225, 296, 300, 301
Erazo, Claudia, 207, 264, 311
Pablo Escobar, 120
Escuela Normal Occidente, 17
Esperanza, Lilian, 6
EU, 249, 316
Eulopio Nixon, Melaño, 178

Facebook, 206, 241, 265
Facussé, Adolfo, 75, 302
Facussé Barjum, Miguel, 48, 58, 60, 61–3, 72, 80, 99, 132, 133, 154, 155, 203, 281, 289–91, 302, 304
Farabundo Martí National Liberation Front (FMNL), 32, 286
FBI, 200
Félix Gallardo, Miguel Ángel, 119
Fernanda, Maria, 253
Fernández, Victor, 121, 122, 183, 192, 300, 313
FHIS (Honduran Social Fund), 75, 76
Ficohsa, 96–9, 297, 316
Figueroa, Ingrid, 236, 309, 315, 316
Flores, Agustina, 87
Flores, Esther, 235, 275, 314
Flores, José Ángel, 156
Flores Facussé, Carlos, 68, 79, 289, 290, 292, 294, 304
Flores Lanza, Tirza del Carmen, 179, 295
Flores López, Austra Berta, 15, 16
FMO (Netherlands Development Finance Company), 95, 96, 296
Fondo de Inversiones Turísticas (Fitur), 160
Forbes, 130
Ford, Charles, 68, 70, 83, 290, 291, 293
Fort Benning, 27, 202
Fox, Vicente, 53, 289
Frente, El (Popular National Resistance Front), 85, 87, 150
FUSINA (National Interagency Security Force), 191, 197, 199, 200, 251, 306, 308, 310

G-2, 26
GAIPE (Grupo Asesor Internacional de Personas Expertas/International Advisory Group of Experts), 222, 311
Galindo, Juan, 162, 198, 199, 304, 305, 310
García, Allan, 116–18, 299
García, Nelson, 194
García, Olman, 237
García, Tomás, 106, 115, 116, 118, 136, 140, 142, 143, 207, 253, 257, 271, 298, 299, 309
García Mejía, Olvin Gustavo, 133, 134, 192, 220, 221, 242, 243, 318
Gerardi, Juan, 27, 287
Global Witness, 164, 280
Globo TV, 124
Gómez, Juan, 127, 301
Gómez, Martín, 102
Gómez Membreño, Tomás, 2, 109, 113, 140, 183, 184, 186, 226, 243, 251, 268, 319
González, Julián Arístides, 129, 298
González, Victoria, 103, 104, 299
Grande Zoo, Joya, 131
Greenspan, Brian, 223, 312
Grupo Continental, 131
Guadalajara cartel, 131
Gualcarque Fraud, 93, 95, 296
Guaraguaos, Los, 167

Guardian, 186, 190, 195, 200, 206, 228, 278, 308, 310, 321
Guillén Vicente, Rafael Sebastián, ('Marcos'), 37
Guzmán, Joaquin 'El Chapo', 126, 278, 313
Gynther, Brigitte, 4, 7, 134, 150, 319

Hasked Brooks Wood, 178
Henry, O., 21
Hernán Acosta Mejía, 79
Hernández, Andrea, 173, 174
Hernández, Antonio 'Tony', 126, 169, 170, 279, 280, 301, 302, 321
Hernández, Donald, 89
Hernández, Dunia, 234, 315
Hernández, Henrry Javier, 201–3, 205, 210–15, 233, 238–41, 255, 258–65, 272, 274, 276, 282, 314, 315, 317
Hernández, Hilda, 124, 275, 300
Hernández, Juan Orlando, 73, 89–91, 104, 123, 124, 131, 160, 161, 169, 170, 172, 175, 231, 251, 275, 278, 279, 289, 293, 295, 301, 302, 303, 306, 307, 310, 320
Hernández, Maribel, 77
Hernández Rodríguez, Henry, 234, 238, 239, 241, 262, 276, 282, 317
Hoey, Colleen, 279, 320
Homeland Security, 279
Honduran Energy Industry, 100
Honduras Solidarity Network, 87, 183
Horcones, Los, 20, 22, 291
Human Rights Defenders, 109, 141, 228, 282, 305, 321
Human Rights Watch, 99, 297

IHSS (Instituto Hondureño de Seguridad Social/Honduran Social Security Institute), 123, 278, 318
IMF (International Monetary Fund), 43, 77, 123, 124, 289
Inclusive Development International, 98
Independent Association of Campesinos, 227
Indignados, Los, 123, 124, 267
Inrimar (Inmobiliaria Rivera Maradiaga SA), 126, 131
Insight Crime, 119, 300, 302, 305
Inter-American Air Force Academy, 202
Inter-American Commission of Human Rights (IACHR), 106, 166, 194, 216, 287, 293, 295, 298, 304, 305, 308, 310
Inter-American Court of Human Rights (IACrtHR), 26
International Commission against Impunity (CICIG), 124, 128
International Finance Corporation, 96
International Labour Organization (ILO), 41, 94, 103, 105, 106, 160, 222, 280, 281, 295, 298
Inversiones Aropolis, 128
Inversiones Las Jacarandas, 97, 100, 296, 313

Jackson Ambrosia, Juana, 178

Jaguars, 197
La Jiribilla, 87
Jovel, Colonel, 200
Juárez Bonilla, Juan Carlos, 8, 184, 226, 308, 313
Justino, Don, 135, 242, 318

Kafie, Schucry, 72
Kawas, Jeanette, 163, 305
Kennedy, John F., 26
Kissinger, Henry, 23
Kubiske, Lisa, 110, 111

Laínez, Jonathan, 95, 296
Lakhani, Nina, 229, 250, 321
Lara, Karla, 121, 122, 303
Lemus, Ismael, 188, 191, 308
Lezama, Hilda, 178
Liberal Party, 15, 39, 41, 61, 67, 75, 79, 88, 130, 131, 150, 293–5, 300, 301
Libre (Liberty and Refoundation), 68, 151, 157, 288, 300, 303–5, 310, 311
Lito, 143, 144, 146, 185, 186, 188, 191, 253, see also Aureliano Molino
Llanitos, Los, 74
Llorens, Hugo, 79, 82, 83, 293
Lobo, Fabio, ('El Comando'), 126, 127, 131, 133, 158, 280, 301
Lobo Sosa, Porfirio 'Pepe', 67, 75, 80, 88–91, 100, 110, 126, 127, 128, 154, 155, 161, 166, 203, 278, 279, 289, 292–4, 298, 301, 306, 320
London Press Gazette, 228
López, Gladis Aurora, 101–4, 296, 303, 311
López, Jair, 245, 250, 254, 309, 317
López, Lilian, 186, 206, 245, 271
López, María, 103
López Arellano, Oswaldo, 23, 61, 297
López Castellanos, Etelinda, 236
López Lone, Guillermo, 92, 168, 295
Lutopas, 128

MACCIH (Mission to Support the Fight against Corruption and Impunity in Honduras), 248, 280, 301, 302
Mack, Ryan, 180
Madrid, Cristian, 118, 207
Maduro, Nicolás, 86
Maduro, Ricardo, 148, 149, 293, 297, 303, 309
Maldonado, Wendy, 247, 248
MAO (Environmental Movement of Olancho), 163
Marconi, Alba, 55, 144
Martínez, Emerson, 178
Martínez, Suyapa, 143
Matta Ballesteros, Juan Ramón, 25, 119, 120, 300
McClintock, Michael, 25, 27, 171
Mejía, Arístides, 71–3, 292
Mejía, Francisco, 128, 129
Mejía, Héctor García, 114, 193, 226, 227, 248
Mejía, Ivan, 114

Mejía, Roberto Arturo, 129
Menchú, Rigoberta, 38, 218
Méndez, Rolando, 243
Mesoamerican Initiative of Women Human Rights Defenders, 228
Meza, Dina, 165-7, 229, 307
Meza, Víctor, 71, 79, 81, 83, 176
Micheletti, Roberto, 66, 68, 75, 79, 83, 88-90, 93, 161, 292-4
Milla, Fausto, 187
MILPAH (Independent Lenca Indigenous Movement of La Paz), 102, 104
Ministry of Agriculture, 104, 275
Miranda, Miriam, 41, 47, 49, 65-67, 75, 87, 148, 149, 158-60, 181, 187, 227, 288
Molina, Aureliano 'Lito', 143, 187, 191, 237
Moncada, Rixi, 73, 74, 93, 293
Mora, Yuri, 224, 249, 316
Morales, René, 63, 154
Morales, Soraya, 121
Morales, Tommy, 167, 193, 305
Morales, Vidalina, 32
MS-13, 170, 172, 211
MUCA (Unified Campesino Movement of the Aguan), 152, 155-7, 290, 304, 310
Murillo, Margarita, 161, 164, 305

Nájera, Óscar, 158
Násser, Fredy, 72
National Agrarian Institute (INA), 48, 62, 290
National Anti-Corruption Council, 128, 306
National Association of Prosecutors, 121
National Party, 12, 30, 67, 80, 84, 101, 102, 104, 121 124, 127, 131, 158, 169, 188, 275, 278, 293-5, 300, 301 311, 320
National Penitentiary Institute, 282
National Resistance, 32
National School of Fine Arts, 44
National Violence Observatory, 167
Nealon, James, 200, 201, 310
Negro, El, ('Smiley'), 168, 205, 311; see also Urbina Soto, Arnaldo, 169
Negroponte, John, 23-5, 33, 200
Nelson, Lucio, 178
Nicolás, Jacobo, 225
Noé Pino, Hugo, 69, 72, 104, 159, 290, 291
Noriega, Roger, 83
North, Oliver, 24, 286
North American Free Trade Agreement (NAFTA), 37

OAS (Organization of American States), 279, 290, 291, 294, 295, 299, 301
Obama, Barack, 81, 174
Obed Murillo Mencías, Isis 66, 86, 291
Odebrecht SA, 74, 293
Office of Public Works, 128
OFRANEH (Honduran Black Fraternal Organization), 41, 48, 75, 148, 288, 304
Olvin, Armando, 134, 221
OPEL (Patriotic Student Organization of Lempira), 29, 30
Orellana, Ivy Luz, 29, 30
Oxfam International, 98

Pacheco Reyes, Roberto, 63, 129, 203, 310, 311
Pacheco Tinoco, Julián, 72, 73, 127, 189, 215, 229, 266, 278, 293, 301, 305, 320
Padre Melo (Ismael Moreno), 7, 22, 28, 87, 88, 148, 149, 167, 187, 286
Padre Tamayo, 163
Palmer, Larry, 133
Pascuala Vásquez, Pascualita, 40, 41, 45, 46, 274
Pastor, Rodolfo, 130, 132
Paz, Elsia, 106, 250, 316
PCI Inc., 205, 207, 215, 239, 315
Pelosi, Nancy, 180
PEMSA (Potencia y Energía de Mesoamérica SA), 100, 247, 297, 310, 316
PEN Honduras, 165
Penabad Pages, José Manuel, 189, 192, 193, 243, 308
Pentagon, 32, 81, 83, 287
Perdomo, Jesús, 156, 238, 240, 241, 304, 311
Pérez, Bernardo, 136, 242
Petrocaribe, 70-2, 292
PHAZ, 255, 256, 308
Pineda, Tasiana, 246, 315
Piñero, Zahra, 249
Planeta Verde, 104, 303
Pompeyo Bonilla, Captain Oswald, 102, 116, 298
Pope Francis, 44
Pred, David, 98
Proderssa (Producción de Energía Solar y Demás Renovables SA de CV), 100, 129, 310, 316
Progress of Honduras, 60
Promotion of Community Development, 89
Public Ministry, 95, 191, 218, 25

Ramos, Dominga, 152
Ramos, Felipe, 226
Rápalo Orellana, Elvin 'Comanche', 201, 211-13, 233-6, 241, 249, 255, 263, 272, 274, 276, 282, 317
Reagan, Ronald, 19, 23, 24, 287
Reina Idiáquez, Carlos Roberto, 39, 41
Renewable Energy Projects Unit (UEPER), 128
Reporters Without Borders, 228
Resumen Latinoamericano, 161
Reyes, Carlos H., 76, 77, 82, 86-8, 124, 149, 151, 293
Reyes, Germán, 100, 101,
Reyes, Mario, 24
Reyes, Samuel, 200, 302, 310
Rice, Condoleezza, 70
Rights Action, 52, 289
Rights of Indigenous Peoples, 42, 281
Rivas, Francisco, 265, 299
Rivas, Yoni, 62, 153-8, 198, 227, 230, 314
Rivera, Dimas, 255
Rivera Maradiaga, Devis Leonel, 125-7, 129, 133, 278, 301, 320
Rivera Maradiaga, Javier, 126, 127, 158, 278,